SPANISH INFLUENCE ON ENGLISH LITERATURE

BY

MARTIN HUME

C. DE LA REAL ACADEMIA ESPAÑOLA Y DE LA REAL ACADEMIA DE LA HISTORIA
EXAMINER IN SPANISH, AND EXTENSION LECTURER IN SPANISH
LITERATURE IN THE UNIVERSITY OF LONDON

HASKELL HOUSE

Publishers of Scholarly Books

NEW YORK

1964

published by

HASKELL HOUSE

Publishers of Scholarly Books

30 East 10th Street • New York, N. Y. 10003

Library of Congress Catalog Card Number: 65-15903

PRINTED IN UNITED STATES OF AMERICA

PREFACE

IT has always appeared to me as impossible adequately to study the history of a literature as an isolated entity, as it is to follow intelligently the political progress of a country without regard to the concurrent events and actions of other nations in relation to it. Literatures, whilst in their origin the outcome of distinct national and racial circumstances, nevertheless act and react strongly upon each other at certain periods; and the student who seeks to unravel the literary history of his own country with real understanding, should possess, at least, some knowledge of the foreign literatures that have influenced his own, and of the reasons why their influence has been exerted at the periods, and in the directions, that it has.

It is, therefore, not with the idea of presenting another history of Spanish Literature that this little work has been written: that has been admirably done in English already; and the subject, moreover, is one that could only be treated properly in a book of much greater dimensions than the present. My object has been rather to provide for English readers, what I venture to call a comparative study of Spanish literature, in special relation to its points of contact with the literature of our own country. Such a study cannot, of course, pretend to be exhaustive, since the ground covered includes generally the productions, over centuries, of two of the most fertile literatures in Europe; but the line of study indicated, and the broad principles laid down, it is hoped, may stimulate English readers to resort to the original Spanish texts referred to, as a means of gaining a fuller appreciation of some of the influences which have helped to make our own literature what it has become.

These views, with regard to the utility of a comparative study of literature, have found a ready response from the University Extension Board of the University of London, by whose commission a Central Course of ten lectures on the subject of *Spanish Literature and its Influence in England* was delivered early in the present year. Since the conclusion of the course many inquiries have reached the writer, with regard to the publication of the lectures in book-form. The result of these inquiries has been to encourage me to rearrange and partially rewrite the substance of the lectures, and to offer it in its present form, in the hope that it may thus reach a larger number of students than I could possibly address verbally, in the scant leisure allowed to me by my other literary work.

MARTIN HUME.

LONDON, *December* 1904.

CONTENTS

CHAPTER I

THE INFLUENCE OF SPAIN UPON EUROPEAN CULTURE IN THE MIDDLE AGES; AND THE BIRTH OF CASTILIAN LITERATURE.

CHAPTER II

DIDACTIC SENTENCES, PROVERBIAL PHILOSOPHY, AND EXEMPLARY APOLOGUES

CHAPTER III

THE CRONICAS, HISTORIES, AND RECORDS OF PERSONAL ADVENTURE

CHAPTER IV

THE ROMANCES OF CHIVALRY AND PASTORALS

CONTENTS

CHAPTER V

THE SPANISH NOVEL : ITS ORIGIN, TENDENCY, AND INFLUENCE

CHAPTER VI

THE PICARESQUE AND PERIPATETIC NOVELS
IN ENGLAND

CHAPTER VII

THE LITERATURE OF TRAVEL AND OF WAR

CHAPTER VIII

DEVOTIONAL, MYSTICAL, AND POLEMICAL LITERATURE

of Spanish mysticism in elevating religious ideals, and reacting upon the semi-pagan sensuousness of the Italian renascence.

THE SPANISH REFORMERS

CHAPTER IX

THE SPANISH THEATRE AND THE ENGLISH DRAMATISTS

CONTENTS

CHAPTER X

THE SPANISH THEATRE AND THE ENGLISH STAGE AFTER THE REFORMATION—CONCLUSION

DECADENCE OF SPANISH LITERATURE IN THE EIGHTEENTH CENTURY

SPANISH INFLUENCE ON ENGLISH LITERATURE

CHAPTER I

THE INFLUENCE OF SPAIN UPON EUROPEAN CULTURE IN THE MIDDLE AGES; AND THE BIRTH OF CASTILIAN LITERATURE.

THE literary form in which facts and fancies are presented may be defined as a revelation of the individual intellect which the writer has by descent derived from the mingled idiosyncrasies of countless progenitors, broadly controlled by racial and national influences. Just as no two persons are facially so much alike as to be undistinguishable, and as the convolutions on the epidermis of all the thumbs in the world vary in pattern, so two human minds never work exactly in the same groove, though thumbs and minds may both be classified into large characteristic groups. Nations and races are but aggregates of individuals. All Chinamen, and for matter of that all Englishmen, bear the natural physical resemblance to each other that distinguishes them from other races, yet each individual possesses characteristics that distinguish him from other members of the same ethnical group. A similar rule may be applied to racial or national intellects, which, owing to antecedent circumstances, differ in the aggregate as much from one another as do the more superficial physical peculiarities; and thus the evolutionary study of a national literature can only be satisfactorily pursued simultaneously with a consideration of the various influences, racial and political, which have operated upon the people who produced it. This is doubtless a truism, but the need for thus widening the scope of literary study is frequently lost sight of by superficial readers who are content to regard each literary masterpiece of any nation as the spontaneous production of an isolated individuality. It is true that the great work appears to the unthinking to have burst upon the world mature and splendid from the brain of one genius. But such is never the case. The genius who produces the work does but focus and mould the elements from within and without which have been working silently, and perhaps unnoticed, for many years before the culminating point of fruition has been reached. All literature is but evolution, and to understand and enjoy any literature fully it is necessary to adopt the same methods as those employed by the philosophical historian. He is not content to tell the blank facts of what happened in the past; he needs to trace the reasons why they happened by searching for their genesis in previous happenings. So in the study of a literature, or indeed of any one important work of literature, it is necessary to understand how and why, historically considered, it took the form it did.

Broadly speaking, there are three sets of influences which may act upon the literary development of a nation : first, and most fundamental, is the dominant character of the race that produces it, springing from natural conditions and racial vicissitudes ; second, the influences exercised by other nations or by foreign invasion ; and third, the individual genius of some great master. It may be safely predicated that, whenever the second of these influences is exercised upon a literature, the first influence, namely, that of the dominant character of the native race, rapidly transforms the foreign element introduced, and, whilst receiving influence from it, colours it in accordance with the native character.

I am anxious to make these primary principles clear, because I shall attempt to apply them in tracing the development of Castilian literature (especially prose literature, for reasons which I will explain later), and to mark how, and where, and why the literature of our own country received at certain periods impregnations from that of Spain. This will necessitate a progressive consideration of the natural and political causes which gave to Spanish literature its peculiar characteristics, its strength and its weakness, and enabled it only to exert appreciable influence upon our own literature at certain distinctly specific points of contact.

The Iberian peninsula has undergone perhaps greater racial and social changes than any other country in Europe. Wave after wave of human inundation has swept into and over it, Iberian, Celt, Phœnician, Carthaginian, Greek, Roman, Afro-Semite, Goth, Frank, and Vandal, and the mixed hordes of Islam have left deep traces upon the race we call Spaniards, and have profoundly modified thought and literary form. But though languages might change, masters come and go, and cultures from other lands introduce new features into Spanish letters, the native spontaneous character of Spanish literature, derived from the sturdy root-races of prehistoric times, has retained always certain qualities which have distinguished it from all others. These qualities may be summed up as being a vivid, exuberant invention, florid verbosity, mocking satire; and, above all, the keynote of the racial character, that overpowering sense of individuality that leads each man to look upon himself as the centre of the universe, in some sort in mystic communion with the higher powers. As Rome grew more corrupt and splendid, and the dependencies richer and more cultured, the provincial influence in the metropolis grew greater, and imperial Rome thenceforward was doomed to decay. Spain, one of the richest of the provinces, with a population which had seized almost fiercely upon Latin civilisation, and was now largely mixed with Roman blood, after centuries of domination, contributed perhaps more than any other to the apparent grandeur but inevitable decay of the empire. In the purer days of the later Republic the Roman exquisites, Cicero amongst them, whilst praising the irrepressible literary skill of Spaniards, scoffed at their strange provincial pronunciation of Latin. But in later days the best of the Cæsars were Spaniards. Trajan, Hadrian, and Marcus Aurelius, though they spoke with the Spanish brogue, ruled the world. Spanish authors infused their peculiar spirit into Latin literature, and set the fashion of exuberant preciosity that led it to decay. The elder Seneca (*b.* 54 B.C., *d.* 39 A.D.), profoundly imbued with the tradition of the best period of Latin literature, was a pure Spaniard, and wrote his critical collection of gems of oratory before the florid tendency of his countrymen had corrupted Latin letters. Of his more famous son, the younger Seneca (5 B.C.—65 A.D.), Mr. John Morley says : ' There is none of the ancient moralists to whom moderns, from Montaigne downwards, owe more than to Seneca. He touches the great and eternal commonplaces of human occasion — friendship, health, bereavement, riches, poverty, and death—with a hand that places him high among the divine masters of life. Men have found more abundantly in his essays and letters than in any other secular writer words of good counsel and import.' This is true, but already in the beautiful ornate and polished periods of the younger Seneca the Iberian love of fine words to clothe didactic thought began to assert itself. In his nephew Lucan

(*b.* 39 A.D., *d.* 65 A.D.) (especially in the *Pharsalia*) the
tendency to oratorical ornament is still more marked.
Martial (43-104 A.D.), like many a Spaniard after him,
set off all the world into scandalised laughter at
the wit and shameless effrontery of his vehement
satires. Quintilian, of Calahorra, gave to the world
one of its noblest pieces of literature. All of these
were Spaniards born, living in the first century of the
Christian era. All of them, except the first, showed
the ineradicable qualities of the race, and though in
them their genius gilded their exuberance, their hosts
of imitators, possessing all their floridness without
their genius, piled ornament upon ornament, one far-
fetched conceit upon another, and one eccentric new-
coined word upon another, until the Latin literary
style was debased to the pompous flatulence by which
it was distinguished when the imperial city fell a prey
to the Gothic invaders (400 A.D.). The splendour of
the Roman empire, the glittering and showy character
of Latin civilisation, and the rotund magniloquence
of the Latin tongue, had captured the inmost heart of
the Romanised race that populated the Peninsula, and
the pervading Iberian spirit aided the empire's fall.

The newcomers to Spain, the all-conquering Goths,
a military autocracy that for generations had fought
their way from east to west, were the very antipodes
of the native Spaniards. They were not a literary
race; they had little poetry or imagination; their
satire was administered with a sharp sword rather

than a stinging tongue; and they were boorish men of few words. They formed an aristocracy whose hereditary lands were inalienable, and they were forbidden to marry native Spaniards. So, though they lived and ruled in Spain for wellnigh three hundred years, they left little trace upon the literature of the land. So far from influencing Spaniards, they themselves long before they finally fell were obliged to adopt the Latin tongue of their subjects, and to submit to the Athanasian form of Christianity, which the Spaniards had fiercely seized upon at the bidding of the orthodox priests. There are few instances in history that show more strongly than this the absorbing and assimilative power of even a conquered and vassal majority, when the latter are mentally the more subtle, as the Spaniards unquestionably were, than the Goths. So the Goths passed in Spain and left little trace, other than a code of laws adapted in Latin from the great code of Theodosius. Spaniards, with their irrepressible love of written speech, continued during the whole of the Gothic domination to write in florid, over-loaded Latin. They had a higher inspiration than ever now. Christianity had appealed to them with a force greater than to any other people. That each man was equal in the sight of God, and that the Almighty took an interest in the humblest of His creatures, was a revelation of the truth of their strongest racial instinct, their self-conscious individualism, and the first Christian Latin poet to

write upon sacred themes was Juvencus, a Spaniard
(330 A.D.). Prudentius, a still nobler poet of Christianity, a Spaniard of the Spaniards, wrote his glowing religious verse, and thirsted for Christian martyrdom,
whilst full of love and yearning for the beautiful forms
and sweet indulgence that paganism had taught
him to admire. Orosius, too, a Spaniard, was the
first writer of history who brought into his writings
the general note of universality that came with the
Christian doctrine of human equality. These, and
such as these, kept still flickering the light of Latin
literature in Spain, whilst the Teuton kings held their
barbaric court at Toledo.

Perhaps the Spaniard whose influence upon European culture was greatest at this period of decadence
was Saint Isidore, Bishop of Seville from 600 to 636 A.D.,
the last of the great Latin writers before the dark
curtain fell. His principal work, in addition to his
History of the Gothic Kings,[1] was a sort of encyclopædic
dictionary called the *Etymologies,* summarising an
enormous mass of learning upon every known subject,
taken from previous authors, many of them now
unknown. Christian bishop as he was, he was obliged
austerely to condemn in words the delight of the
eye and the senses—'the vain fictions of the poets,
who with fables move the soul to levity'; to thunder
against showy, empty eloquence of the pagan authors,
in comparison with the staid simplicity of the Gospels.

---

[1] *Historia Gothorum, Wandalorum, etc.*

But Isidore was a Spaniard after all, and could be as florid an admirer of beauty in the abstract as any of his pagan forefathers. The work of Isidore, didactic above all things, profoundly influenced thought outside the Peninsula, especially in France. Men began dimly to understand, that much as beauty, and harmony, and elegance might be condemned officially, as leading minds to revere other things than the true God, yet that, properly and humbly regarded, they might serve as handmaids to religion itself; and, indeed, might be recognised as good gifts of God to His creatures. This idea, or a development of it, spread from Spain to France and Italy, and made itself felt later in the Italian renaissance. But not in Spain. There an event happened in 711 that swept the stage clear and turned Spanish culture into other channels.

From across the narrow strait there swarmed the Moslem conqueror—the savage Berbers, themselves but recently won to the faith of the prophet, and like all converts frantic in their zeal, the cultured Syrian, and philosophical Persian. Men of all the Eastern races, sons of Shem for the most part, close kinsmen, many of those from Africa with the root stock of Spain ; they spread northward without resistance, and in a few short months looked from the slopes of the Pyrenees upon a country over the whole of which the green flag of Islam waved, and the Crescent had abased the Cross.

Thenceforward for centuries the Christian ideal in Spain was changed. From the extreme Celtic north-west, the reconquest of the country began; and a tiny band of irreconcilables pushed forward, foot by foot, the territories of the Christian king. Most of the Spaniards were content to live in peace and safety, at first, under their Moslem overlords; for there was no intolerance. Human arms alone would never have sufficed for the little band in Asturias, to have conquered the conquerors. Religious fervour, mystic communion with divine powers, voices in the air, and guiding stars; fasting, penance, and austerity, combined with the inborn belief of every Spaniard in a special selection of himself as one of God's favourites: these were the sources from which the Christian reconquest obtained its impetus. All that was clean and sweet and beautiful was odious, because the infidel revelled in cleanliness and luxury and beauty. Christian Spain was too busy and too austere during the first three centuries of the reconquest to do any-thing for literature, except to write a few priestly lives of saints and the like. And so, in Christian Spain, as in the rest of Europe, overrun by the rough Teutons, all culture slept where it had not been deliberately destroyed.

But not so in Moorish Spain. There one caliph of Cordova after another, polished, enlightened, and learned, gathered around them all that money, taste, and knowledge could obtain of the culture of the ancient peoples. From the first caliph, Abd-er-Rahman, late in the eighth century, through his son, Al Hishám, his grandson, Al Hakám, his great-grandson, Abd-er-Rahman II.; and later still the greatest of the caliphs, Abd-er-Rahman III., and his son for two hundred years down to the end of the tenth century, Cordova alone of European cities it was that kept the ancient learning alive. Palaces more splendid than a poet's dream; a mosque that stands to-day almost peerless amongst the beauteous buildings of the world; luxury and fastidiousness that ultimately led to enervation and decay—all these had Cordova under the caliphs. But this was not all. Cordova, in Roman times the patrician colony, had been the home of literature and the birthplace of poets and writers without number. But under the caliphs it became the centre of the learning of the world. Students from all parts of Europe flocked to her private schools, and sat at the feet of the learned men who taught in them: not Arabs alone, but Jews and Mozarabic Christians too. Duns Scotus came to learn and spread through Europe the philosophy of the great Jew poet and philosopher Avicebron (*d.* 1070). Literature, philosophy, and rhetoric were mainly taught at first, and later every branch of science was studied, especially medicine and surgery. Astronomy, geography, chemistry, natural history, horticulture, and the fine arts all had their literature, their teachers, and their devotees.

The great library of the caliph Al Hakám was the wonder of the world. In every city of the East his agents were vigilantly seeking and collecting for him rare manuscripts in the Oriental tongues, in Persian, Hebrew, and in Greek. Bagdad, Damascus, and Cairo were ransacked for treasures to send to Cordova; and copyists in the pay of the Spanish caliphs transcribed, in the libraries of the East, those texts which money could not buy; and before the learned Hakám died in 961, over 400,000 precious manuscripts were at the service of the scholars of Cordova. Though the over-luxury brought disaster to the caliphate, and the Moslem fanatics destroyed much of the precious library, yet the tradition of culture clung still to Cordova. Even the Christian Spaniards there, for the first two centuries at least, spoke and wrote Arabic as often as the Latin dialect which had descended to them from their fathers; and the Hebrews, who had followed the Moors in vast numbers, were in danger also of losing their ancient speech through the cultivation of the courtly Arabic, when the caliphate fell and the reaction came.

As the Christian conquest gradually advanced, and religious fervour on both sides grew, each people in Moslem Spain resumed the use of their own speech whilst mostly speaking Arabic as well. The provincial cities of Moslem Spain, now capitals of petty kingdoms, Toledo, Saragossa, Seville, Murcia, Badajoz and others, became in their turn centres of culture;

and from them, and especially from Cordova, with
its learned traditions, there sprang the first Greek
renaissance in the twelfth century, before that of
Italy was dreamt of. During the caliphate Cordova
had especially been the home of poets and of poetry,
for the fatalistic creed of the Arabs did not encourage
them at first to study the exact sciences. It was not
therefore primarily to the Arabs that the Spanish
renaissance was due. To the Jews of Spain must
be given the credit of opening the way, though
Mozarabes and Arabs followed them usefully afterwards. Astronomy had slumbered from the times
of ancient Greece until the discoveries of the Spanish
Jews and Arabs carried it to a height never attained
before. Averroes, one of the greatest philosophers of
all time, was a Cordovese (1116-1198). He translated Aristotle's works, not from Greek, but from
Hebrew into Arabic. Oxford, Padua, and Paris
eagerly sent, copyists to turn the revived text into
Latin, and all the schoolmen in Europe, in the
thirteenth century, were discussing the doctrines which
Averroes had deduced from Aristotle. The doctrine,
when applied to Christianity, was in favour of the
idea of natural or revealed religion, which needed
no justification by reason ; and it unquestionably in-
culcated a more implicit acceptance of religious dogma
than that formulated from Spain some years after
Averroes's death by another Spaniard, Ramon Lull
the Majorcan. He travelled the world over, teach-

ing and preaching his philosophic theory that the truths of Christianity were to be demonstrated by reason and logic. His influence upon the mediæval universities was enormous, and to him is due primarily the study of the Oriental languages at Oxford and elsewhere. What is now called rational Christianity, and appeals so strongly to the modern mind, is first due to the Spaniard Ramon Lull, whom the Roman Church has alternately banned and blessed, and who, notwithstanding the Inquisition, has already been placed upon the step that leads up to full sainthood.

Poetry as well as the sciences also spread up north from Moorish Cordova and Toledo, thanks mainly to the Jews. Other Spaniards besides the writers and teachers carried to the world echoes of the lore which the Spanish cities had preserved. These were the Hebrew physicians, necromancers, and poisoners, who for centuries were to be found in every court in Europe. Toledo especially was regarded as the home of their occult and esoteric science; and the secrets of the ancient peoples were carried by them to the world, until the new learning ousted the old in the sixteenth century. Moses Ben Maimon (Maimonides), the greatest of European Jews, was offered the post of physician to Richard I. of England, but preferred the service of Saladin. He sought in his famous book *Yad-ha-Hazakah* ('The Strong Hand'), and in his *Guide to those who are travelling perplexed as to the right road,* to give a rational interpretation to the

Talmud, much as Lull did for the Christian gospel. A dozen other great names of Spanish Jews might be mentioned to show how they spread learning in the world: less in Spain than elsewhere, be it said, in consequence of the religious fanaticism by which zealots kept the Spanish peoples apart; but I have written enough to show that but for Moslem Spain much of the knowledge of the ancients would have perished. The Greek, Persian, and Coptic manuscripts gathered from all quarters by the enlightened liberality of the caliphs and kings were turned into Arabic at Cordova and Toledo, and by the Jews and Mozarabes translated into Hebrew and Latin. After the fall of the caliphate, in the twelfth and thirteenth centuries, Philosophy was studied in all the smaller capitals, the petty kings of which competed with each other as patrons of art and letters. Medicine and surgery were carried to a perfection unknown before, by the most famous professors of the age, Abd el Kamín and Aben Zoar of Seville. Botany was the province of Aben Abaithar of Malaga, who wrote a book called *Collection of Simple Remedies*, anticipating many discoveries of later medicine, and describing scientifically two hundred new species of plants. Mathematics and astronomy were eagerly pursued, and observatories were to be seen in all the centres of culture where the heavens might be studied. The most important observatory then in Europe was that famous tower that still stands unrivalled in beauty

after eight centuries, the Giralda of Seville. Travel
and descriptions of far countries claimed many Arabic
and Jewish professors. Tales abu Hamid Algarnati
of Granada, and Aben Chobair of Valencia, travelled
through the East and described what they saw. El
Abdari of Valencia visited and wrote of Egypt, Arabia,
and Chaldea, and Benjamin of Tudela's travels are
still quoted. Philosophy, the earliest manifestation of
the culture of Cordova, continued to divide scholars
throughout the world long after Cordova fell. Avem-
pace (*d.* 1138), who preceded the great Averroes,
wrote his *Regime of the Solitary* on the lines of Plato's
Republic, and no mediæval school was without a copy
of the book. *The Fountain of Life* of the Spanish
Jew Solomon Ben Gabirol (1021-1070) produced a
profound influence throughout Europe. Abraham
Ben David of Toledo wrote works on astronomy ; and
his philosophical attempt (*Exalted Faith*) to reconcile
philosophy with revealed religion claimed followers
by hundreds in Italy, France, and England. Literature, and especially poetry, flourished exceedingly,
as the numerous original texts of poems and tales in
Hebrew and Arabic now in the Escorial Library
testify, and the printed works of Gabirol, Judah Ben
Levi, and others further prove.

And so from the eighth to the twelfth century
Moslem Spain remained the home of learning and
literature, whilst the Christian kings from the north
pushed onward and ever onward the frontiers, too

busy in fighting, too fervid in their religious faith of special selection to seek to learn much from infidels ; or to adopt, to any great extent, the tongue of their enemies. The conquest had developed into two main branches: one of Frankish and Provençal origin in the north-east of the Peninsula ; the other, Gothic and priestly as to leadership, had drawn to the Celtic north-west all those Romanised Spaniards whose attachment to their masters, or their love of independence, had led them to refuse Moorish domination. The realm of the north-east, Aragon and Cataluña, continuing the ancient connection with the peoples of the same blood and sovereignty on the Gulf of Lyons and in the south of France, spoke the dialect of Latin which we call Provençal ; whilst the kingdoms of Galicia and Leon spoke a cognate tongue akin to the Portuguese. As for the Christian Mozarabes who, as we have seen, in the earlier years of the Moslem domination, had to a great extent adopted Arabic as their language, bigots on both sides had influenced race and religious hatred to such an extent by the eleventh century that, as the Christian kingdoms were pushed forward, and the Cross supplanted the Crescent in province after province, the men of Spanish descent again took up universally the peculiar dialect of Latin that the Romanised Spaniards of Cordova had spoken, greatly modified now, as may be supposed, by two or three centuries of Arabic propinquity. With each advance of the

Christian frontiers a larger number of people who spoke this dialect were included in Christian Spain, and these were people, for the most part, much more advanced in civilisation and accomplishments than the other inhabitants of the Christian kingdoms. In the meanwhile the more settled condition of the northern part of the Peninsula, distant from the fighting frontiers, was causing poetry and dramatic interludes to be cultivated even there. But the impetus in this case came from the Provençal troubadours and juglars, who lived in the courts of kings and nobles, and travelled from house to house, ever welcome guests to sing and recite their epic verse and dramatic dialogues ; to chant and jest and tell stories in the Provençal tongue, which most could understand. Out of these, and the imitations from them in the Galician tongue (the court language of Castile), grew Spain's poetry. But the influence was less native than French even in the earliest specimen of Castilian poetry, the famous *Poem of the Cid* clearly owing its form to the *Chansons de Geste* which had been carried across the Pyrenees by the troubadours.

Here, then, we have no less than three, if not four, distinct dialects of Latin spoken in Spain ; as, indeed, is the case even to this day. Two of these, the Langue d'Oc or Romance and the Galician, were, and are, tongues capable of much poetical expression and with a considerable poetical literature ; but they were languages in which, for political reasons that I have pointed out, little scientific or philosophical learning had been written. Their sound, moreover, was less sonorous and majestic to the ear than was the dialect that had grown grave by being spoken for centuries side by side with guttural, emphatic Arabic. This dialect was richer too, and more flexible, for many Arabic words had crept into it, and its grammatical construction had grown far less rigid than the Low-Latin forms of Galicia or Provence. With the conquest of the imperial city of Toledo by Alfonso VI., in 1085, the first step towards the generalisation of the Mozarabic dialect was taken. The severities of Moslem fanatic sects that had seized power in the Mohammedan districts, had already driven vast numbers of Christian and wavering Mozarabes to settle within the territories of Castile; and the establishment of the court of Alfonso VI. at Toledo surrounded him and his nobles with people who spoke that dialect, which, thus became familiar to the ear. It was only fifty years afterwards, in the middle of the twelfth century, that the first and greatest Castilian epic poem was written, the *Poem of the Cid*; but, as the epic and lyric poetry of Spain exercised little or no influence upon our literature, I purpose to speak at present only of the development of Castilian prose.

When Cordova was conquered by St. Ferdinand in 1241, he found it necessary to promulgate the code of laws that had grown out of the Gothic code during the four centuries of the re-conquest, not in Latin or in Galician, but in the dialect that the Mozarabes of Cordova spoke; and, though doubtless many charters to newly occupied Moorish towns had been drawn up in the same language before this, only two fragments are known to exist in prose undoubtedly earlier.[1]   In Seville, again, in 1248, when St. Ferdinand established his capital there, the same thing happened; and the conqueror's edicts were couched in the dialect of the Mozarabes.   Thenceforward even some of the chronicles and history began to be written in the same tongue, for the information of the newly conquered people.   Rodrigo Ximenez de la Rada, Archbishop of Toledo, had written in Latin a *History of the Gothic Kings*, and so anxious was St. Ferdinand to remind the Christian Mozarabes of their pre-Moorish descent, that he ordered the bishop to translate his own book into their dialect.

---

[1] The first of these is the *Disputa del Alma y el Cuerpo*, in which the soul of a man recently dead upbraids his body for the troubles into which it had led the imperishable part of him.   The fragment begins thus :

> 'Si quereedes oir lo que uos quiero dezir
> dizre uos lo que ui, nol uos i quedo fallir,'

by which it will be seen that early as the text is—probably the middle of the twelfth century—the language was already fully formed.

The second fragment is part of a sacred auto representing the visit of the three kings of the East to the Infant Saviour, and is of similar date. The first lines, which are a soliloquy of the first king, Caspar, when he sees the star of Bethlehem, begins thus :

> 'Dios Criador ! qual maravila
> No se qual es achesta strela !
> Agora primas la e ueida
> Poco timpo a que es nacida.'

But with the death of St. Ferdinand in 1252 the great change came that decided the battle of the Peninsular tongues, and made what we now call Castilian the predominant language of Spain. The new king, Alfonso X., was one of the most bookish kings that ever lived, a born *littérateur*, with an insatiable thirst for knowledge. He had heard at his father's court, from Jewish, Mozarabic, and Mudejar sages, of the past glories of the caliph Al Hakám's great library at Cordova, of the hoarded wisdom of centuries that had formerly made the city of the caliphs the intellectual capital of the world. He saw now how the fairy palaces, the imperial libraries, and the busy schools had been cast down by ignorance and fanaticism. He was himself a sweet poet, in his own familiar tongue of Galicia, as well as in the Mozarabic dialect, which he wrote as well as his own. He had two languages to choose from at least, if not three ; and in his vast project to form a national literature he must have been guided in his choice by many considerations. The Mozarabic dialect was unquestionably the richer in words, and more facile in the adaptation of compounds than Galician. It was the dialect of the most lettered men of his realm, as well as of the larger number of his Castilian subjects ; and, above all, it was a pure Spanish speech evolved on Spanish soil, and owing nothing to Provence. When the giant Edward Plantagenet, with his crowd of English and French nobles, came to Burgos in 1254 to wed his beloved

Blanche of Castile, Alfonso's sister; and when in the splendid entertainments that accompanied the wedding and the knighting of the English prince in ancient form, the princes and nobles of both countries forgathered, there can have been little difficulty in their understanding each other's speech, for the Low-Latin of Galicia and the Low-Latin of Aquitaine were akin. But consider for a moment if, instead of Provençal or Galician, Alfonso and his courtiers had spoken the Mozarabic dialect, with its many Arabic and other exotic elements, how unintelligible they would have been to their Anglo-French guests. It is clear then that Alfonso X., when he chose the Mozarabic form of the language as the vehicle for the formation of a new national literature, must have been conscious that, with all the advantages of sound and flexibility it possessed, it would shut off Castile from the main current of European culture much more than would have been the case if he had adopted Galician or Provençal, which were more closely allied to the other literary Latin tongues. Why, then, did he deliberately choose it?

In the first place, it was the common speech of most of his people in the richest part of his realms, now that Toledo, Cordova, and Seville and most of Andalusia had been added to Castile. This is made clear by the introduction to one of the crude prose poems on sacred subjects written by Gonzalo de Berceo, one of the earliest known writers in Castilian. He was a Benedictine monk living at Calahorra, and begins thus a sacred poem evidently intended for recitation, and written before 1260:—

> ' Quiero far una prosa in Roman paladino,
>   En qual suele el pueblo fablar á su vecino
> Ca non so tan letrado á far otro Latino
>   Bien valdra como creo, un vaso de bon vino.'

> ' Such prose I wish to make in common speech,
>   As friends and neighbours use in talk and trade.
> No other Latin, 'faith, did they me teach ;
>   A cup of wine for it may well be paid.'

But a more important reason than the general use of the dialect, probably, was that Alfonso's great project depended mainly upon the translation, adaptation, and utilisation of the Hebrew and Arabic texts, which had survived the Berber fanaticism in Moorish Spain. Gonzalo de Berceo, in his many rough verses, the writer of the *Libro de Alexandre*, and the author of the *Poem of Jusuf* (Joseph and Potiphar), the writer of the *Poem of the Cid*, and many others, had been writing popular Castilian poetry for recitation, sacred and profane, for many years before the accession of Alfonso X., though the treatment and subjects of all this crude verse were derived from French or Provençal sources. The *History of the Gothic Kings* had been translated from Latin into Castilian, and during the latter years of Alfonso's father, St. Ferdinand (1252), many Arabic and Jewish translators had been busy adapting to Castilian the moral works which the Jews and Arabs had originally derived from the

Sanskrit (which will be the principal theme of the
next chapter). It will thus be seen that the way was
prepared on the accession of Alfonso X. for a great
forward literary movement, such as he had in view.
Perhaps no other king that ever lived conceived so
vast a scheme as Alfonso X. To extend mere
dominion is a vulgar dream, for dominion passes
away as it comes ; but the creation on a fixed plan of
a new national literature, and deliberately to choose
the dialect in which it shall be written, is a work
that may set its mark upon civilisation for all time
to come ; and this is what Alfonso did.

To the natural inherited tendencies of this new
literature, and to its influence in England, I shall
devote the greater portion of this book. My concern,
however, for the moment, is to show how the literature
itself was created. In the first place, it was clear that
a native Spanish literature should not be drawn from
France, which had hitherto influenced Spanish poetical
form so greatly. Alfonso was therefore obliged to turn
to the rich mine of Arabic, Hebrew, and Greek texts,
which had been studied and written in Spain under
the Moslem domination. To aid him in his immense
task, ignorant clerics like Berceo, writing but one
language, were of no use. So to him he called, as he
was obliged to do, a host of learned Jews, Arabs, and
Mozarabes, to compile and arrange for him, in the
only Spanish tongue with which they were familiar,
the learning which was enshrined in the Eastern

tongues of their forefathers. No branch of literature was neglected by Alfonso the Learned. No social narrowness or religious prejudice stood in the way of his great project. The plan of a universal history of the world had never been conceived before. The learned king now set about writing such a work, aided by scholars who searched the writings of the ancients and the lore of the Bible. *La Grande et General Historia* reaches only down to the dawn of the Christian era, and would fail to satisfy a modern historian, but it is a high achievement nevertheless, and a still greater idea. I had the delight of discovering perhaps the most ancient known text of it, in the Duke of Wellington's library at Strathfieldsaye, dated not many years after Alfonso's death, and what strikes the intelligent reader, besides the catholicity of the text, is its curious modernity. This is seen also in *La Estoria de Espanna*, written undoubtedly by Alfonso himself. An example of the style may be of interest. Taken unquestionably from the seventeenth chapter of the *Korán*, this extract will be understood by any one who can read modern Spanish. Recollect that it was written in 1260 or 1270, and then try a passage from the original of Chaucer, who wrote more than a century later, and you will see how much more English has changed in 650 years than Castilian has. The extract relates Mohammed's dream.

'Tomó me el angel Gabriel (decia Mahoma) et leuome suso fasta el primero cielo, et los angeles que

y estavan, venieron contra mi, et recisbieronme muy
bien, et fueron mui alegres conmigo. Et con el gran
plazer, que ende ouieron, cataronse unos á otros et
decian. Ay que bien! Ay que bien es este! Et
orauame todos, todo el bien et toda salud. Synon
uno que estava ahy, que non se alegrava conmigo nin
se reya como los otros. Et yo pregunté entonze al
angel Gabriel, qué quien era aquel ó porqué se fazie
aquello. Et Gabriel me dixo. Sepas q'ueste angel
nunca se reyó, nin se reyera. Que este es el angel
guardador del fuego.'

If Alfonso's historical ideas were before his age,
so too were his services as a legislator. I have
already spoken of the great Gothic Roman code of
laws drawn up in Gothic Latin, and promulgated in
the seventh century in Spain. Six hundred years had
passed, and the Moslem domination had altered the
whole country ethnologically and socially. Alfonso
set to work to recast in Castilian this code in seven
parts, called the *Siete Partidas*, dealing exhaustively
with the duties and rights of every class of citizens
of Castile, from sovereign to serfs. This tremendous
work was begun in 1255 and finished in 1263, and
remained the basis of all Spanish law until the great
Napoleonic upheaval. Nothing can exceed the freedom, and yet the correctness and beauty, of the
language of this code. This will be seen by the following specimen of it, dealing with the rules with
regard to the places where high schools or universities

might be established. It is so clear that any modern Spaniard could understand it without difficulty.

'Las escuelas del estudio general, deben seer en logor appartado de la villa, las unas cerca de las otras, porque los escolares que hobiessen sabor de aprender aina, puedan tomar dos liciones, ó mas si quisieren, en diversas oras del dia, et puedan los unos preguntar á los otros en las cosas que dubdaren; pero deben las unas escuelas seer tan acredradas de las otras que los maestros no se embarguen oyendo los unos lo que leen los otros.

'De buen ayre et de fermosas salidas debe seer la villa do quieren establescer el estudio, porque los maestros que muestran los saberes, et los escolares que los aprenden, vivan sanos, et en él puedan folgar et rescibir placer á la tarde quando se levantasen cansados del estudio: et otro sí debe seer abondada de pan et de vino, et de buenas posadas en que puedan morar et pasar su tiempo sin grant costa. Et otro sí decimos que los cibdadanos de aquel logar do fuere fecho el estudio deben mucho honrar et guardar los maestros et los escolares,' and so on for many pages, no point being missed. Besides this code, Alfonso wrote another juridical book, called *The Mirror of Laws*.

But great as all this is, it was a mere tithe of Alfonso's vast literary activity. With the aid of Jews and Mudejares he compiled a multitude of scientific works. The *Alfonsine Tables* were a complete recalculation and correction of the astronomical tables of

Ptolemy, and were in use until the late eighteenth
century; *La Sphera Redonda*, the *Astrolabe*, and a
dozen other works, translated or adapted from the
Eastern languages, placed in the hands of Spanish
speaking people—and through them the rest of the
world—the cosmographical, astronomical, and philosophical knowledge that had been hidden in the
libraries of Moslem Spain.   Most curious of all are
Alfonso's books upon the properties of minerals, adapted
from the *Lapidarios* of the Jew Abolays, and of the
Arab Mahomed aben Quich.   Alfonso tells us, indeed,
in one of his poems (*Versos de Arte Mayor*), that he had
actually learned and successfully practised alchemy,
and gives the secret as it was taught to him by an
Egyptian philosopher.   Another direction in which
Alfonso's literary activity was employed, was in guide-
books of various sports and games, chess, dice, and
draughts, books on hunting, and others of the same
sort; and to crown his services to posterity he
collected a mass of poetry, the first *Romancero*, some
of the poems by himself and some by others, all of a
religious and mystic tendency, which is beyond price in
showing the development of Spanish verse (*Cantigas de
Sancta Maria*).   Here, then, was a national literature in
a practically new language, created during the lifetime
and by the efforts of a single man.   Even in these, its
first days, the indelible stamp of the race is upon it; a
stamp which, as we shall see later, remained until our
own times, and left its impress upon the later literature

of Europe. These qualities of race were exuberant fertility of expression and devotional personal mysticism, derived from the Romanised Celt-Iberian, supplemented now by the sententious didacticism which had been the tradition of the Hebrew and Oriental letters that had given birth to the new Castilian literature. From the specimens of early prose given above, it will have been recognised that before Alfonso's death Castilian had become practically the same fine language that it has remained ever since, although doubtless the pronunciation was different, probably the guttural j and x being later developments, and certainly the lisping of the c and z.

In this first chapter I have confined myself to the circumstances that underlay the first appearance of Castilian literature. This has been necessary in order that the direction in which its influence was subsequently felt upon English literature might be understood. In the following chapters I shall dwell not only upon the development of the literature itself, but upon its influence on the prose and dramatic writings of our own country.

CHAPTER II

DIDACTIC SENTENCES, PROVERBIAL PHILOSOPHY, AND EXEMPLARY APOLOGUES

THE preceding chapter traced the origin and birth of Castilian prose literature in the thirteenth century, and showed that the character of the root-race of the Peninsula had set its stamp upon its previous literary product. This was seen in a tendency for any chosen literary form to degenerate into extravagance of imagination and over-floridness and affectation of diction. This tendency was traced in the decadence of Latin letters under Spanish influence, and in later chapters we shall witness exactly the same process of degeneration of the Castilian letters, at whose birth we have assisted, and whose development we are now to follow. Under Alfonso the Learned, Castilian prose literature was born pure, terse, and simple. But there was one great and remarkable characteristic both of its matter and its manner to which I must direct very careful attention. I mean its sententious didacticism. Every one of Alfonso X.'s books had for its one object the teaching of something by short, authoritative pronouncements, which were sometimes glossed or expounded, as texts might be in brief sermons. It was always the sage or elder instructing youth or inexperience. Long before the coming of the Moors, Seneca the younger, and many other Latin and Greek authors before him, had written in didactic aphorisms in this way. The classical forms which had dominated all cultured Europe before the Roman empire crumbled, had of course been derived originally from the East, where the didactic sentence, proverb, or short parable was the traditional form taken for the conveyance of wisdom and experience ; and it was one of the few traditions that still existed in Europe in the dark ages that succeeded the disappearance of the Roman power. But, as was seen when the Italian renaissance began, the austerity and direct simplicity of the parable or apologue had been lost during the many centuries that had passed since it had left its Oriental home. In Spain it was otherwise. There, as we have seen, when Christian culture was at a standstill, and old forms had been lost, the Arabs and Jews introduced straight from the Orient again, pure and strong, the simple tradition of the conveyance of wisdom and experience by means of authoritative sentences, or parables, each containing a separate moral lesson. The new Castilian prose literature created by Alfonso, therefore, at once took a much more didactic and sententious form than did any other European literature, because the king was obliged to turn for models and originals to the only learning his subjects knew, namely the Hebrew, Arabic, Sanskrit and Persian texts that had for four centuries been the intellectual food of the southern Spanish scholars of various races. This, consequently, was a fresh introduction of Oriental influence into European literature through Spain, and, as we shall see later, it vastly strengthened the didactic proverbial form throughout the civilised world, and not least in England.

We will trace how a few of the earliest of these works came from the East to Spain, and thence carried the taste for proverbial wisdom to the rest of the world. In early ages a collection of Eastern fables, written in Sanskrit and called the *Fables of Pilpay* (or Sindabad), was carried to Persia and translated into old Persian. Thence it found its way to Syria, and throughout the near East, and became a popular book. Hebrew and Arabic versions of it existed in Cordova in the time of the caliphs, and in 1251 Alfonso the Learned, whilst he was a prince, ordered the Arabic version of Abdallah ben Al Mocaffá to be translated into Castilian. I may say that two centuries previous to this the book had been translated into Greek, and many years afterwards the Greek version was made use of by Italian and other scholars to reintroduce the stories into Europe. But the Spanish translation, which was called *Kalila and Dimna*, the names of the persons who alternate in telling the story, was the first in any modern language, and at once became a popular book both in Spain and abroad. Each story, as usual, is used to enforce a particular moral or lesson, and the Spanish version is extremely brilliant and interesting. If any one will take the trouble to read the Spanish tales in it, and will then turn to Mr. Keith Falconer's English version of them, taken straight from the Syriac text (Cambridge, 1885), it will be seen how unmistakably the Spanish spirit had infused itself into the Oriental body of the work in its *Kalila and Dimna* form. The tales are mostly too long for quotation here, but sometimes little subsidiary anecdotes are introduced to enforce some secondary moral. The following is a specimen :—' Once there was a young man beloved by the wife of another man, and the woman, the better to be able to entertain her lover, made a subterranean passage from her house to the street, near the well whence they drew their water, so that, if her husband surprised them, the young man might go into the passage and the door be shut upon him whilst he made his way into the street. One day when her lover was with her the woman heard her husband coming. " Run," she said to her lover, " and get into the passage by the well." He went to the well, and found it broken down, and so turned back to the woman and said, " I went to the well, and I see it is broken down." " I did not tell you the well," she said, " but the passage by the well. I only mentioned the well incidentally to guide you. Make haste, for Heaven's sake, and go, or we shall get into trouble." " Well, then, you ought not to talk about wells when

C

you mean passages," said the lover. "If you want me to go into a passage, why not say so plainly?" "Go, go," she cried; "don't stay talking nonsense there, we shall be discovered." "I can't go now that I have upset you so about the well," he replied; and so the simple fellow continued talking until the husband came in and took them both for punishment before the king.' The lesson here is, in matters of importance, not to dispute about details, but to go to the main point.

Many of the apologues are fables of animals, not unlike those of Esop, whose fables also are originally Oriental; and throughout the Spanish version of *Kalila and Dimna* the Eastern influence is undisguised. Almost contemporary with this collection was another which became even more popular. This was the adaptation by Prince Fadrique, Alfonso the Learned's brother, of a set of moral stories from the Sanskrit through Arabic, called the *Book of Sindabad, or the Seven Sages*. Fadrique gave to his collection the ungallant name of *Tricks and Wiles of Women* (of which a translation in English has been published by the English Folklore Society). The fashion for proverbial philosophy and moral examples thereafter became a perfect craze throughout Europe. This *Book of the Seven Sages*, for instance, was translated into every modern language, and the stories, transformed to suit the manners and views of various peoples, became part of the lore of every country. The same may be said of the books which grew out of these moral tales. Such books took the form of collections of the tit-bits and aphorisms, culled from the discourses contained in the larger books, and in many cases also of collections of original didactic proverbs from the Hebrew. Within a few years of the death of Alfonso the Learned, *Poridad de Poridades*, *El libro de Buenos Proverbios*, *Flores de Filosofia*, and *Bocados de Oro*, appeared, and *Bocados de Oro* was afterwards translated into English by Lord Rivers, who was in Spain during the long siege of Granada. When Caxton began printing, one of the first books he published was a collection of these proverbs, called *Dictes and Sayings of the Philosophers*, many of which were taken from Lord Rivers's translation of the Spanish, and many more from the Spanish Oriental books already mentioned translated into French. Thus these Oriental pearls of wisdom, easy to learn and easy to recollect, became a part of the common knowledge of life possessed by all educated persons; and until the end of the seventeenth century, as we shall see later, it was considered a fashionable accomplishment for a gentleman to be able to compile a collection of sentences, as they were called, either original or extracted from the works of some stated author. Indeed there has been a revival of the fashion quite recently in England, where it is now common to see 'Birthday' books, or 'Beauties' from modern authors. But it was mainly from Spain, in renewed touch with the Orient, that the impetus for the sentcntious form came. So strong was the hold of the sententious proverb upon Spaniards, that even their florid satirical poetry was embroidered with it. The great satires of Lopez de Ayala (Rimado de Palacio) and of the Archpriest of Hita, an earlier Rabelais, were full of wise saws to enforce their moral. Perhaps the two most notable instances of the rhymed proverb are the world-famous collection of *Moral Proverbs* of the Spanish Jew, the Rabbi Sem Tob of Carrion, whose six hundred and eighty verses were written for Alfonso XI. in the fourteenth century, and the collection of *Proverbios* of the Marquis de Santillana written fifty years later.

A specimen or two of each set may be quoted, and it will be seen how, either directly or indirectly, the moral has become familiar to us. A thought, however trite and obvious it may seem to us from our familiarity with it, was not trite when it was first put into circulation. Read, for instance, this quatrain of Sem Tob's :—

'Quien los vientos guardare
Todos, non sembrara.
Quien los nubes catare
Jamas non segara.

'Who fears the winds, howe'er they
  blow,
Can never hope his grain to sow ;
And if he watches for the rain,
His sickle ne'er will reap the
  grain.

El oficio al hombre
  Es joya prestada.
Costumbre buena y nombre
  Es suya apropiada.

Our rank is but a jewel light
  Borrowed from day to day ;
Good actions and a record bright
  Possessions are ours for aye.

Al Rey solo conviene	Only the king should dare
Usar de franquesa,	His mind to speak to all,
Que segurança tiene	For he is free from care
De non venir en pobreza.	Lest poverty befall.
El fino acero sano	Forth from a broken case
Sale de rota vayna	Leaps there a shining blade ;
Y del fino del gusano	Out of the maggot base
Se fase seda fina.'	The glittering silk is made.'

More confessedly didactic in object were the other set of rhymed proverbs mentioned. They were by a great noble and poet who lived fifty or sixty years after Sem Tob, and died in 1458, Iñigo Lopez de Mendoza, Marquis de Santillana, who also came from Carrion. Of his lyrics, inspired as they were by Italian models, it is not necessary to speak here; but he shows himself in his folk-tales, *Rhymes that old women tell in the Chimney-corner*, and in his *Rhymed Proverbs*, a true Spaniard with the old traditions still strong upon him. These proverbs were written for the instruction of the Castilian prince, who afterwards became Henry IV. the Infirm ; and, like all the others that I have quoted, each verse inculcates a lesson. There is one point in connection with them, which shows how persistent was the Oriental tradition of instruction conveyed by maxims. It will be noticed in the *Book of Examples*, in *Kalila and Dimna* and others, that the mere enunciation of the example was not sufficient to enforce its own lesson; there must always follow (or, as in the *Book of Patronio*, precede) the illustration or text, a sort of sermon enlarging upon the lesson conveyed. It is the same here in Santillana's proverbs.

One would think, for instance, that this little verse carried its lesson clearly enough for anything—

'No rehuses recibir	'Spurn not contrition
al contrito.	with a frown.
Ni te plega al aflito	Beat not those down
Afligir.	in sore condition.
Que flaqueza es perseguir,	A coward chases
al que huye.	foes that fly.
y animo al que destruye	True courage high
resistir.'	Mercy graces.'—

and yet the writing of half a dozen classic philosophers, not to say holy writ, is ransacked for pages of 'gloss' or exposition of the simple, sufficient lesson.

The example of the bookish king—not a very encouraging one, for politically he was most unfortunate—was of course followed by his successors. As usual in such cases, it became in the late thirteenth and fourteenth centuries the fashion amongst gentlemen to write something, and that something had of course for the most part to be imitations of existing models. Alfonso's son, Sancho the Brave, busy as he was all his life fighting, yet found time to write books. Besides the translation of some Latin and French works that he ordered, he himself wrote two books which will illustrate the trend of Spanish culture soon after the death of Alfonso the Learned. The first book of Sancho the Brave is called *Lucidario*, and the object of it is to compare divine and human instruction. The plan of the work supposes a scholar living in a place where there are many schools of various branches of learning, desiring to investigate the questions and doubts that occur in the classes. This he seeks to do by discussing the points with his tutor, who endeavours to elucidate what the scholar finds difficult or obscure to understand. Every science and art, from theology to rhetoric, is brought under review by the curious scholar, and expounded by the omniscient tutor, and the type of this and many other such books written in Spain from the thirteenth to the fifteenth century may be seen with little change in our *Sandford and Merton* and similar works. Sancho the Brave wrote another book, notable as the forerunner of a school of didactic literature which afterwards flourished exceedingly, not only in Spain but also in Italy, though never to any very great extent in England. I refer to the books intended specially to teach morality, statesmanship, and perspicuity to young princes and nobles. They were often given as a rule of life by old or dying sovereigns or high ministers to their sons. Sancho the Brave's book, which is called *El Libro de los Castigos y Documentos*, or *Book of Punishments and Proofs*, was written three years before his death in 1292, for the guidance of his son Prince Ferdinand. It contains fifty chapters, in which is unfolded a complete moral and religious guide of conduct in all relations of life, public and private, rules for the guidance of political affairs, for management of men, and for behaviour in peace and war. As a specimen

of the tone of these counsels I will quote, in Spanish
and English, one of Don Sancho's chapters :—

' *Que fabla quant buena cosa es cordura, é como es
fija del buen entendimiento.*'

"Mio fijo: mete mientes en quant buena cosa es
cordura. La cordura es fija del buen entendimiento ; ca
ningund home non puede ser cuerdo si entendido no es.
Por cordura es el home guardado de muchos peligros,en
que podria caer á su gran danno. Cordura da al home
grant açosiego : primeramente en su corazon é en los
movimientos que face en su cuerpo, é en sus manos, é
en los fechos de su facienda. Asi como la cobdicia es
raiz de todos los males, asi el contrario desto, la
cordura es la raiz é aumento de todos los bienes. Por
cordura enriquesece el home : ca ninguno non puede
ser rico si asosiego de cordura non ha en si, é en la su
facenda. Pues por ende la cordura en si mesma da
asosiego al home con su verdat é non anda con ella
bulliendo. Por cordura se da el home por firme en las
cosas que ha de decir é de facer, é extrémase por ella
del arrebatadizo et movedizo que se mueve liviana-
mente con mal seso. La cordura es peso de balanza,
en que pesan al que la su pro ó su daño trae. La
cordura tuelle las cosas peligrosas, é de gran ventura,
é da las provechosas. La cordura da al home buena
fama y tuelle le de la mala. La cordura endereza la
facienda del home en esto mundo é la pro desu alma
para el otro mundo que muera en buen estado. La

cordura tuelle los malos pensamientos, é desvia los males que dellos podrian nascer,"—and more to the same effect. In English it may be rendered thus :—

' Chapter telling how good a thing moderation is, and how it is the daughter of good sense.'

" My son, take heed how good a thing is moderation ! Moderation is the child of good sense, for no man can be moderate unless he be of good understanding. Moderation shields a man from many dangers, which may otherwise bring him to grave trouble. Moderation gives to a man great peace, first in his heart and the movements of his body and hands, and secondly in his estate. Just as greed is the root of all evil, so is its opposite, moderation, the root and enlarger of all good ; for no man can be rich unless the peace which comes with moderation be with his body and estate. Besides, moderation itself gives peace to a man, and prevents him from giving way to excitement. Moderation gives a man confidence in what he has to say or do, and holds him aloof from the rash and fickle who are moved by levity and foolishness. Moderation is the weight on the balance that weighs the effect that good and bad bring to a man. Moderation averts risky and dangerous things, and brings profitable ones. Moderation gives a man good repute, and banishes evil repute. Moderation sets straight a man's goods in this world, and his soul in the next. Moderation stops bad thoughts and the evils they bring." Here you see that upon one moral proposition a series of separate aphorisms is hung, and the whole of Don Sancho's fifty chapters are worked out in the same way. First a truth is enunciated, and then it is set forth sententiously in its various phases. Any one of these aphorisms is such as you may see in intricate Arabic characters inscribed on Eastern doorways, or ornamental friezes, and even upon Oriental pottery or brass ware, to this day ; whilst the best and most epigrammatic of such aphorisms have been crystallised into the proverbial philosophy that has been fashionable in Europe from the time of the caliphs of Cordova to Martin Farquhar Tupper.

From Spain these didactic aphorisms, and a little later, as we shall see, the short moral tale or fable, extended to every corner of Europe.

I have spoken of Alfonso the Learned, his son Sancho the Brave, and his brother Prince Fadrique, and their literary activity. There was, however, another member of his family whose pure literary genius far exceeded that of any of them—Alfonso's nephew, the Prince Don Juan Manuel, who, following the example set to him, or rather improving upon it, wrote a series of didactic books of the highest importance, and one which must always be held as marking a great epoch in literary history. I refer to the *Libro de Patronio*, or, as it is usually called, *Count Lucanor*. Before dealing with this book at length, however, I wish to refer to some others of Don Juan Manuel's works, which exercised a far-reaching influence outside Spain. The author was born in 1282, and, although he was plunged in turbulent intrigue, war, and politics all his life, yet he managed to write fourteen books, of which nine still are known to exist; namely, the *Book of the Chase*, the *Book of the Knight and Squire*, the *Book of the Assumption*, the *Book of Three Reasons*, two chronicles, the *Book of the States*, the *Book of Punishments*, or *Castigos*, and, of course, the never to be forgotten *Count Lucanor*. It will be evident by the titles that they are all didactic, though freer in manner than the undisguised Oriental adaptations that had preceded them.

I wish to direct attention mainly to the three last books I have mentioned—the *Book of States*, *Castigos*, and *Count Lucanor*—the last two written for the instruction and amusement of his son. Don Juan Manuel's *Book of States* offers us several very interesting points. The book is, of course, didactic; and is supposed to represent the education of a pagan prince by his tutor, who, being unable to answer the boy's questions satisfactorily, begs the aid of a Christian priest. In the discussion and settlement of the various doubts suggested by the pupil, every possible point of political and religious ethics is dealt with; and the book was held to be a monument of wisdom both in Spain and abroad. But the most interesting thing about it is this: most of the illustrations are taken naturally from Oriental sources, which had filtered through the Jews and Moors of Spain, and amongst others is the famous legend of Barlaam and Josaphat. The book of Juan Manuel's was popular throughout Europe. The story was held to be true, and the Holy Saints and Martyrs Barlaam and Josaphat of India were canonised. Don Juan Manuel, in common with another author of his day, appears to have borrowed the idea of this legend from an Arabic version of a Sanskrit Buddhistic work. Josaphat (or rather Yudasatf) is the Arabic form of Buddha. This gives an idea of the extraordinary way in which these Oriental legends spread through Europe, and the strange mutations they underwent in changing from Buddhistic to Mohammedan, Jewish, or Christian mediums. Before passing to the consideration of Don Juan Manuel's famous *Book of Patronio*, reference may be made to another author who wrote in a similar vein to Don Juan Manuel somewhat later, and who also utilised this Arab Buddhistic version of Barlaam and Josaphat more unmistakably even than Juan Manuel. I refer to Clemente Sanchez in his *Book of Examples* (*Libro de Enjemplos*). This *Book of Examples* is perhaps the most interesting of the series. Many of the stories, most of them perhaps, are taken from a book in Latin called *Disciplina Clericalis*, by Petrus Alfonsus, who was really a converted Jew of Huesca, in Spain, named Rabbi Moses Sephardi, whose book Caxton printed in English. The *Libro de Enjemplos* contains an immense number of short tales, mostly religious; and in it may be found the germ of many tales of Boccaccio, the French fabulists, and Chaucer, though perhaps in most cases they came to us through the French and Italian rather than the Spanish version. Each tale is preceded by a little rhymed couplet, setting forth the moral which the story illustrates. One of the shortest may be chosen to give an idea of the style :—

> ' La limosna da gran crescemiento,
> Que por una cosa trae ciento.'

> ' Charity doth increase our store,
> For it returneth a hundred more.'

'There was a woman in England so sorely poor that all the gear she had in the wide world was one cow. One day she was in church, and the priest preached that God had promised to repay a hundred-fold what was given in charity. So she sold her cow and gave to the poor all it fetched, being covetous of the increase that was promised to her. One day, whilst she was standing with many other poor people at the bishop's door waiting for alms to be given to them, the bishop himself stopped for a moment and gazed upon them. And he noticed that this woman was carrying a lighted candle, which made him marvel greatly, thinking that perhaps she did so out of some special saintliness. He had her brought to him, and he questioned her as to who she was. "Alas!" she said, "I am a poor sinful woman, and I have no pro-

perty at all but a herd of cows that are coming to
me." "How is that?" asked the bishop. "I heard
a priest in church say that God would return a hundred-fold that which was given in charity, so I sold
my cow and gave its price to the poor, for I knew that
God would keep His promise, so I am sure of my
hundred cows soon." The bishop marvelled much at
her simple faith, and judged that God's will had led
him to notice this poor woman, in order that by a
miracle the Scriptures might be fulfilled. So he called
his steward, and, to the great delight of the woman,
ordered him to give her a hundred cows.'

We may now return to the Castilian prince, Don
Juan Manuel, and to his great book *El Libro de
Patronio*. It will have been remarked that up to this
time the Oriental apologue or moral tale, in inferior
hands, did not change very greatly when it was
turned into Spanish. It was simple, direct, and
biblical. But Don Juan Manuel was one of the great
literary geniuses of his age, and this book of his,
written, be it recollected, at the beginning of the
fourteenth century, is one of the epoch-making
books of the world. Apart from the brilliant, racy
Spanish in which it is written, the tales themselves
have in many cases taken a Spanish garb; the mind
behind them is no longer that of the simple, patriarchal
sage who speaks his words of wisdom in figura-
tive parable, but of a man of the world, who has done
and seen much, a keen intellect with a Spaniard's

characteristics of satire, subtlety, and floridness. The first, or completed, part of the book, consists of fifty-one stories, supposed to be told by the philosopher Patronio to a prince (or Count Lucanor). The stories afford the germs of many later ones that have become popular.[1] Boccaccio, who wrote only a few years later, probably did not borrow directly from Juan Manuel ; but the honour of being the forerunner of the real modern short story must be awarded to the Spanish prince. The book was enormously popular, and versions of it soon found their way to France and Italy, and thence many of the tales drifted to England. In more than one of the *Canterbury Tales* the influence of Don Juan Manuel may be seen. Calderon, the Spanish dramatist, borrowed plots from him, and of course Le Sage and other similar Frenchmen told the tales as their own. But the instance of most interest to us is the germ of the story of Shakespeare's *Taming of the Shrew.* It is extremely unlikely that Shakespeare can have had the story direct, but long before his time the tales of Juan Manuel had been translated, adapted, and copied extensively in France and Italy ; and there is no difficulty whatever in believing that the following story from *Count Lucanor* is the

---

[1] Don Juan Manuel's tales are clearly all from Oriental sources, though many of them cannot now be traced to the originals. Four of them are evidently taken from *Kalila and Dimna*, two from *Disciplina Clericalis*, by the converted Jew of Huesca, Rabbi Moses Sephardi, several from *Al Makkari*, and one from the *Book of Punishments* by Sancho the Brave.

origin, indirectly at least, of the *Taming of the Shrew.*

After detailing the circumstances that led up to the marriage of the young Moor with the termagant, the story continues thus :—

'Now, being left alone, the young couple sat down to supper, when the bridegroom, looking behind him, saw his mastiff, and said to him, "Bring me water wherein to wash my hands." The dog, of course, took no notice of this command, so the young man became angry and ordered the dog, more harshly than before, to bring him water for his hands. But still the dog heeded not, and his master rose in a great fury, drawing his sword and attacking the dog cruelly. The poor animal tried to escape, but finding no retreat, jumped upon the table and then to the hearth, his master still pursuing him until at last he caught him, hacked off his head and paws, and slashed the body into strips, covering everything with blood. Then, raging and bloodstained, the bridegroom returned to the table, and looking round saw a cat. "Bring me water for my hands," he cried loudly to the cat, who heeded him not. "What, false caitiff," he cried, "do you not see how I treated the mastiff for disobeying me? If you do not do as I tell you immediately, I will serve you the same." The poor cat stared innocently, taking no notice, and the master seizing him dashed him against the wall and killed him. Still roaring with fury he again took his seat at table, looking about him as if to find some other creature to attack, whilst his wife, thinking he had taken leave of his senses, held her peace. Soon his eyes caught his horse, the only one he had, and he called fiercely to him an order to bring water for his hands. The animal did not obey him, and he called out in a rage, " How is this ? Think you that because I have no other horse you can dare to disobey me ? Your fate shall be the same as that of the others : no creature living shall disregard my commands and escape my vengeance." Saying this he struck off the horse's head and hacked the body to pieces.

' When the wife saw this, knowing he had no other horse, she felt that he was really in earnest, and was dreadfully frightened. He again sat down to table raging and dripping with blood as he was, swearing that he would kill a thousand horses, or even men or women, if they dared to disobey him. Holding his bloody sword in his hand he glared around until, fixing his eyes upon his wife, he ordered her to bring him water to wash his hands. She, expecting no other fate than to be cut to pieces if she demurred, immediately rose and brought him the water. " Ha ! thank God, you have brought it," he said; " if not, I was so irritated by these senseless brutes, I should have served you the same." He afterwards ordered her to serve him with meat. She complained ; but he warned her in a threatening

D

tone of voice to take care, as he felt as if he was going mad. Thus passed the night, she not daring to speak, but meekly obeying all his orders. After letting her sleep for a short time he said to her, "Get up; I have been so much annoyed that I cannot sleep; take care that nothing is allowed to disturb me, and in the meantime prepare for me a good meal."

'While it was yet early the following morning, the fathers and mothers and other relatives came stealthily to the door of the bride and bridegroom, and hearing no movement feared that the young man was either dead or badly wounded; and they became still more alarmed when the bride came to the door alone. She, seeing them, went tremblingly on tiptoe towards them, and exclaimed in accents of fear, "What do ye, ye traitors? Dare not approach the gate; hold your peace and make no sound, for if you wake him we are all as good as dead!" When they heard this they marvelled greatly, and on learning what had passed the night before, they esteemed highly the young man who had made so good a beginning in the management of his house. The wife from that day grew docile and complaisant, and they led a very happy life.'

Although the machinery of these tales is similar to that of the other collections I have mentioned— namely, the didactic sage that teaches a young prince by fables, it is plain that here the story rather than

the application that follows it is the main point, the
moral being confined to a note at the end saying
that Count Lucanor was pleased with the lesson read
to him by Patronio; and as Don Juan found the
example a good one he had set it down in his book
with this verse, and then follows a couplet enshrin-
ing the moral. It will be useful to compare the
manner of Don Juan Manuel with that of Chaucer.
It will be noticed that in each case the presentation
is racy and personal, and though the works differ as
widely as the personalities of the authors, it is evident
throughout that the fashion of the story had reached
Chaucer from a source where the influence of Don
Juan Manuel had been strong. The Spanish Oriental
apologue with its applied lesson was the indirect inspiration, rather than the Italian story without a
moral, which had come down from the classic authors,
and had been shorn of its application in the descent.

Another curious instance of the international exchange of these stories, and the prevailing fashion
for them in all countries at the time, is the case of a
book called *El Libro de los Gatos*, a most popular book
of moral apologues which was produced in Spanish
in the early fourteenth century, but is a translation of a certain collection written in Latin by an
English monk named Odo of Cheriton. Where he
found his inspiration one knows not, but it is probable that it was from the Latin. Anyhow, the
Book of the Cats, which is the name of the Spanish

version, is extremely Spanish, though quite Oriental in the insistence upon the moral of each story. One story relates how a man came upon another who was ploughing and had yoked some beetles to his plough as well as the oxen. In reply to the surprise expressed at this, the ploughman says that every little helps. But the moral is that when the ploughing was done and the beetles unyoked they obstinately refused to return home to the comfort of the farmhouse with the man and his oxen, but preferred to stay in the field. Just, so the moral runs, like some men who, though they may have been chastised by God, prefer to remain in their sin rather than return to goodness. As a specimen of this class of story, which formed a large part of the reading of the fourteenth and fifteenth centuries, one other short apologue from this *Book of the Cats* may be quoted, showing the transformation of the Oriental apologue after it had passed through a Spanish as well as an English medium. 'In a certain convent there was a cat which had killed all the mice in the house but one, which was a very big one she never could get hold of. The cat mused in what manner she might beguile the mouse and kill him ; and she thought so long and deeply that at last she made up her mind that she must take the veil, and, clothed in a nun's garb, take her seat at the table with the rest. So she did as she had thought, and the mouse when he saw the cat demurely eating with the nuns rejoiced greatly, thinking that since the cat had now become a religious sister she would do him no harm. Mr. Mouse came and frolicked about where the nuns were eating; and the cat turned up the whites of her eyes as one who had abandoned all earthly vanities and follies. When the mouse saw how peaceful and pious her countenance looked, he ventured nearer and nearer in his play; but once when the cat saw him near enough she pounced upon him with her claws and began to choke him. So the mouse cried out: "Fie! thou a nun, to be so cruel as to want to kill me." Whereupon the cat replied: "Think not thy cries will make me let thee go; for know, my son, that when it suits me I am a nun, and when I like I am a lay sister."'

Odo of Cheriton was not the only Englishman whose works were turned into Spanish in these early times. There was one Roger Hoveden in the twelfth century who wrote in Latin a book of didactic form, and of this book there is in the Escorial Library a Spanish translation of the fourteenth century called *El Espejo de Legos* (*The Layman's Mirror*), and in the chapter upon pastoral literature it will be shown that John Gower's famous *Confessio Amantis* in English was also translated late in the fourteenth century into Spanish.

Thus we have in Spain, and percolating thence through Europe, from the thirteenth century onward, a great mass of didactic and proverbial literature in more immediate touch with the original Oriental sources than was the similar literature of the Italian renaissance, which drew its inspiration through earlier Greek and Latin adaptations. But even the Italian forms were partly coloured by Spanish Orientalism. The *Prince* of Machiavelli, the *Cortegiano* of Castiglione, the *Maxims of State* of Botero, and many other similar works intended for the instruction of young Italian princes, and popular throughout Europe as the quintessence of wisdom, are clearly inspired by the similar works in Spanish already mentioned. All this, of course indirectly, influenced English literature, in common with others. But there came a time in the sixteenth century when the influence of Spanish thought and form over English letters was direct and extensive.

The coming of Catharine of Aragon to England brought hither Spanish bishops, professors, and courtiers with Spanish books and modes of thought, though Latin was the tongue in which they mostly wrote and spoke in England. One of them, the famous Latinist Luis Vives, who was the great friend of Sir Thomas More, a professor at Oxford and tutor to Mary, Queen of England, wrote all his books in Latin, and two of them particularly had an immense popularity when they were translated into English by Sir Richard Moryson and Richard Hyrde. The most famous of them was called *Instruction of a Christian Woman*, which was published in English by Hyrde in

1540, and ran through at least four editions before the end of the century. The *Introduction to Wisdom*, translated by Moryson, was also very popular in England; and together these books, and above all Vives's direct personal influence on English scholars, did much to introduce the fashion of Spanish didacticism into the courts of the Tudors. But there was another man whose influence was much greater everywhere, and especially so in England, even than that of Vives. This was Antonio de Guevara, Bishop of Mondoñedo, the Confessor of the Emperor Charles V. To modern readers that influence appears to be quite inexplicable at first sight, for the books of his which were such a rage in England are certainly not wiser than the long series of didactic works that we have already noticed. After saying something of the books themselves, it may be possible, however, to suggest a reason for their popularity other than the subject-matter they contain.

The most famous of these books was in the form of a literary mystification, and was called *The Dial of Princes*, though subsequently it became better known as *The Golden Book of Marcus Aurelius*. Guevara pretended to have found certain manuscripts of the Spanish Cæsar, and upon them he bases his book—a set of moral apologues, infinitely tedious they seem to us now, in which Marcus Aurelius is made to show his wisdom, by improving the occasion whenever possible, and reading a lesson suggested by events. The book was considered in England as the fine quintessence of political subtlety, and its maxims were collected and repeated in the court of Elizabeth by every one who aspired to literary taste. The first man of note to set the fashion of Guevara in England was Lord Berners, who translated the *Book of Marcus Aurelius* through a French version in 1534. Then Sir Francis Bryan, Henry VIII.'s favourite, translated another of Guevara's books called *Dispraise of the Life of a Courtier* (*Menosprecio de la Corte y Alabanza de la Aldea*), which was afterwards republished as *Looking Glasse for the Court*. Thenceforward edition after edition of Guevara's works was published in England. *The Golden Book of Marcus Aurelius* especially caught on, and allusions to it, and extracts from it, abound in Elizabethan literature. One of the stories in it, referring to the Serf of the Danube, was so familiar that everybody in Elizabethan England was supposed to understand it. For instance, in the curious *Chronicle of Henry VIII.*, written by a Spanish merchant then resident in London, the author tells how a London butcher came to complain to the Privy Council of the enclosures of common land by the nobles, and says that he evidently intended to imitate the Serf of the Danube when he addressed the Senate. Casaubon, in his prologue to *Marcus Aurelius*, truly says: ' Hardly another book in the world except the Bible has been so often translated and into so many tongues, or has been so frequently reprinted.' It may be interesting to tell in a few words what this famous story was.

The plan of the Serf of the Danube part of the book is to bring a noble barbarian from the banks of the Danube to Rome, to complain of the oppression and cruelty with which his native land is being ruled by the Roman officers; and into his mouth is put an address to the Senate containing all the subtlety, eloquence, boldness, and philosophy of which Guevara was master. It is in its substance a great oration in favour of liberty. The scene is supposed to take place in the tenth year of the reign of Marcus Aurelius. The emperor was ill and surrounded by doctors and sages, who were deploring the decay and degeneration of Rome, which they attributed to the hosts of idle flatterers who surrounded the governors. Marcus Aurelius then tells his tale of how the Danubian serf had come to Rome some years before. This is how the emperor is made to describe the eloquent serf:—' His face was small, with thick lips and deeply sunken dark eyes. His hair was rough and stubborn, his head uncovered. He wore sandals of porcupine skin, and a tunic of goat's hide, and a girdle of sedge rushes confined his waist. His beard was long and thick; and his neck and chest as hairy as those of a bear; and in his hand he carried an olive staff. Surely when I saw him enter, I thought him to be some animal in the guise of man, but when I heard him speak it seemed to me that he must be one of the gods.' The discourse, in the highest and most pompous style of eloquence, pleads the old, old cause of the contented peasant against the great conquering empire. 'I ask you, O Romans! what had you, bred upon the banks of the Tiber, to do with us who lived in humble peace by the rushing Danube? Did you see us join your foes or declare our enmity to you? Did the lying rumour reach you here in Rome that we were seeking conquest? Did you hear that we had dared to raise our hands against our lords, and bend our necks to the unvanquished barbarian? Did you send any envoy to us to ask for our love, or did we send defiance unto you?' and so, after exhausting possible reasons for the Roman conquest and oppression of his native land, the serf breaks out into an impassioned appeal for freedom, his eloquence being rewarded by his being given full Roman citizenship and the oppression he complained of remedied.

Other chapters of this famous book tell how Marcus Aurelius's wife Faustina asks him for the key of his study, and the emperor improves the occasion. No woman or child had ever been allowed to enter. 'I would with a lighter heart,' he said, 'be robbed of my treasure-chest than have my books disturbed.' Faustina had set her mind upon going in, and wept, and prayed, and railed in vain. The emperor replies in a tremendous speech, crammed with philosophy and epigrams, which, unless Roman women were different from those of to-day, Faustina must have thought quite inapplicable to the case, and he winds up with a set of eighteen rules by which wives may live happily with their husbands. The first is: 'A husband should be patient and tolerant when his wife is angry, for there is no serpent so poisonous as an affronted woman.' The fourteenth is: 'The husband should take care that, even if his wife is ugly, he should pretend that she is beautiful; for there is nothing more likely to raise strife between them than for her to think that the husband disregards her for want of comeliness.' But it is to be noted that after he has laid down in seventeen rules how much the husband is to consider his wife, he ends rather ungallantly. 'The husband ought to give way in things of *no* importance and grant his wife her way even if she is wrong, for a woman would rather be acknowledged right even in a lie than have a revenue of six thousand a year.' But after all this philosophy Faustina had to go without the key.

Guevara's *Familiar Letters* was also much admired and read in England. What was the reason that caused this great fashion for Guevara's turgid, inferior philosophy throughout Europe? It always happens, and particularly in Spain, because of the vehement literary floridness of the race, that any given literary form becomes by familiarity trite to readers. The constantly recurring commonplace phrases to describe the same things become wearisome and conventional, and then extravagance of diction, eccentric expressions, compound, manufactured words, and strange preciosity take the place of direct simplicity, and are hailed as the highest of literary excellences by the thoughtless. Then, unless stern good sense prevails, and a pure standard is maintained by some, the literature becomes artificial, overloaded, and top-heavy, and falls into ridiculous bathos. This is what had begun to happen in sixteenth-century Spain, and Guevara's far-fetched images, and platitudes clothed in extravagant language, appealed to a jaded literary taste. There was really in England no natural tendency that way yet, because, far from being decadent, we were just entering upon the most vigorous and splendid of our literary epochs; but there are always some exquisites who love eccentricity and can set the fashion. This is exactly what happened in Elizabeth's court with regard to Guevara. The proverbial philosophy in terse maxims or epigrams, culled from his writings and those of others, appealed to a large class in England and elsewhere, and kept alive the fashion of proverbial philosophy so conspicuous in Shakespeare and his contemporaries. But there was another class to whom Guevara's extravagant and artificial style was the principal attraction; and the result was the formation of a school which found its first expression in the famous novel by John Lilly called *Euphues*. The affected style of this book attracted disciples, and euphuism was one of the literary bogies of the sixteenth century. But this strange eccentricity, which ran its affected course without great harm in

England, found a firmer footing in Spain. There Gongora, a poet of high rank, carried affectation to an absurd length. Quevedo, whilst laughing and sneering at the fashion, followed what he called the *Latiniparla* as much as anybody. Lope de Vega himself fell into the bad habit; and by and by the fertile orchard of Spanish literature was choked with the weeds of affected pomposity.

Guevara's influence in England in the direction of obscurity and involution of style was great, as any one who reads the letters of Queen Elizabeth and her imitators may see; but it was still more remarkable in fixing the fashion of the proverbial form of philosophy. Bacon's *Apophthegms*, Lord Burghley's *Maxims for the Guidance of his Son*, Sir Walter Raleigh's *Maxims of State*, Sir Francis Walsingham's *Legacy*, and a dozen other similar works of the period which will occur to the reader, prove how universally the minds of scholars and statesmen at the time ran upon the Spanish form of thought derived from the sententious learning of Hebrews and Arabs reintroduced to modern Europe through Moslem Spain. Perhaps a more direct influence even than Guevara upon English literary fashion in the same direction, was that of the exiled minister of Philip II., Antonio Perez, who wrote his books and letters in his extravagantly affected style at Essex House in the Strand. He too was so much in love with his own gems of wisdom that he culled them himself from his various books and letters, and printed them as an addenda to his *Relations*. Perez was the pet for a time of the greatest literary set in England, that which sat under the shade of Essex and the Bacons, and his affected wit and preciosity, as well as his sententious philosophy, set its mark upon most of the English writing of the end of the sixteenth century, side by side with the similar impress produced by the books of his countryman Antonio de Guevara.

CHAPTER III

THE CRONICAS, HISTORIES, AND RECORDS OF
PERSONAL ADVENTURE

THE Spaniard is, and always has been, personally the most independent of all Europeans. The accident of poverty or lowly station does not, in the mind of the average Spaniard affected by it, connote any personal inferiority on his own part; and whatever political or social changes may have been effected in the country, the base principle of Spanish ethics never has changed, and never will change, to any great degree ; namely, that one free man is as good as another under a supreme power, great and sacred enough to dwarf all minor distinctions, whilst each individual, high or low, rich or poor, in some sort focusses upon himself the admiring regards of his Maker. This proud mysticism, and the conviction of individual centralisation natural to the Celt-Iberians, was greatly strengthened by the long centuries of the reconquest over the Moors, which owed its principal impetus and strength to priestly incentive, urging the Christians ever forward with the idea they were the chosen people to vanquish the enemies of God and of His evangel. When the learned King Alfonso x. in the thirteenth century summoned to him the sages and scribes of the land to form a literature in the Castilian language, and when thereafter the Spanish people was seized with a fever of literary production, in imitation of their king, it is not so surprising as it looks at first sight, that history in the Castilian language should assume a form more closely connected with the doings and personality of the sovereign, than was the case in any other European country. Even before the time of Alfonso the Learned, his father had ordered Ximenez de la Rada, Archbishop of Toledo, to write in Castilian his *History of the Gothic Kings*; and the material for the book was drawn doubtless from the official records kept by order of the kings themselves by churchmen. But when Alfonso the Learned set about his task of compiling a *History of Spain* down to his own accession, he broke through a tradition that had up to that time been universal; namely, that records of events should be written by clergymen, mostly monks. Thenceforward the chroniclers of the Spanish kings were high palace officials, with the rank of chancellors, knights and nobles, who themselves took active part in the stirring scenes they recorded.

How differently would such a man, a literary noble layman, in a bookish court, record the history of his time than would a monk in his cell, depending upon old charters, official diaries, and personal recollections for his information. Glance for a moment at the chronicles and early histories of our own land, and see how great is the difference between the two classes of historians. Take the *Saxon Chronicle*, as it is called, of which the main portion was written in the tenth century. There the king, of course, is mentioned incidentally, for he was the most important person in the realm ; but the events in the *Chronicle* are not grouped around the personality of the king in any way. At random I have translated from the *Saxon Chronicle* the entries for five successive years, which will explain the distinction :—

829. This year died Archbishop Wulfred ; and Abbot Fologild was afterwards chosen to the See on the 25th April, and consecrated on Sunday the 11th June. On the 13th of August he was dead.

830. This year Coelnoth was chosen Archbishop on the death of Abbot Fologild.

831. This year Archbishop Coelnoth received the pall.

832. This year the heathen men overran the Isle of Sheppy.

833. This year fought King Egbert with thirty-five pirates at Chartmouth, where a great slaughter was made, and the Danes remained masters of the field. Two bishops, Hereford and Wigan, and two aldermen, Dudda and Omond, died in this year.

Any one can tell at a glance that a churchman must

F

have written this, and that the personal actions of the king are not the central point of the history. Take two other very early English monkish chroniclers, Gildas and Bede. Although the latter was in advance of his age, and really had an idea of writing a broader narrative than could be gathered from his monastery records, and sets down the acts of kings when they come into his story, his chronicle is far more concerned with religious affairs than with royal adventures; whilst that of Gildas is almost confined to ecclesiastical matters. It is true that two chroniclers in the twelfth century, Geoffrey of Monmouth and William of Malmesbury, wrote professedly chronicles of kings. But Geoffrey of Monmouth's *Historia Britonum* was merely a translation of an ancient Welsh or Celtic book, written under the Roman domination of Britain ; and the character of the native Britons was like that of the Spaniards, with whom they were akin, mystically devoted to a sovereign religiously sanctified, quite different from the Saxon and Norman idea of a military chief ruling by consent of armed nobles. William of Malmesbury, who wrote his *Gesta Regum Anglorum* about 1135, and depended for most of his facts of early times upon previous narrators, was a man of genius who tried, like Bede (whom he copied), to write a real history of the times ; and it was obviously the most convenient way to tell his national events by reigns of kings. But even he does not make the personal adventures or movements of the king his central point, and constantly strays far away from the king altogether to tell some legendary tale or old prophecy, to give an account of St. Dunstan, to describe the great abbey of Glastonbury, or to copy old monastic charters. These chroniclers bring us down almost to the time when the real kingly chronicle took root in Spain. Later on we shall see how English chroniclers of the fourteenth century and after were influenced, as I believe, by the more directly personal heroic chronicle of the acts of sovereigns as the central point of historical narrative, which was so fashionable in Spain for two centuries after the days of Alfonso the Learned.

Alfonso's grandiose but impracticable plan of writing a universal history from the Creation to his own times, remains mainly as a monument of the vastness of his ambition, for no trustworthy material existed for its realisation ; but his *History of Spain* was a really creditable attempt to produce a faithful record of events. In the compilation of such a book at the instance of a sovereign, the authors would naturally seek their information from palace records, either in the original or in the writings of previous compilers who had had access to them. We have it on the authority of another chronicler who lived some years afterwards, and of whom I shall speak at length presently, that 'King Alfonso X., wishing that the deeds of the kings before him should be set down, ordered the records to be searched, and found that the acts of the kings from the coming of the Goths to the fall of Don Rodrigo, the last Gothic king, and from Don Pelayo to Don Ferdinand, had been written in the books of the Privy Chamber.' These sources, together with court traditions and juglars' recitations, furnished Alfonso X. with the material of his first chronicle or *History of Spain*. It is obvious that a history drawn from such founts must necessarily develop on heroic personal lines with the monarch as the central figure; quite different from the history growing out of a churchman's records, where ecclesiastical personages and affairs would loom large, and where battles, invasions, famines, and pageants would probably be mentioned, with the sovereign as an actor in them; but where the king would not be followed from day to day, as the centre from which events radiated. At the very birth, therefore, of Spanish historical writing, it assumed a knightly and heroic personal form quite different from that of other countries. It was another instance where the influence of the mystical and devotional Celt-Iberian character was seen; and another new cast back to the Hebrew, Persian, and early classical tradition, which made the king the centre of all movement, as you may see it was by the Book of Kings in the Bible, and by the works of Herodotus and Josephus. The example of the learned king made culture fashionable in Spain; and princes and nobles vied with each other during the later thirteenth and fourteenth centuries in writing verses, didactic treatises, and sets of apologues, proverbs, and sentences, such as those mentioned in the previous chapter. Don Juan Manuel, the nephew of the king, was the greatest *littérateur* of his time ; the king's brother, Don Fadrique, wrote several books ; the learned king's son, Don Sancho the Brave, wrote and inspired the important works I have mentioned ; and at a period when, in England at least, a knight or a noble scorned the art of reading and writing as only fit for a shaveling monk, the gentlemen of Spain—not ecclesiastics—were busy creating a national literature. Even in the other Spanish kingdom of Aragon the nephew of Alfonso the Learned, the great James the Conqueror, was caught by the infection of the kingly chronicle, and wrote a vigorous and heroic record of his own reign.

Don Juan Manuel's chronicles are merely summaries or abbreviations of Alfonso's *History of Spain* ; and it was left to the initiative of Alfonso XI. (1297-1350), the learned king's great-grandson, to continue the compilation of the kingly chronicles. He for the first time appointed a regular royal chronicler, a high state official and noble with the rank of chancellor. The man appointed was in all probability Fernan Sanchez de Tobar, and at the command of the king he undertook to write a history of the kings from the death of St. Ferdinand (1252), when Alfonso X.'s chronicle had ended, down to his own day ; namely, the reigns of Alfonso the Learned, King Sancho, his son, King

Ferdinand IV., his grandson, and Alfonso XI. himself
—in all, about eighty years. Some short chapters of
this and succeeding chronicles may be quoted in order
that we may follow the development, or rather the
degeneration, of the style. The chronicle written by
Alfonso the Learned had been terse, and evidently
sincere, with a desire to record the deeds of the kings
plainly from official sources or from trustworthy
knowledge. That this was still the influence under
which Sanchez de Tobar began his work at the
instance of Alfonso XI. is evident from the preamble
of his chronicle:—

"By many means the ancient sages thought well
that the things which were said and done in bygone
times should be made known, both because they were
important in themselves, and that they might serve as
examples for those who came afterwards, for all time
to come. This was done also for the science of
astronomy and other sciences, to relate the stories of
the prophets, the coming of Christ, and the laws of
God. It is therefore desirable that the deeds of the
kings who are the lieutenants of God on earth should
also be written down, especially those of the kings of
Castile and Leon, who by the decrees of the Almighty,
and for the increase of the Holy Catholic Faith, strove
so worthily and faced so many perils in the struggle
against the Moors. The most noble King Alfonso X.,
wishing that the deeds of the kings before him should
be set down, ordered the óld records to be searched,

and found that the deeds of the kings from the time of the Goths to the fall of Don Roderick, and those from Don Pelayo to St. Ferdinand, had been written in the books of the Privy Chamber. As many deeds have been done by the kings since then which have not been chronicled, and as Don Alfonso XI. thought that these worthy deeds were falling into oblivion, he determined that the things that befell in the time of his great-grandfather, the learned king, his grandfather King Sancho, and his father Don Ferdinand, should be written down in this book so that posterity should know what had happened in those reigns."

When Alfonso the Learned endeavoured to get himself elected Emperor of the West in 1275 he left his second son, Sancho, as his regent during his absence from Spain. The eldest son, Ferdinand, had died, leaving two sons, the Infantes of La Cerda, as they were called. According to the Roman law these children were the heirs to the crown, but the Gothic elective principle, and the Oriental tradition of the rights of the oldest surviving member of the family, were still strong; and Sancho during his father's absence got the nobles around him to fight the Moors, and obtained their support to his claim to the heirship. This is how Sanchez de Tobar tells what happened thereupon :—

'*How the king* (i.e. *Alfonso X.*) *returned from the Empire, and how he mustered his people to consider the demands of Don Sancho.*

" In the twenty-fourth year of the reign of this king
(*i.e.* 1276), the King Don Alfonso arrived at Requena,
having come through the realm of Valencia, and so
passed by Cuenca to Alcalá de Henares. There he
learnt that the Infante Don Sancho, his son, and the
nobles, had defended the country well in his absence,
and he much rejoiced at what Don Sancho had done.
He had always cherished him as a son, but thenceforward he loved him more than ever. He departed
towards Camarena, near Toledo, where he remained
for the greater part of the year, as he did not choose
to enter the city, but sent word to Don Sancho that
he had come. As he had no means of making war
and was ignorant of the state of his realm, he tried to
make peace with Aben Yusuf, and with the King of
Granada. Aben Yusuf rejoiced thereat, for the
Christian fleet that Don Sancho had sent to the coast
had cut off the Moor's supplies and his people were
nearly starving, and also because he coveted the ports
of Algeciras and Tarifa, which he then held and
wished to keep, to enable him to take ship whenever
it pleased him. He also induced him to join in the
two years' truce which he signed with Don Alfonso.
Thereupon the Infante Don Sancho and the nobles
who were with him went to Toledo to see the king,
and when they were all assembled, Don Lope Diaz
spoke to them all frankly in the name of Don Sancho,
asking them to demand of the king that Don Sancho
should inherit the crown after his father's death,

as they were all satisfied with what the son had done during the king's absence. And as Don Sancho was the eldest (living) son, they agreed to this; and Don Lope Diaz spoke to the king, saying how well Don Sancho had acted in his absence in defending the honour of the realm and protecting it from the Moors, after the Infante Don Ferdinand had died. He said that Don Sancho was now the eldest son living, and that all the assembly were agreed in praying the king to make him his heir. He prayed that the king would send to all the cities, ordering them to send representatives with powers to agree to this. It would be, said he, a favour to Don Sancho, but a greater favour to his own state and authority, as well as filling the hearts of his people with joy at Don Sancho's elevation. The king replied that he dearly loved and esteemed Don Sancho, who was well fitted to be a king, but he must take time to consider their petition, and would give them an answer later. So he summoned the Infante Don Manuel and the rest of his council, to tell them what Don Lope had said, and ask their advice thereupon. All the councillors present murmured, and doubted much what advice to give. Then up and spake Don Manuel thus: Señor, the tree of kingship may not be blighted by arrangements thus, nor can he be disinherited who by Nature's self is chosen for the crown. If the first-born die, the inheritance must pass to his children

one by one. There are three things that no compromise can change : the law, the king, and the state ;
and if in any of them an alteration be made, the
act is illegal and may not be respected. And in
the accounts that exist of this council, there is no
record of more words than these having been spoken.
As soon as the king learned that the truce had
been signed with the Moors, he travelled to Segovia
accompanied by his nobles. From thence he sent
orders to the towns to send their representatives to
Segovia fully authorised to pay homage to Don
Sancho as heir to the crown."

The next chapter tells in a similar direct style the
story of the famous Cortes of Segovia, in which
Sancho's usurpation was confirmed by the conni-
vance of the feeble king ; the escape of Alfonso's wife,
Violante of Aragon, with the rightful child heirs and
their mother, Blanche of France ; and the execution
of some of the Castilian nobles who had conspired
in their favour. But the chapter already given will
suffice as a specimen of the arid simplicity of the
narrative. Yet compared with the more impersonal
chronicle of Alfonso X. himself, written three-quarters
of a century earlier, the development in individual
interest is remarkable. The intensely individual
character of the Spaniard was already manifesting
itself, and the court chronicler, a layman and an
aristocrat, was even thus early developing the
chivalric, romantic element in history, which differ-

entiated the Spanish form from that which grew out of monastic records in other countries.

The lines in which the same chronicler tells of the death of King Sancho, demonstrate how personal and vivid the relation became when the events related happened within the observation of the writer:—

"And Don Nuño Gonzalez, son of Don Juan Nuñez, who was there, and other nobles, with all the gentry and people of Toledo, made very great lamentation ; and you or any other man could not think how great it was. And the Archbishop Don Gonzalo with all the clergy, and with the priestly knights and all the nobles, took the body on the same day in the morning, and they carried it to the church of Santa Maria in Toledo, and the Infante Don Enrique and Don Nuño, with the queen, made very great lamentation. And the Archbishop straightway said mass, and when it was finished, they interred the body in a stone monument which he had ordered to be made during his lifetime."

This, artless as it is, plainly discloses the spectator and courtier, to whom the person of the sovereign is the centre of interest. In the later chronicle by the same writer, written after the death of Alfonso XI. (1350) by the order of Henry II., the personal note is carried still further. The chronicler is telling how the young king Alfonso XI., at the age of fourteen, threw off the tutelage of his uncle Don Manuel by a *coup d'état*, and took the government into his own hands :—

'How the king set up his household, and what men he took for his councillors, and what he did afterwards.'

" In the realm there were two gentlemen who have already been mentioned in this history. One of them was a Castilian called Garcilaso de la Vega, and the other a Leonese whose name was Alvar Nuñez de Osorio. Both of them were able and worthy men in all things. Before the king had reached his fourteenth year, and had left Valladolid, these two gentlemen had caused him to be spoken to on their behalf, and they also sought some plan by which they might gain audience of the king. They agreed when the king should leave Valladolid they would meet him on the borders of their lordships. As soon as the king attained his fourteenth year and left Valladolid, they did as they had agreed ; and, although the king knew that they and their bands had harried the land, their wisdom was great, and he admitted them to his council. And inasmuch as for many years it had been the custom for kings of Castile to have in their households Jews as treasurers, the king at the instance of his uncle, Don Felipe, took for his almajar (treasurer) one Yusuf de Ecija, who had a great place in the household and much power in the kingdom by the king's favour to him." Then follows an account of the organisation of the council, and Alfonso's speech to the nobles and

representatives, saying that he would take the government in his own hands, reduce taxes, reinforce the
border castles, and go through the realm on a justice
assize.—*Chronicle of Alfonso XI.*

These chronicles, you will observe, were so far un-
adorned records of royal adventure, but abounding
in personal interest, and quite different in tone from
the monkish and priestly chronicles that at the same
time were being produced in England. But a genius
was at hand who was able to make the kingly
chronicle interesting as history, whilst still retaining
its heroic and personal character. I shall dwell upon
this historian at some length, because I conceive
that his example, or at least the same spirit that
animated him, was soon afterwards felt in the writing
of English and French history.

The man to whom I refer was the chancellor and
official chronicler of Peter the Cruel and Henry II.,
Pedro Lopez de Ayala (1332-1407). He was a noble
of very high lineage, cf great powers of observation,
a keen satirist, and a charming writer in prose and
verse. He had studied classic models, especially Livy,
and was learned in other tongues than his own.
His career was as extraordinary as his talent. A
friend and favourite of Peter the Cruel, he deserted
him in the great civil war which ended in the triumph
of the king's bastard brother, Henry of Trastamare.
He was in the thick of the fighting when the Black
Prince and all the chivalry of England were battling

on the plains of Castile for the evil cause of Peter the Murderer. It was said, indeed, that when Lopez de Ayala was taken prisoner by our Plantagenet he was carried to England, where he wrote some of his works. This I do not believe ; but that he was held prisoner by the English in Gascony is fairly well established. Under four kings Lopez de Ayala served, and he saw all that two eyes with a big brain behind them could see through a long life in courts and on battlefields. He witnessed and recorded not only the war of Peter the Cruel against his brothers, but the marriage of Peter the Cruel's daughter to John of Gaunt, and the long series of wars which followed the Duke of Lancaster's claim to the crowns of Castile in the right of his wife. He saw the final settlement of the struggle by the marriage of an English princess, Catharine of Lancaster, to the king of Castile, and English knights and nobles received at her court with open arms. This was the man who gilded the kingly *Chronicle* of Spain with his own genius, making of the records of four monarchs not dry statements of royal movements, but vivid representations of the events that passed around the king. A few specimens of Lopez de Ayala's prose may be quoted, in order that we may see, first, how it influenced the writing of history outside Spain, and secondly how, by its very brilliance, it marks in one direction a decline. This is how Lopez de Ayala tells of the marriage of faithless Peter the Cruel with

his wife, Blanche of Bourbon, and his prompt desertion
of her for his mistress Maria de Padilla :—

"When these things had passed, the King Don Pedro
celebrated his nuptials with Doña Blanca at St. Mary's
at Valladolid. There was much rejoicing, with brave
jousts and tournaments. And on that day Don Pedro
and his bride were dressed in garments of gold and silver
tissue lined with ermine, and they were mounted on
white chargers. The best man to the king was Don
Juan Alfonso de Albuquerque, and the queen was given
away by Queen Leonora of Aragon, who rode upon a
mule and was dressed in white woollen cloth with grey
feathers. By the side of Queen Blanca there walked,
holding the reins of her palfrey, Count Enrique [here
there follows a long list of nobles]. The Infante Don
Ferdinand of Aragon held the reins of Queen Doña
Leonora, his mother, whilst the king's mother, the
Queen Doña Maria, rode on a mule led by the Infante
Don Juan of Aragon, she being dressed in white silk
brocade trimmed with fur and feathers,"—and so on,
with a description of the dress, or some characteristic
touch of all the members of the court.

"On the Wednesday after the wedding, the king
dined in his palace, which was the house of the Abbot
of Santander, where he was staying, near to the
monastery that is now called the Huelgas. He was
alone and in private, seated at table, when his
mother, Doña Maria, and his aunt, Queen Doña
Leonora, entered the chamber weeping bitterly. The

king rose, and the queens took him aside and said:
Sir, to our grief we have been told that you are going
away at once to join Doña Maria de Padilla, and we
beseech you not to do so." Here follows a long
speech, setting forth how wrong such a course would
be, and how it would offend everybody, and especially
the king of France; and the narrative continues: "The
king assured them that he had no such intention, and
would not go away. So the two queens left him,
though they did not believe what he said; and they
knew he was going away, though they were powerless
to stop him."

More spirited still is the story told by Lopez de
Ayala of Peter the Cruel's murder by his brother, the
bastard pretender, Henry of Trastamare.

'How Don Pedro sallied from Montiel and died.'

"When Don Enrique had defeated the enemy at
Montiel and saw that Don Pedro had taken refuge in
the castle of Montiel, he took great care to surround
the castle with stone parapets, and posted guards by
night and day all about, in order to prevent the escape
of Don Pedro. In the castle with Don Pedro there
was a gentleman called Rodriguez de Sanabria. And
Rodriguez came out in the night to Mosen Beltran,
who commanded the guard on the side of the camp
where Rodriguez and his band were stationed, and spoke
to him thus: "Señor Beltran, Don Pedro, my master,

ordered me to speak to you, and to say that you were always a noble gentleman, who prided yourself upon doing great deeds and worthy. You see the sore strait in which he is, and he bids me tell you that, if you will get him away from here and place him in safety and you will keep faithful to him, he will give you the towns of Saria, Almazan, Atienza, Monteagudo, Deza, and Seron for you and your heirs for ever, and he will also give you 200,000 gold Castilian doubloons as well. I, on my own part, pray you heartily to do this, for the honour that will redound to you in having succoured so great a king, and all Christendom shall know that from your hand he has recovered his realm and his life. Mosen Beltran replied to Rodriguez : Friend, well you know who I am, and that I owe allegiance to my native sovereign the King of France, and by his orders I came hither to Spain to serve King Enrique, since our enemies, the English, have espoused the cause of King Pedro. I am therefore in the service of King Enrique, and am paid by him, and I cannot, in honour, do anything against him or his interests; and you, on your part, ought not to ask me to do such a thing. If you have ever received any kindness or courtesy at my hands, I pray you not to press me further. And Rodriguez answered Mosen Beltran : I well understand that my proposal to you may not be altogether honourable, and I can only beg you now to give me your counsel on the matter. And so together they went to the lodging of Mosen

F

Beltran, where Rodriguez dismounted from his jennet, and, after a few minutes, the latter said : Come, mount, it is time we were gone; but Beltran replied not a word. Don Pedro himself was hidden in the lodging of Mosen Beltran, as King Enrique had been told, and when Don Pedro heard that Beltran made no reply, he began to doubt and to fear that the plan had gone awry. So he tried to mount the jennet upon which Rodriguez had come and escape, but one of Mosen Beltran's men held him, and said : Wait a bit," and so they prevented him from going. . . . When the king, Don Enrique, learnt that Don Pedro had been stopped in the lodging of Mosen Beltran, he was all ready armed from head to foot, with his helmet on his head, awaiting the news. And so he came to the lodging of Mosen Beltran, and as soon as he entered he came up close to Don Pedro, whom he did not know, for he had not seen him for a long time. And one of Mosen Beltran's men cried out to him : Take care, that is your enemy. But King Enrique still doubted that this was true; and it is said that King Pedro himself cried out twice, It is I! it is I! And then Don Enrique knew him, and he wounded him in the face with a dagger, and they say that both kings in the struggle fell to the ground, and whilst they wrestled on the ground King Enrique struck other wounds in his brother. And so Don Pedro, the king, died thus on the 23rd March of this year (1369). And soon there was a great outcry in the camp that the king, Don Pedro, had escaped from Montiel ; but soon we learnt that he was dead."

It will be remarked how much more vivid this presentation is than the earlier chronicles I have quoted before. Here the king, or kings, are the centre, it is true ; but you get the background as well. You can see the camp outside the castle, the French gentleman in King Henry's army in command of one side of the besieging forces. You can see first the Spanish gentleman approaching him with offers of a bribe, and whilst he was thus talking, the despairing King Pedro and his faithful band of nobles themselves leaving the castle, and, as a last hope, going to the Frenchman's tent. Then the murderous struggle between the two brothers, and Peter the Cruel lying dead, whilst the fratricide bastard of Trastamare is hailed as the puppet king of Castile by the nobles who have decided to make him pay them for his shadowy kingship to the utmost farthing. But something else you can see besides the vividness in all this. You can see the Spaniard's all-pervading love for telling tales of personal adventure, to make the world gape at the story of how one king killed another, and the proudest crown of Christendom was won by a fratricide.

But the next development in the hands of an inferior artist shows this tendency even more strongly. This is in the anonymous *Chronicle of Juan II.* Juan II. was the son of Catharine of Lancaster and Henry III. of Castile. His was the most chivalrous

and luxurious court in Europe in his time. The craze
for writing, for poetry, pageantry, and high-flown
adventure had once more in Spain become wellnigh a
disease. Everybody of position wrote something. It
is clear they could not all write about the king, so
they had of necessity to write about other important
personages in the same strain of heroic personal
record. The more marvellous were the stories told,
the more overwhelming the valour, the more splendid
the hero, the greater would be the attention given to
the work ; and so rapidly downhill the kingly
chronicle went towards stories of inflated adventure.

Take this instance of the *Chronicle of Juan II.*—an
official chronicle, be it recollected :—

*' What happened to certain Cavaliers of Carmona and
Marchena with the Moors.*

' At this time there sallied from Carmona and
Marchena forty-two horsemen and twenty-eight footmen to raid the tower of Al Hakem and Ayamonte.
And when they were near to the Sierra of Agrazalema
they were discovered ; and forth from Ronda and
Setenil there rode to encounter them two hundred and
forty Moorish horsemen. As the Christians beheld
them approaching they posted their footmen on a
steep hillside, which the Moors endeavoured to capture. But as Paynims stormed up the slope, the
Christian horsemen fell upon them so doughtily that

forty Moors fell at the first onslaught; whereupon
they began to fly, the Christians following in pursuit,
wounding and killing them as they went until they
were within the walls of Al Hakem. Seventy Moors
were slain in the fight, amongst whom was the Al-
guacil of Ronda, whilst eight of the best gentlemen of
Ronda were captured. The Christians also captured
a great booty and eighty horses, and so returned
rejoicing and triumphant to their town of Olivera.
And as they rode along they asked one of the Moorish
prisoners how it had come to pass that so large a
band of Moors had allowed themselves to be defeated
by so few Christians. The Moor replied that he
would swear by the Prophet that the Christians who
had fought them numbered at least four hundred
horsemen. It is evident, he said, that forty-two horsemen could not have vanquished two hundred and
forty; and he was sure that God had sent succour
to the Christians, or that the apostle Santiago had
come and joined them. The Christians bore before
them two pennons they had captured in the fight,
one white, the other red, and these were hung in the
church of Olivera; and six Christian horsemen and
one footman alone perished in this battle.'

Throughout this *Chronicle of Juan II.*, which was
written in the middle of the fifteenth century, the
tendency already indicated for chronicle to degenerate into heroic narrative is plainly discernible. The
contrast between the staid record drawn from official

documents set down by Alfonso X. and the marvellous tales of personal adventure which overlie the
Chronicle of Juan II., two hundred years later, is very
great ; but history once started upon this steep decline
was forced to degenerate still further, since each fresh
chronicler, being a Spaniard, found it necessary, in
order to centre attention upon himself or his hero,
to go beyond his predecessors in the wondrous deeds
he recorded.   New heroes, too, had to be found or
invented, since there were not enough kings to go
round, and the central individual hero was primarily
necessary.   Prominent personages in the State or in
warfare were eagerly seized upon, either to bulk largely
in the general kingly chronicle or to be made subjects
of separate chronicles of their own.   The greatness
and power, as well as the dramatic fall, of the famous
favourite of Juan II., Don Alvaro de Luna, was made
the theme of numberless moralisings, to which reference will be made in a later chapter ; but chroniclers
also recorded his doings in prose so florid as almost
to recall the ancient *Chansons de Geste,* in which the
Provençal juglars sang the prowess of their legendary
champions.   The following extracts from the later
portion of the *Chronicle of Juan II.* with reference to
Don Alvaro de Luna will show how the personal note
was already dominating even official history, to the
extent of placing national affairs in a secondary
position after the doings of a royal favourite :—

' Of a Joust that was celebrated at Valladolid on the
1st May of that year (1434).'

"The king departed from Medina in April, and
travelled to Valladolid, where the Constable Don
Alvaro de Luna ordered a great joust to be held on
the 1st May. He himself entered the lists with thirty
gentlemen of the king's household and his own—
fifteen being dressed in garments of green and fifteen
in yellow. And albeit the whole thirty rode into
the lists with him, the green band tilted against the
yellow band. The king himself entered the lists as
an adventurer, and broke a lance on Diego Manrique,
son of the Adelantado Pedro Manrique, who was one
of the challengers, and another lance on Juan de
Merlo. This was a very fine joust in which many
notable encounters took place. The feast was given
by the Constable, and the whole of the tilters and
many other gentlemen of the court supped with him
that day. From there the king went to Medina,
where, by the advice of his nobles and the representatives of the towns, he issued the following
decree."

The decree was an extremely important one for the
suppression of lawless disorder; and yet it and the
parliament that passed it were evidently in the eyes
of the chronicler much less interesting than the
chivalrous entertainments of Don Alvaro.

The last lines of this chronicle recount the disgrace

and execution of the favourite, and thus moralise upon his fall :—

"Oh! John Boccaccio, if you were alive to-day, I cannot believe your pen would fail to set forth in writing the thunderous fall of this valiant man, as famous as any prince whose life you tell. What greater example than this was ever presented in any State before? What greater warning was ever displayed before our eyes? What greater proof of the changes and chances of tricky fortune? Oh! blindness of the human race! Oh! the unforeseen happenings of this world! Who could believe that a man, basely born of a mother of low degree, though of virtuous and noble sire, a son unrecognised as such until his father's death ; without inheritance, without influence, and without worldly prospects, a foreigner in a strange land, far away from his kin, abandoned in his early youth, could have arrived at such a pitch of grandeur as this?"

And here follows a magniloquent statement of the Constable's titles, offices, and possessions. The insistence upon the personality of the actors in the chronicles is seen also in this writer's almost photographic description of Don Alvaro :—

"The Grand Master," he says, "was very short of stature, with a thin face. His limbs were well proportioned. He was bald, his eyes small but very keen ; he had a cavernous mouth and bad teeth. His heart was great, his courage high, and he was energetic, astute, and suspicious. He was much given to his pleasures; was a fine rider in all kinds of horsemanship, a dexterous swordsman and tilter, and sang and danced well."

The same tendency of a desire to emphasise the personality of history is seen in the works of the nephew of Lopez de Ayala, Fernan Perez de Guzman (1378-1460), whose attempt to compile a great universal history—*Mar de Historias*—may be placed in the same category as that of Alfonso the Learned. But when he comes to describe the great personages of the court of Spain who had been known to him, he shows how good an artist he was. People in his day were fond of comparing him with Petrarch, and certainly he must have been conscious of Italian models; but his keen satirical touch, his crispness— I may say his waggishness—mark him for the true Spaniard that he was.

That Fernan Perez de Guzman, literary artist as he was, fully recognised the evil tendency that was dragging history in Castile down to the level of bombastic fable, may be seen in the first page of his celebrated book *Generaciones y Semblanzas*, which contains some marvellously vigorous word portraits of the principal personages of the Castilian court in his time. 'It very often happens,' he says, 'that the chronicles and histories telling of the memorable deeds of powerful kings, noble princes, and great cities, are held in suspicion and doubt, little belief

being given to them. The reasons for this are prin-
cipally two: first, because some of the men who
undertake to write about bygone times are impudent
rascals, who prefer to write about strange and marvellous things rather than to tell true and well-
authenticated events. They think that no history
will be considered remarkable unless it contains some
prodigious stories hard to believe. These writers care
not, so long as the things they relate move people
to wonder rather than to belief. In our own times a
presumptuous knave called Pedro de Corral has done
this in a chronicle that he calls *The Saracen Chronicle*,
but which should more properly be entitled a book
of lies and frauds.'

But this growing tendency to the marvellous,
although to some extent arising from the character
of the root-races of Spain, was, as I have endeavoured
to show, mainly fostered at this time by the persistent introduction of the personal note in history ;
and of this love for personal and satirical detail
Perez de Guzman himself is an excellent specimen.
He hits off in *Generaciones y Semblanzas* one personage after the other, biting in the likeness with little
touches of acid that show up the truth unmistakably.
This, for instance, is how he describes the Queen-
mother Catharine Plantagenet, daughter of John of
Gaunt: 'This Queen was tall and very fat, with an
exceedingly fair red-and-white complexion. From
her height and the movements of her body she looked

more like a man than a woman. She was very virtuous and discreet, jealous of her good fame, besides
being very liberal and open-handed. But unfortun-
ately she was much given to allow her favourites to
rule her, which is a common failing of monarchs.
She was careless of her person, and she had a bad
attack of paralysis which prevented her from speaking
plainly afterwards and affected her body. She died
in Valladolid, aged fifty, in 1418 on the 2nd June, and
she is buried in Toledo in the chapel of the kings by
the side of her husband Don Henry.'

Although Perez de Guzman in his own history
does his best to correct the abuses that had crept into
the chronicles, in inferior hands to his the degeneracy
continued. Men were so eager to attract attention by
writing wonders, that truth and even verisimilitude
were of secondary importance. Pages and followers
began to write accounts of the romantic adventures
and gallant deeds of their lords and of each other. A
good specimen of this vicious development of the
courtly chronicle is the chronicle of Don Pedro Niño,
Count de Buelna, a great noble who rejoiced in
the services of a literary standard-bearer who must
have been a veritable Boswell. Whilst John of Gaunt
was struggling for the crown of Spain, and Castile
was at war with England, the Count de Buelna went
to the wars both by land and sea, and his standard-
bearer recorded his deeds. No one ever could have
been so brave, so wise, and so good as the Count is

represented to have been by his admiring scribe. This Gutierre Diez de Gamez, the standard-bearer, amongst other things describes the wonderful invasion of England by his master, his capture of a town in Cornwall he calls Chita, his unsuccessful attack upon Plymouth, his sacking of Portland against tremendous odds, his great battle at Poole; and finally his entrance into Southampton Water, and his visit to Southampton, which he seems to confuse with London. All this and much more is told by Gamez, in a style so romantic and pompous, as to make his chronicle resemble already the latest stage of degeneration which the courtly chronicle reached, namely, the purely imaginary tales of chivalry which soon afterwards swamped Spain.

The account of the famous embassy of Gonzales de Clavijo to Persia, called *The Life and Deeds of the Great Tamerlane*, of the same period (1412), is a similar book. The great effort is to surprise. And a further drop still towards the inflated and completely fictitious romances of chivalry, to which I shall refer in my next chapter, is the *Libro del Paso Honroso*, by Rodriguez de Lena, who held a bridge with nine knights against all comers for a month in 1434, and fought six hundred combats, apparently for no reason at all but to satisfy his personal vanity.

It will be seen thus that the personal note of the kingly chronicle in Spain had, by the middle of the fifteenth century, degenerated in one direction to

almost fictitious tales of marvels which were soon to
end in inflated and foolish romances.

Before we pass to its development in another
direction, we will consider what influence this exuberant fashion had outside Spain. In the same wars
that Lopez de Ayala took part in and recorded, there
was another recorder of genius, mixing with Spanish
nobles and writers, hearing their romantic style
of recounting events, and doubtless reading the
chronicles which in that literary court passed from
hand to hand. He was a Frenchman named Froissart,
whose chronicle telling of these wars between England and Spain, of which he was a spectator, is
written on the Spanish lines of personal interest,
romantic adventure, and vivacious characterisation.

Froissart's chronicle has been popular from the
days in which it was written until the present hour,
and did much to introduce into the rest of Europe the
knightly personal, or heroic, chronicle form of history,
rather than the ecclesiastical form that had previously been dominant. During all the war period,
with English armies in Spain, sometimes as friends,
sometimes as foes, the Spanish chronicles must have
been familiar to such English knights as could read.
When Constance of Castile, daughter of Peter the
Cruel, became Duchess of Lancaster, Spanish manuscript chronicles, telling of the deeds of her forefathers, must have gone with her to England ; and the
nobles who went backwards and forwards during the

time that Catharine of Lancaster was Queen of Spain must have known such chronicles. In these circumstances, it is not surprising that from the end of the fourteenth century onward, a change came over the form in which history was written in England. From time immemorial, monks like Gildas and Bede had written chronicles of their times; and other churchmen in later days, like Geoffrey of Monmouth, William of Malmesbury, Matthew of Westminster, and Richard of Cirencester, had collected and continued them. Those that had been produced before the coming of the Saxons, like the chronicles translated by Geoffrey of Monmouth, were to some extent imbued with the Celtic spirit of the sacredness surrounding the sovereign, and the British chiefs and Roman commanders usually took the centre of the stage, but there was no attempt at attractive description or at characterisation. The first conspicuous change of manner is found at the end of the fourteenth century, in the so-called *Chronicle of St. Albans.* Here the public and warlike events, like the pillage of Roxburgh by the Scots, and its recapture by the Earl of Northumberland; the riots in London, the entrance of the mob into the Tower; the destruction of the Hospital of St. John at Clerkenwell, and the like, are related clearly and vigorously, and the first note of modern history is struck. But there is in this case no hero-worship, no centralisation of events around a personage in a way that would disfigure the events themselves, such as was taking place in the development of Spanish chronicles. But, withal, the broader view, the satirical touch, the gaiety, that the lay chroniclers had introduced were already influencing English historical writing. Froissart had caught the trick and passed it on; and a further development of the chronicle in the direction of picturesque narrative, to some extent grouped around the person of the hero, was rapidly seen both in France and England. With Fabian in the fifteenth century, the fashion of thus writing history may be said to have become permanently acclimatised in England. The English form varied from the Spanish, as the national characters varied. There was less striving after the marvellous, for the stolid Saxon had to some extent swamped the Celtic element in our race; there was less assertion of the individuality of the sovereign around whom the national events revolved, because he was a feudal king held in check by barons, and was not sacerdotal; but thenceforward it was the layman, the student, the courtier, the soldier who wrote history, instead of the churchman in a monkish cell, and the purview was broader, the style more virile, and the grouping of events more attractive. The fashion of picturesque historical narrative had thus been, more or less directly, set to us from Spain, and our countrymen had adopted the fashion whilst avoiding its abuse.

CHAPTER IV

THE ROMANCES OF CHIVALRY AND PASTORALS

THE Kingly Chronicle in Spain, written by knights or palace officials, may be traced in two directions: first to the serious modern history continued by scholars and churchmen like Zurita and Mariana ; and secondly, to the far-fetched and marvellous adventures which were grouped around the figure of the hero of the personal chronicle. From this latter development to entirely imaginary stories, unfettered by any pretence of truth, or even of probability, was only a step. As we have seen, the character of the people had always led them to develop their literary forms in the direction of the marvellous. Their imagination was as fertile as their language was florid. Their Celtic admixture had filled them with a mystical and sacrificial devotion towards any exalted abstraction which appealed to them, and by the fifteenth century, when the power of the Moslems had been reduced to a mere shadow in one corner of the Peninsula, and the romantic episodes of border warfare failed, the Christian Spaniard turned, with the avidity of a famished man to a meal, towards the heroic fables which had already become trite and tiresome to the rest of Europe. These marvellous adventures of impossible prowess by impossible knights, for equally impossible princesses, were not very much more extreme than the Spaniard's own later personal chronicles had been ; and they gave infinitely greater scope for imagination, because they re-introduced the paraphernalia of sorcery and enchantment, of pure-hearted, self-sacrificing Christians, battling undaunted against the supernatural powers of evil ; and for the most part they were located in vague foreign countries, where anything extraordinary might presumably happen. We have already seen that previous to the fifteenth century Spain had been too busy in real romantic adventures with the Moors to pay much attention to the purely fictitious tales of knight-errantry. The juglars and reciters had introduced from France the epic poems about Roland and Charlemagne ; and the heroic poem of *The Cid*, in which marvellous adventures are grouped around a real person, had been a close imitation of them. But of *native* Spanish forms, as I have shown in earlier pages, the main outcome of literary activity had been the didactic apologue, the sententious aphorism, and the kingly chronicle. We will for the moment postpone the consideration of the development of the romances of chivalry in Spain, and the extraordinary influence they exerted in reviving the dying cult in the rest of Europe, and will endeavour to trace how the germ of the stories came to Spain at all.

G

There always has been much difference of opinion with regard to the origin of the magic element in these tales. Many authorities have urged that the dragons, and magic rings and amulets, and enchanters, did not make an appearance in Europe until after the Christian warriors had returned from the Crusade in the twelfth century; whilst from the earliest known form of Eastern story, they had been part of the regular machinery, as you may see in *The Arabian Nights*. The dragon, they say, was only the winged horse of the ancient Persians, which had been carried by the Moors to Spain as an element of fiction, and through France had reached the rest of Europe. With this opinion I, for one, cannot agree, for reasons which I shall state later. Others allege that the tales of magic, in connection with self-sacrificing knightly heroes, are the direct descendants of the sagas sung by the pagan northmen around their heroes dead and alive, which songs, they say, were carried into Normandy and Brittany by the Normans when they came south. For centuries previous to the Crusades the Norsemen sang of fairies and of dragons, and of the intervention of their pagan deities in the daily affairs of men. On the other hand, the institution of knighthood, as a chosen order of proved self-sacrificing warriors, was undoubtedly Germanic, arising naturally out of the circumstances of a race organised on military lines pushing its way for centuries through opposing peoples, and consequently calling frequently for individual sacrifice to the common weal. By far the most probable source of the magic element in the tales is prehistoric Celtic tradition. This is not quite incompatible, however, with the Norse contention, because many believe that the Norsemen were of Celtic origin. In any case, the stories, both of magic elements and of heroic knights, were told in Celtic Ireland, and also probably in Celtic Britain, centuries before the Crusades or the Norman invasion of Britain, as may be seen by Lady Gregory's two fine collections of such stories recently published, *Cuchulain* and *Gods and Fighting Men*.

Out of these traditional fables, whatever their origin, repeated from father to child over untold centuries, there grew in the twelfth century onward in England a concrete connected set of legends, set down in Latin and later in French, by Anglo-Norman scribes. Whether there ever was really a King Arthur of Britain is even yet uncertain. *The Chronicle of Britain*, adapted or translated by Geoffrey of Monmouth in the twelfth century from an older British book, builds up a regular history of a certain wonderful King Arthur, with the magician Merlin as his adviser; and so does Richard Wace the Norman in the previous century in his *Roman de Brute*. Both of them had introduced into their story of the king the strange legend of St. Joseph of Arimathea, who was supposed to have possessed, and lost, the holy cup

filled with Christ's blood, called the Sangreal or
Holy Grail. The saint was said to fall into a
trance at the end of each century, and to awake re-
juvenated ; and, indeed, it was asserted that thirteen
centuries after the Crucifixion, at which he had been
present, St. Joseph appeared in England and dined
at the table of a bishop. The Glastonbury thorn is
said to have been his walking staff, which he struck
into the ground where he founded the first Christian
church in England. Anyhow, he is inextricably
mixed up in the legends with the more or less real
King Arthur and his minister Merlin ; and Arthur
is said to have kept a space vacant at his table for
the Holy Grail when it should be found and recovered. This legend, or set of legends, first popular-
ised in writing by the Anglo-Norman and French
scribes of the twelfth century, was made the subject
of a regular *Life of Merlin* in the thirteenth, written
in French prose by one Barron. He tells how the
devil, being alarmed at the great number of Christian
converts being made by St. Joseph in Britain, calls
a congress of his diabolical fellows to discuss the
situation. They decide to send one of their number
to England to marry a Christian maiden and become
the father of a child that shall in time destroy the
human race. The devil is represented as staying in
the house of a noble Briton, with three lovely
daughters, and after much ingenious but ineffectual
strategy, he manages to obtain possession surrepti-

tiously of the eldest. The girl is shut up in prison for her supposed unchastity, and there her babe is born, and christened by the priest with the not inappropriate name of Blaise. When the child Merlin is a month old the mother is condemned to die for her supposed offence; but the child consoles her with the promise that he will save her; and goes himself before the judges, and in an eloquent harangue, for a child of a month old, confounds the court with the proofs that the Chief Justice's own birth is not beyond reproach; the result being that the Chief Justice, unwilling to bring his own mother in question, lets Merlin's mother off. A civil war is raging between Britons and Saxons at the time; and the British usurper, Voltigern, who has ousted the two native princes, builds a high tower for his defence; but time after time, just as the last stone is being placed on the top, the tower falls down. Instead of leaving it without the top stone, Voltigern summoned a meeting of astrologers, who tell him that the tower is bewitched by a child engendered by no mortal man; and unless this child be found and his blood used to mix the mortar the tower would never stand. Orders are sent that the child must be searched for throughout Britain, and Merlin, hearing this, presents himself unbidden, and informs the usurper that the reason for the instability of his tower is that two dragons, one white and the other red, are engaged in deadly combat in the earth underneath. On digging this was found to be true; and the

terrible combat of the mythical beasts is interpreted
by Merlin as signifying the rivalry of the two brother
claimants to the throne, the Princes Pendragon and
Uther.   Soon afterwards these two princes land in
England from Brittany, where they had taken refuge,
conquer Voltigern, and burn him in the ruins of his
tower.   Pendragon mounts the throne, but is soon
killed in battle with the Saxons ; and Uther becomes
king, with Merlin the enchanter as his prime minister,
the Christian birth and baptism softening somewhat
his diabolical tendencies, so that he is represented as
a personification of the powers of evil weakened by
Christianity.   By his advice, King Uther founds the
society of the Round Table, where are seated with the
king fifty or sixty knights, with a space left for the
Holy Grail when it shall be found.   When Uther dies,
Arthur, his illegitimate son, seizes the throne, to the
great discontent of the people.   But he shows himself
so doughty a knight as to be able to wrench from the
solid rock the sword which the magician Scalibur had
embedded in it, though two hundred and one of the
best knights of Britain had previously tried to extract
it in vain, and he is greeted by the British people as
the hero king worthy to reign over them.   Merlin
becomes Arthur's prime minister, changing his shape
at will to suit his purposes, now a dwarf, now a
harpy, now an animal, employing his magic powers
in the service of Arthur, and to defeat his enemies.
Merlin's wife Bibiana has been let into some of the

secrets of his sorcery, that she may use them in case of emergency; and, apparently because she is anxious to see how the thing works, she practises one of the incantations; but by means of some mistake she consigns Merlin himself to the inside of a whitethorn tree in the midst of a deep wood, where his terrible cries and wails resound for leagues around thenceforward, without any one being able to locate him. This was the Frenchman Barron's first connected version of Merlin's life, written in the thirteenth century; and I have told the story in detail, that we may see how it was growing by imagination and be able to trace its further development. Up to this time there was not much chivalrous element in the story. Arthur here was a strong figure, like a Norse demi-god; but the ideas of heroic righting of wrongs, and pure self-sacrifice, were not yet a special feature. That was to come a century later, and was perhaps more Germanic or Frankish than Celtic.

In the fourteenth century, Thomas Lonelich, later a scribe at the court of Henry IV. of England—a contemporary of Chaucer—wrote in verse, which was afterwards put into French prose, the first of the real Arthurian cycle of tales, called *The Sangreal*. There the legend begins by telling how St. Joseph of Arimathea had obtained the holy cup from the hands of the Saviour and had filled it with the blood that gushed from His wounds. The Jews were so

much incensed at this that they shut St. Joseph up
in prison, where Christ appears to him and restores
the cup. On the capture of Jerusalem by Titus
Vespasian forty-two years afterwards, St. Joseph
regains his liberty, and travels through the world
preaching the Gospel. The powers of evil plot
against him, and obtain possession of the cup; and
Merlin advises King Arthur to found a society of
knights, who shall sit with him round his table,
their purpose being the recovery of the cup, each one
swearing to spend his life, if necessary, in filling the
vacant space that is left at their table for the Holy
Grail. The history of Arthur and the knights of
the Round Table consists mainly of the heroic deeds
of the knights to regain the cup. Here we see the
purely knightly and self-sacrificing element added
to the marvels and magic of the Celtic legends. The
story appealed strongly to the English mind of the
fourteenth century, and was followed by sequels by
various writers; the most important of which is
Sir Lancelot of the Lake and his son Sir Galahad.
Sir Lancelot of the Lake is supposed to be the son
of a king of Britain, who being besieged in his
castle flies with his wife Helen and his child
Lancelot. Turning when he reaches a hill-top to
look upon the realm he has lost, he drops dead
with grief; and his wife, laying the infant on the
border of a lake, runs to her husband's aid. The
moment the mother's back is turned the Lady of

the Lake, Bibiana, the wife of Merlin, whose mishap with her magic has resulted in enclosing her husband in the whitethorn, rises from the waters of the lake, wherein she lives, and seizing the child, dives into the lake with him. When Helen turns she finds her child has disappeared. Lancelot is brought up tenderly and well by the Lady of the Lake, and at the age of eighteen is taken to King Arthur's court to enter into the order of knighthood. When he has been knighted, Arthur's wife, Queen Guinevere, falls in love with him : and their loves and intrigues fill a large space of the book. The Queen sets to Lancelot all sorts of seemingly impossible tasks and perilous deeds, as the price of her love ; and he faces a thousand perils, human and supernatural, to please her, conquering kingdoms and seizing crowns to lay at her feet.

Here we have first clearly set as a motive, heroic sacrifice of a man, simply to comply with the caprice of the lady to whom he has devoted his life. Guinevère certainly does not appear to us either an amiable or a worthy heroine, to demand such sacrifices ; but that probably heightens the sacrifice of the man, who is not bound by duty to serve her at all, and only does so for her love. Guinevere invades Northumberland, and captures the castle of Berwick ; but learning that Arthur suspects her fidelity, she and Lancelot decide to dethrone Arthur, and crown Guinevere Queen. Guinevere's falsity is disclosed to Arthur by Morgana his sister, through a knight of the Round Table called Sir Gawain. Arthur in his rage musters his forces and marches against Lancelot at Berwick. Whilst he is fighting his rival, Arthur learns that Mordred his son has risen in rebellion against him, aided by the Spanish Saracens. He hurries back, but is met on Salisbury Plain by his son and the rebels. Here he falls, and his body is never found: Lancelot in revenge of him killing Mordred the son; and, instead of crowning Guinevere, he raises to the throne a kinsman of Arthur. Lancelot then becomes a hermit, and is joined by the last surviving knight of the Round Table, whilst Guinevere becomes a nun, and finally Sir Galahad, son of Lancelot, with Sir Percival, recovers the Holy Grail.

This is the second development in which chivalric love is made the main motive for self-sacrifice. In French, and later than *Sir Lancelot*, there came *Tristan de Lyonesse*, much the best of the series, considered as literature. Most of the action passes in Cornwall; and again Merlin's enchantments, faithless wives, and tremendous adventures of their loves to please them or rescue them from peril are repeated. These are the principal Arthurian stories[1] which in

---

[1] It is true that at a later period (1450) Malory's beautiful story *Morte d'Arthur* was written in English; but before that time chivalry as a living force was disappearing in England, and discipline and the reign of law had taken its place as a r eans of social restraint. Malory's book was read, as it still is, but as story, not a gospel.

the thirteenth and fourteenth centuries absorbed the minds of such readers as existed in Europe, with the exception perhaps of Spain. Others there were of purely French origin founded upon the apocryphal chronicle attributed wrongly to Bishop Turpin, relating to the deeds of Charlemagne and the twelve peers of France, especially the knight Roland: but this series is concerned with the supposed deeds of the French in forcing Christianity upon Spain at the sword's point, and the stories are evidently inspired by, or descendants of, the *Chansons de Geste* or recitative epics relating to the same events, rather than real tales of altruistic individual heroism. I will consequently not dwell upon them; but will keep to the theme of the true chivalric magic romance, which grew up, as I have explained, mainly in England from mixed Celtic aud Germanic elements.

These absorbing, but utterly unreal romances, satisfied a need in stimulating imagination, and provided, so long as it was necessary, an altruistic incentive to action, and an exalted or spiritual reason for attachment to a leader, both of which were very necessary in the wars, such as the crusades, where each knight led an almost independent band into battle, and where there was little organised cohesion in an army. But this was not the case for very long in England. The battles of the Black Prince in France, and even more so those of Henry v., were

gained mainly by disciplined and combined movements, rather than by heroic personal encounter; and,
as discipline and law became stronger, the sense of
duty replaced the idea of chivalry as a motive for
action. Although, therefore, the Arthurian romances
of chivalry continued to be read as literature, and
especially Malory's *Morte d'Arthur*, chivalry itself,
as a living force, declined in England before the
fifteenth century had far advanced.[1] In Spain, however, it was quite different. Wonders always appealed
to the people. They had been starved of literature
until the end of the thirteenth century, and, as I
have pointed out, they promptly thereafter showed
their irrepressible bent by turning their history into
romance in the course of a century and a half; and
when the moment came, they seized upon the
chivalric idea more strongly than any other country
had done.

How did these Celtic tales reach Spain to begin

---

[1] This is seen by the contemptuous way in which the Host interrupts
Chaucer in the *Canterbury Tales*, when, in answer to the invitation to
add to the entertainment of the company by telling a story, the poet
begins the chivalric rhyme of Sir Thopas. The Host soon loses patience
with the absurdity of the tale, and breaks in with—

> ' No more of this, for Godde's dignitee,
> Quod our hosté, for thou makest me
> So weary of thy very lewedeness
> That also wisly God my soulé bless,
> Myn earés achen at thy drasty speech,
> Now such a rhym the devil I beteech.'

and he continues by bidding the unfortunate reciter to tell the company
something sensible ' in which there shall be some mirth or doctrine.'

with? There was no printing, recollect, but somehow the English legends that I have described were current in Spain in the fourteenth century, and probably long before. Perhaps the Cluny monks who flocked into Spain in the thirteenth century brought them from France; perhaps the crowds of pilgrims to Santiago told them to each other and to their hosts in Spain ; perhaps the English knights and soldiers who came with Edward I. and his great-grandson the Black Prince spread them ; or, finally, perhaps they had also clung unforgotten from prehistoric times to the Celtic peoples of the west of the peninsula, to be revived by the echoes of the tales that had been woven out of them by their far-away kinsmen in Brittany, in Wales, and in Ireland. In any case, they came; and the dissolute poet-priest, the Archpriest of Hita, mentions these British tales in the middle of the fourteenth century. About the same time, a poet named Ferrus, writing a jocose rhyming letter to the famous Pero Lopez de Ayala, the chronicler and satirist, mentions Arthur, Lancelot, and Tristan of Lionesse. The *History of Merlin*, we know, was translated into French, Italian, and Latin, perhaps into Spanish, in the fourteenth century; and *Lancelot of the Lake* was certainly turned into French or Spanish at about the same time, because Lopez de Ayala, in his famous rhymed satire *Rimado de Palacio*, mentions it by name. All this argues that the Arthurian tales had, by the middle of the fourteenth century, become well

known to people who could read in Spain, and formed
the intellectual attraction of the day.

Whether there was a French or English tale, now
lost, called *Amadis*, we do not know. But what is
certain is that, some time early in the fourteenth
century, there was a book called *Amadis of Gaul* (or
Wales) current in Spain, which is usually mentioned in
conjunction with the Arthurian books, and which
appears to have been written in Spanish. Who wrote
it, or when, nobody knows, or perhaps ever will know;
but the book, or rather series of books, for there were
nine in all, were evidently inspired by the Arthurian
series, which I have described. The first copy of
Amadis known to us is in Portuguese, adapted or
prepared for a Portuguese prince late in the fourteenth
century, by one Vasco de Lobeyra, who, in all probability, must have had before him a Spanish version,
now lost, since Lopez de Ayala in his old age deplored
the time he had wasted over reading *Amadis* in his
youth, and it is improbable that Lobeyra's version can
have been written so early as that. All we know of
the matter is, that *Amadis of Gaul* in the fifteenth
century became a perfect craze in Spain; and, as had
been the case with the Arthur series in England,
sequels were added to it by various hands, until
a regular literature of Amadis grew up, and imitations by the dozen followed rapidly one after the
other.

Here was a form which gave to Spanish writers full

scope for their love of the marvellous, and their overflowing imagination. Neither probability of incident,
unity of action, nor precision of locality bound them.
But to these recommendations there came late in the
fifteenth century, and almost simultaneously, two
great factors, which operated more than any others in
fixing firmly upon Spain the chivalric idea which
thenceforward was sc powerfully to sway the fate of
the Spanish people. These factors were, first, the
invention of printing, and secondly, the deliberate
policy of Ferdinand and Isabel of unifying the loosely
connected kingdoms which went to make up Spain, by
fostering the pride of exclusive religious orthodoxy,
by arousing in the breasts of all Spaniards, from the
Celtic Gallego to the half African Murcian, that
spiritual exaltation and thirst for personal distinction
by sacrifice, which was already deeply ingrained in the
national character.

So when *Amadis of Gaul* was first printed in 1508 it
fell on fruitful soil. The last Moorish ruler had been
expelled from Spain, and throughout the kingdom the
fires of the Inquisition were burning Jews and heretics.
With the condemnation of every backslider from the
true faith the spiritual pride of each individual
Spaniard of the majority grew. All men but himself
were suspect. He was of the true aristocracy of God,
anxious to distinguish himself in the sight of the
Almighty by sacrifice and suffering. Hermits, seers,
and dreamers macerated their flesh and rejoiced in the

misery, cold, and squalor by which they sought to draw the notice of God upon themselves. Self-sacrifice was the national note. Personal distinction by patient suffering in the cause of good against evil was the heart-beat that sent the blood coursing throughout the nation's members. The literature of chivalry, issuing from the printing press at the moment that it did, sounded a note to which every soul found an echo. Here was set forth, in the form of marvellous story of personal adventure, the lesson that faith and steadfastness to divine or human love was in the end irresistible, that patient and undaunted valour ensured the pure-minded battler for the right against all the wiles of the devil and his host of evil sorcerers. Here was mental food which satisfied to the full the love for marvels; here was spiritual food that made every Spanish heart glow with the knowledge that though the way of heroic sacrifice was hard, yet in the end it was sure to bring happiness and distinction to those who suffered bravely and strongly. It was a pure, a beautiful, and a noble ideal. But it was an ideal, and never could be real, because each man was left to be judge of what *was* good, and conduct in life was divorced from religion. An exalted devotion, mystical assurance of divine favour, the faithful acceptance of a fixed doctrine and ritual, were held to cover all sorts of evil, or what we should judge evil, conduct. And so Spain became for the next hundred and fifty years a country where religion was a thing apart, and not closely connected with worldly behaviour; and high professions, perfectly sincere, were constantly accompanied by low morality.

Amadis of Gaul itself, and its eight or nine sequels, were modelled almost exactly on the lines of the Arthurian legends, so far as regards locality and incident, but with certain alterations of spirit which I shall point out presently. The story of Amadis is as follows. Perion, King of Gaul, or Wales, is married to Elisene, Princess of England. He has an illegitimate son named Amadis, who, upon the king's marriage, is abandoned by the seashore, an infant, where he is rescued by a knight and carried to Scotland. On growing up he calls himself the Knight of the Sea, and enters the service of Lisuarte, King of Britain, with whose beautiful daughter Oriana he falls in love. Fate brings him into contact with his half-brother Galaor, Prince of Gaul, with whom, after fighting, he becomes the fast friend and learns his relationship. Thenceforward they seek adventure together, fighting enchanters, rescuing their lady-loves from countless perils; and finally Amadis becomes King of Gaul, and marries the peerless Oriana. The text, as it has come down to us in the Spanish of Montalvan, is rich in incident and overflowing in imagination. To the readers of the present day the adventures will appear tedious and childish, and they will wonder how the book and its many imitations should have seized upon Europe as it did.

Of the sequels and imitations of *Amadis* I need not say much. *Palmerin de Oliva* and *Palmerin de Inglaterra* are perhaps the most famous. *Sergas de Espalandrin*, and *Artus de Algarve*, are hardly less so. But the machinery was always the same: wandering knights, usually princes, went through countless adventures, and finally killed all the giants and sorcerers opposed to them and their lady-loves whom they married, and with whom they lived happily ever after. It is incredible with what force these tales fixed themselves upon the imagination of Spain in the sixteenth century.

When Philip II. came to England to marry Queen Mary, several of his courtiers wrote accounts of what they saw, and the main delight of these Spaniards was to identify the scenes of Amadis's and Arthur's imaginary adventures. At Winchester the principal object of interest with them was the so-called Round Table of the knights, which still hangs on the wall of the castle. When the Spanish ambassador in England wished to say something excessively bitter about Elizabeth and her government, he could think of nothing more effective than to compare them with some of the characters in *Amadis*. The constant reference to these books in the correspondence of the time shows that a knowledge of the stories was considered to be a polite literary accomplishment. You have only to look at the first book of *Don Quixote*, which finally pricked the over-inflated bubble and 'laughed Spain's chivalry away,' to see how deeply they had entered into the national life. The whole of the sixteenth century saw Spain dominated by an impracticable idea. The search was not so much for worldly gain, although that was not lost sight of as an accompaniment of glory; but the source of Spain's greatness, a temporary and a fleeting one, was the pride of special selection and distinction by fidelity to an exalted mystic ideal, religious or amorous; and all the nation went helter skelter after an illusive Will-o'-the-Wisp, which, though they bore all before them in their rush, landed them finally into the bog of idleness, ostentation, high-faluting profession and low moral standard, to national ruin and decay.

It is now time to turn to the influence exerted in England by this curious craze. It has been pointed out that chivalric idea (as apart from the mere literary recreation of such books as the *Morte d'Arthur*) had lost its potency in England by the middle of the fifteenth century. English life had by that time become practical. The feudal powers of the nobles had decayed, the middle class had grown rich and strong, and the visionary attachment to an abstraction did not appeal strongly to the pervading Saxon racial character. But almost simultaneously with the popularisation of the chivalric romances in Spain, there mounted the English throne a king of Welsh blood, whose hereditary rights to the crown were weak or non-existent. Henry VII., conscious that this was the case, promoted the assertion that he was descended from the ancient British kings. Elaborate genealogies were constructed for him, and to strengthen his hold upon the imagination of the people he did his best to revive the ancient British tradition, and, above all, the stories of the heroic King Arthur, from whom he claimed descent. In pursuance of this he had made that great wooden table at Winchester, with the names of the king and his knights painted thereon. He called his eldest son Arthur, Prince of Wales, and such patronage as he could give to literature was given to the revival and spread of the chivalric idea. In this, to some extent, he was followed by his son Henry VIII.; but it was too late for the heroic chivalric idea to catch on. In Elizabeth's reign Anthony Munday, a most industrious mediocrity, translated some of the Spanish chivalric romances, and the characters in *Amadis*, and even more so *Palmerin de Inglaterra*, were well known in England by name; but their effect upon national thought was almost nothing, for English life had become too real for such visions.

But there was a variant of the chivalric, altruistic romances that came from Spain to England, and artificial though it was, had a considerable influence upon English literature. I mean the pastoral romance. At first sight nothing would appear more incongruous than the mixing up of shepherds and shepherdesses with the stories of heroic knights, fair ladies, and fearsome demons. The impetus was unquestionably not of native Spanish origin, but classical; for the *Eclogues* of

Virgil and his school had been fashionable centuries before, and had in the hands of Sannazaro become popular in Italy by the beginning of the sixteenth century. There was in Spain before this a slight trend towards the pastoral form in a most popular book written by San Pedro called *La Carcel de Amor*, which tells the story of a youth being led in chains through the deserts of the Sierra Morena by an enchanter of evil aspect, who is supposed to represent 'desire.' The youth is led by Desire to the Castle of Love, where he is made to suffer cruel tortures. At last, softened by his sorrowful tales of true love for the shepherdess of his thoughts, his jailer releases him ; and after undergoing much adventure he dies of love at the feet of his lady. This *Carcel de Amor* was translated into English by Lord Berners, and published in London in 1540, becoming a favourite book. But the true pastoral romance did not appear until the middle of the sixteenth century, when the Portuguese Montemayor produced a book called *Diana*. To modern readers it will seem more artificial than even the knightly romance ; but, false as it was, it kept a high place for nearly two centuries, and set the fashion, jointly with the Italian works of the same tendency, until the middle of the eighteenth century, at least in France, where the simpering beribboned and satin-clad shepherdesses of the Watteau period perpetuated the imaginary loves of Chloe and Strephon.

This *Diana* of George Montemayor was a distinct

improvement on the insipid Italian models he copied. It is partly in prose and partly in verse, and mixes magic and sorcery with the tales of the love-lorn shepherds. Why the style should have caught on in England is not far to seek. Knights in search of adventure were quite out of date in the England of Elizabeth, and some quite fanciful vehicle was needed to convey works of pure imagination. Shepherds and shepherdesses in impossible Arcadian conditions were an ancient classical tradition. They might be made to undergo any adventures without offending probability, since they themselves were improbable, and yet they carried more conviction than did wandering knights with altruistic ideas that no one could understand in strenuous England. So when Bartholomew Young wrote his translation of *Diana* in English in 1583, it at once attracted attention, though it was not published until 1598, when it became exceedingly popular. The second book of *Diana* was made up of an interpolated story called 'The History of the Shepherdess Felismena,' which sets forth how a love-sick lady deserted by her fickle sweetheart follows him to foreign lands in the guise of a page, and sacrifices herself to him to the extent of serving as his messenger to woo his new flame. The latter falls in love with the lady, who is dressed as a youth; and the complications that ensue are numerous and intricate. In the chapter on the Drama I shall point out the indebtedness of Shakespeare for his plot of

the *Two Gentlemen of Verona* to this incident, which
you will see is identical with it.

Shakespeare must have seen Young's manuscript,
or have heard the tale told, for the book was not
printed in English until after the *Two Gentlemen of
Verona* had been written. But others than Shakespeare were stricken with the pastoral craze by reading
Diana. *The Shepherd's Calendar*, where Colin Clout
and his pastoral mates go the round of the months
with their stories in verse, is clearly inspired by it;
and in France and Spain, as well as in England, the
writing of poems and stories around imaginary shepherds and shepherdesses became universal. When
Sir Philip Sidney went abroad to die, he left instructions that his pastoral story called *Arcadia*, written
for the amusement of his sister the Countess of Pem-
broke, should be destroyed. Fortunately his command was disobeyed, and one of the gems of English
literature was preserved. It is written deliberately in
what is called the euphuistic or affected, obscure, and
precious style which had become fashionable in England, as I mentioned in the last chapter, through the
popularity of Guevara's writings. This style, which
is also that of Montemayor himself, is suited to the
completely artificial pastoral tales, though probably
Sidney's correct taste and judgment had no desire to
link his fame for ever with a style which sins against
simplicity. He has, however, written enough beautiful pure English for us to look with indulgence upon

Arcadia. If you will read Bartholomew Young's translation of *Diana,* and then read Sidney's *Arcadia,* you will see that he copies closely. Indeed, in the lyrics with which the text is interspersed, he much improves upon the Spanish book, which, it must be understood, he did not translate, but imitated. These two verses of Sidney's, for instance, are better than anything Montemayor could write :—

> ' Of this high grace with bliss conjoined,
> No further debt on me is laid.
> Since that is selfsame metal coined,
> Sweet Lady, you remain well paid.
> For if my place give me great pleasure,
> Having before me nature's treasure ;
> In face and eyes, unmatchèd being,
> You have the same in my hands, seeing
> What in your face mine eyes do measure.
>
> Nor think the match unevenly made
> That of those beams in you do tarry.
> The glass to you but gives a shade,
> To me mine eyes the true shape carry :
> For such a thought, most highly prizèd,
> Which ever hath Love's yoke despisèd,
> Better than one captiv' perceiveth ;
> Though he the lively form receiveth,
> The other sees it but disguisèd.'

Throughout the later sixteenth, and all the seventeenth, century in England and France, the pastoral form of romance and poetry continued in vogue. Quite divorced from truth or probability, it yet allowed the sentiment of love, which is always real to be set forth with such ideal surroundings as lent glamour to it on paper. But, as the strong realist school of writing in England gained ground in the early eighteenth century; when the age of Queen Anne brought us writers of strong, natural, English prose; when Swift scoffed at shams; when Addison, Steele, and Fielding looked at life as it was, with open, seeing eyes; then feeble imitations of what, at best, was an artificial style, only earned derision ; and Ambrose Phillips, whose ridiculous nickname has added an expression to the English language, wrote of the ideal loves of wooden shepherds and rag-doll shepherdesses, and the line of pastoral writers ended in Namby Pamby and deservedly died.

CHAPTER V

THE SPANISH NOVEL: ITS ORIGIN, TENDENCY, AND INFLUENCE

IN previous chapters I have led the reader gradually along two different paths to the point where they converge. First the Oriental apologue, or short story to enforce a moral lesson, was traced onward to where (and especially under the influence of Boccaccio and the Italian renaissance) the anecdote was told for its own sake, and the moral suppressed or placed in the background; and secondly the kingly chronicle, which, when we left it, had in Spain degenerated through bombastic narratives of heroic adventures into the unreal and over-inflated romance of chivalry. Each successive romance of this sort, if it was to claim attention, had to make its giants bigger and more terrible than ever before, its sorceries more diabolical, its knights more altruistically heroic, and its afflicted maidens more ineffably beautiful. But for the absence of humour displayed in these stories, they must have burst with laughing at their own absurdity. And yet the Spaniards were in their very nature more apt to satirise by ridicule than any other people in Europe.

122

The only way to explain their having for a whole century overlooked the vulnerability of the romances of chivalry to the darts of their malicious wit, is to acknowledge that the gust of spiritual self-sacrificing exaltation that swept over the nation in the sixteenth century swamped for the time even their keen sense of humour. But the racial trait could not be hidden entirely for very long, and was to assert itself, at first tentatively and rarely, and later boldly, until out of the amusing short anecdote on the one hand, and the top-heavy chivalric romance of wandering knights-errant on the other, there was to spring a new form of fictional literature, the effects of which have remained upon the novels of the whole world until to-day.

But though, as I shall presently point out, the Spanish novel of movement sprang from these sources, yet there were other side influences, both Spanish and universal, that contributed to make the new form of fiction what it was, and added to the vast power that it subsequently possessed in Europe. Side by side with the growth of the chivalric romance there had never ceased to exist in Spain a fashion for satirical verse, whose subjects for flagellation were not imaginary, but were drawn from the observation of the author. It would have been odd, indeed, if the countrymen of Seneca the younger, and of Martial, had forgotten the love of biting mockery of real things and persons that lay so deep in the national character. So, whilst cultured Spain in the fourteenth century was beginning to weep over the troubles of Oriana, and working itself into heroic ecstasies at the valour of Amadis, a dissolute priest, a very Rabelais, called Juan Ruiz, the Archpriest of Hita, was spinning facile verses by the hundred, lashing the vices and weaknesses of his countrymen and countrywomen, and showing himself suspiciously familiar with the dissolute life he pretended to condemn, whilst gloating over its unedifying details. He gathered his illustrations and his tales wherever he found them: in the old books of apologues, in the French fables, in the classical satires. But he applied all their teaching to the foibles of the people who surrounded him. Hypocritical nuns, canting, dissolute priests, thieving servants, poor, proud, pompous hidalgos, cheating gamblers, and mumping beggars pass through his verse, to be lashed and laughed at in the *Libro de Cantares*, by the Archpriest of Hita, who confesses himself to have been as bad as any of them. The book of which I speak must have been written about the middle of the fourteenth century; and some twenty or thirty years later the *Rimado de Palacio* of Pedro Lopez de Ayala, of whom I have so often made mention, presents before us another set of types of Spanish society to be made the whipping-blocks of their times; and later there were other satires of the same sort, which endeavoured in rhyme to present real figures drawn from observation, instead of heroic abstractions. This shows that the eye to see things as they were was in Spain never entirely blinded by the craze for high-faluting heroics, such as never could exist whilst mankind is as it has always been.

The next step towards the creation of a literature of real life was a great, a very great, one. More than a hundred years after the shocking Archpriest of Hita was in his grave, there was printed at Burgos (in 1499), a few years before the first printing of *Amadis of Gaul*, a little anonymous book, which to students of literary evolution must ever remain one of the beacons which guide us from headland to headland across the seas of time. It was a story in dialogue, or dramatic form, called *La Comedia de Calisto y Melibea*. Though written as if for the stage, it was too long (twenty-one acts) and otherwise impossible of presentation entire as a drama. It must not be forgotten that writers were groping in the dark. No one had as yet learned to present a complete connected long story in prose, for the tales of chivalry were only collections of episodes lightly strung together, and the development of character by means of fiction had not been heard of in modern times ; so that, although this story of *Calisto y Melibea* (or *Celestina*, as it became known throughout the world afterwards) may appear crude and childish to us, we must not forget that it was the first connected long story with a complete plot written in modern literature.

The plot is a sad one of lovers pursued by evil fate,

and sensuality meeting with a dire punishment. If we did not know of the Italian origin of *Romeo and Juliet*, we might think that Shakespeare had been inspired by *Celestina*; and, indeed, it is likely that he knew of Mabbe's translation of it in manuscript from Mabbe's friend Ben Jonson. The types are taken mainly from the Archpriest of Hita. A young nobleman named Calisto, of good repute and disposition, falls violently in love with a young lady of high station named Melibea. Finding the lady unassailable to his approaches, Calisto is persuaded by a roguish valet to appeal to an infamous old woman, a procuress named Celestina, evidently inspired by the archpriest's convent trotter, and by her intrigues with servants, and her hypocritical arts with Melibea herself, she contrives to bring about a meeting of the lovers, and the ruin of Melibea. Celestina is killed by Calisto's servants because she refuses to give them a due share of Calisto's reward; and Celestina's infamous friends kill Calisto in revenge, which causes Melibea to commit suicide.

This story is told so vigorously, and with so much humour and observation, and with such a sense of character, as to mark an epoch in fiction. It was almost immediately translated into Italian and French, and in the former language came to England, to be denounced by the grave Oxford professor Luis Vives as being a source of levity to be avoided. In 1530 *Celestina* was translated into English anonymously, and before the end of the sixteenth century the book was in the hands of every cultured reader in Europe. There had rarely been a book so popular as this in all lands. It told in vivid language what might be an experience of any of those who read it. This was life itself, not an abstraction. The quaint translator James Mabbe ('Don Diego Puede-Ser') translated *Celestina* again in that fine Elizabethan English of his, and the recent republication of it in the 'Tudor Reprints' brings it within reach of all English readers. There is no mincing matters about *Celestina*. The infamous old woman and the crowd of immoral rogues that surround her are taken straight from the low quarters of a Spanish city. Vice is not gilded, as it is in the chivalric romances ; it is not in words flagellated, and yet gloated over, as it is by the Archpriest. It is simply presented as it is, and its evil consequences naturally brought out by the development of the story. The following few words of Mabbe's translation will show how here, for the first time in modern literature, the character of the individual is developed by what he says, instead of only guessed at by what he does. The speaker is one of the dissolute women in Celestina's house, and she indicates her recklessness by enunciating the principle of a short life and a merry one. 'As long as we have meat for to-day, let us not think of to-morrow. Let to-morrow care for itself. As well dies he that gathers much, as he that lives but poorly.

We are not to live for ever, and therefore let us laugh
and be merry, for few are they that come to see old
age, and they who doe see it seldom dye of hunger.
I want nothing in this world but meat, drink, and
clothing, and my share of pleasure. And, though
rich men have better means to attain this glory than
he that hath little, yet there is not one of them that
is contented; not one that sayes to himselfe, I have
enough. There is not one of them with whom I
would exchange my pleasures for their riches.'

Thus, even when the artificial romance of chivalry
was at its highest vogue in the sixteenth century,
there arose in Spain a realistic fiction, in which the
habits of low life and vicious people were set down
as they existed, without any heroism at all. A
similar process was taking place in other countries
of Europe at the time, which doubtless, to some
extent, influenced the subsequent production of the
Spanish rogue novel. From the earliest classical
times one of the standing elements of the Greek and
Latin dramas was the roguish tricks of servants who
were used as a foil, or what we now call 'comic
relief,' to the heroes. Petronius in the *Satyricon*
even went beyond this, and presented a type who
lived by the exercise of his ingenuity in getting the
better of his fellow-creatures. Then, side by side
with this element in classical writing, was another
that told of the vicissitudes of a man in the guise
of an animal passing through the service of many

masters, such as the *Golden Ass* of Apuleius. And yet another development had arisen in Europe in the form of a collection of smart tricks or ingenious swindles that had clustered around some favoured jester, or some well-known buffoon or rogue fool. Such, for instance, was the German collection of cheating anecdotes first published in 1519, under the name of *Til Eulenspiegel,* by Thomas Murner, which was soon Englished under the title of *Til Owl-glass,* and was very popular in England. Therefrom sprang quite a list of English collections of similar tales, in which separate roguish anecdotes were strung together on some well-known name:—*The Gestes of Skoggin* (1565), by Andrew Borde ; *The Twelve Merry Gestes of the Widow Edyth* (1573), by Smith ; *The Conceited Gestes of George Peele* (1607); Skelton's *Merry Tales,* and others ; all of which I shall have to refer to at greater length in the next chapter, when I speak of the rogue tale in England. Tales of beggar life were also not uncommon in the sixteenth century all over Europe, giving accounts of ways and subterfuges of vagabonds, their slang, and their haunts. But, be it recollected, none of these were connected tales, nor was any attempt made in them to develop character or analyse motives. They were simply the apologues and classical stories of rogues' tricks, the deceits of servants, and the practical jokes of court jesters, collected together and threaded upon the string of a notorious name.

I

We have thus brought matters down to the middle of the sixteenth century in Spain. There existed, as I have shown, a small literature of satire in verse, upon real live types; *Celestina* with a few imitations, dealing with the life of the vicious classes, actually copied from existing society, without romance, the Oriental and classical short stories derived from the apologues; and overwhelming everything, the top-heavy, unnatural and inflated romance of chivalry, without humour and without reality, growing every year more extravagant. From such a monstrosity as this latter no healthy direct offspring could be derived. The short story, such as those of *Count Lucanor*, or Boccaccio, or like the collections of rogue stories I have mentioned, could go no further except to become more polished, more witty, more pungent. For the essence of these was that each one consisted of a single incident; and a single incident could not be spun out indefinitely. So with the exception of *Celestina*, which told, in more or less dramatic form, a single story consisting of several interlaced incidents and their developments, Spanish fiction had reached an *impasse* by the middle of the sixteenth century.

I have said that no healthy offspring could be expected from so monstrous an artificiality as the romance of chivalry had become. But what happens when that is the case? When degeneracy stops development an entire reaction takes place, and the effete type is not gradually reformed, but is convulsively

reversed. This is what took place in Spanish fiction.
Amadis, Arthur, Palmerin, and all the rest of them,
were artificial from top to bottom. The incidents,
crammed with giants and sorcerers, with maidens
too lovely to live, with knights too self-sacrificing and
brave ever to have been sons of men ; with shepherds
having no work to do but to lie on the grass and
sigh, or tell long-winded stories of their loves and
sufferings ; with shepherdesses who in real life would
not have known a sheep from a calf : these folk had
no relation whatever with real life. They were
abstractions, who had fulfilled an important and
influential part in purifying aims and elevating
altruism to a cult in a rough and violent age ; but
even in Spain the real need for them was passing
rapidly, and since a gradual reform of the stories
to a more reasonable and convincing tone was no
longer possible, the next development took the place
of an entire reaction. *Celestina* and the collections
of smart stories gave the clue. Realism, unmitigated,
must replace florid fancy. Instead of verdant lawns,
jewelled with starry flowers, the gutter of a slum must
be the scene; instead of languishing princesses, too
lovely for words, and with none of the ordinary cares
of humanity (for which indeed her constant tribula-
tions with ogres, sorcerers, and lovers would give her
no time), the woman of the story must be the labour-
ing peasant, or the trull of the streets ; instead of
jewelled palaces, soft music, and heavenly perfumes,

the beggar's hovel, the thieves' den, the blatant sounds and pungent odours of the streets, must be reproduced upon the page. Nothing must be pardoned in the way of inversion. The smart rogue must be the hero, instead of the knight ; and altruistic self-sacrifice must give place to dishonest and immoral selfishness. But, withal, nothing is ever invented in the world entire and new, and one part of the machinery of the chivalric romance was adopted for the framework of the new fiction. All the adventures of the knights of chivalry had been encountered on the way. The heroes were always wandering from one place to another, knights-errant rightly called, to right wrongs, rescue their lady-loves, or conquer kingdoms. But movement from one place to another was always essential to the story. This, then, was taken as the framework of the picaresque or rogue novel, when it was evolved as a reaction from Amadis. The other ingredients were the collections of stories I have already described, dealing with practical jokes or rogues' devices to get the better of other people ; partly derived from the classical cunning servant, and partly from the Oriental Spanish apologue.

This was the genesis of the rogue novel. Let us now look at what the novel itself became. To do this we can find no better way than consider the first, and in many respects the best, of the class—*Lazarillo de Tormes*. Who wrote the book, nobody knows ; but it has generally been ascribed to a great noble and statesman and a sound historian, to whose works I shall have to refer later—Don Diego Hurtado de Mendoza, who was the emperor's ambassador in Venice, and his representative at the Council of Trent in 1546. Having had the opportunity of studying and translating very many of his manuscript writings, and of considering those in print, I am quite convinced that Mendoza was not the author of *Lazarillo*. And yet, from the time of its appearance, there have always been traditions that connected it somehow with the Council of Trent; and it has been asserted that it was composed 'ambulando' by some of the Spanish prelates as they slowly rode on their long journey thither. This is possible, but unlikely; for anything less clerical than *Lazarillo* it is difficult to imagine. It is far more likely to have been written piecemeal by one of the clever Spanish literary men sent to Trent in the trains of bishops and ambassadors, and read perhaps on the way to amuse these great personages. In any case, it must have been written at that period, and it was first published very modestly in Burgos in 1554; the only copy of the first edition known being now in the Duke of Devonshire's library at Chatsworth.

The book is called *La Vida de Lazarillo de Tormes: y de sus fortunas y adversidades*, and tells the story of a young scamp, who says that his father was foreman in a mill on the river Tormes, near Salamanca, and that he was born in the mill. The father is sent to prison for pilfering the meal, and, afterwards going as muleteer to an officer, was killed in the wars against the Moors. The widow then opens a cookshop at Salamanca, and enters into relations with a negro groom, who steals his master's fodder to regale his mistress, and gets into trouble with the authorities. ' One can hardly wonder,' says Lazarillo, 'at a priest or a friar, the one robbing the poor, the other his convent, for the sake of their fair and devout believers, when love can stimulate a poor slave to do the like. All this was fully proved ; for when they came to me, I, like the child I was, and fearful of the threats of punishment, told them all I knew, even about the very horse-shoes that my mother had sent me to the farrier's to sell. My poor stepfather was soundly flogged, and his flesh tickled with drops of scalding fat, whilst my mother was commanded under the severest penalties never to receive Zaide again.' A blind beggar comes to lodge at the house where Lazarillo's mother is a servant, and the boy is engaged to lead him about. Thenceforward the adventures of the hero fill the book. There is but little subtlety of character. The lad is represented as being schooled gradually into cunning and vice ; sometimes in good places, where he prospers, sometimes with beggars, thieves, and rogues, where he starves till he steals. But, whether up or down, he never appears either despondent or elated. The hero, in short, although a real hero and the legitimate centre of interest of the story, is only there for the things that happen to him during his life, not to show how character and effort may mould events. That development came later.

The adventures of Lazarillo are probably adaptations of roguish tales current at the time, and drawn from a multitude of such sources as these I have mentioned. But, even so, Lazarillo is a great advance upon anything else before it. It tells in elegant, copious, and nervous Castilian, the ups and downs, the trials, perils, and adventures of a boy living by his wits, sharpened by adversity; and it enables the writer to portray, in the persons of Lazarillo's companions and employers, the various types that went to make up Spanish society of the day. The broken soldier, the out-at-elbows hidalgo, the hypocritical priest, the pickpocket jostling the overdressed crowd in the Calle Mayor, and the beggars and mumpers living hideously in squalid abundance on the proceeds of their afflictions, real and assumed. The work was a great one, and it first started a school of fiction which is not yet dead. It is difficult in a book of such a length to choose an adequate specimen. Here, however, are a few passages where the lad tells his first adventures with the blind man after they left Salamanca to take to the road :—

" With all this, however, I am sorry to say that I never met with so avaricious and so wicked an old curmudgeon : he allowed me almost to die daily of

hunger without troubling himself about my neces-
sities ; and, to say the truth, if I had not helped myself by means of a ready wit and nimble fingers, I
should have closed my account from sheer starvation.
Notwithstanding all my master's astuteness and
cunning, I contrived so to outwit him, that generally
the best half came to my share. But to accomplish
this, I was obliged to tax my powers of invention to
the uttermost. Of this I will recount a few specimens,
although they may not perhaps tell much to my
credit. The old man was accustomed to carry his
bread, meat, and other things in a sort of linen knap-
sack which was closed at the mouth by an iron ring,
and secured also by a padlock ; but in adding to his
store, or taking from it, he used such vigilance that
it was almost impossible to cheat him of a single
morsel. However, when he had given me my pittance,
which I found no difficulty in despatching in about
two mouthfuls, and had closed his budget thinking
himself quite secure from depredation, I began my
tactics, and by means of a small rent which I slyly
effected in one of the seams of the bag, I used to help
myself to the choicest pieces of meat, bacon, and
sausage, taking care to close the seam as opportunity
occurred. But in addition to this, all I could collect
together either by fraud or otherwise, I carried about
with me in half-farthings ; so that when the old man
was sent for to pray, and the people gave him
farthings, all of which passed through my hands, he

being blind, I contrived to slip them into my mouth, by which process so quick an alteration was effected, that when they reached his hands they were invariably reduced to half their original value. The cunning old fellow, however, suspected me ; for he used to say, How the deuce is this ? Ever since you have been with me, they give me nothing but half-farthings, whereas before it was no unusual thing to be paid with halfpence, and never less than with farthings. I must be sharp with you, I find. Whenever we ate, the old man took care to keep a small jar of wine near him, which was reserved for his own special service. But I soon adopted the practice of bestowing on this favourite jar sundry loving though stolen embraces. Such pleasures were but short lived, for the fervency of my attachment was soon discovered by the deficiency of the wine ; and the old man afterwards, to secure his draught, never let the jar go without tying it to him by the handle. But I was a match for him even there ; for I procured a large straw, and, dipping it into the mouth of the jar, renewed my intimacy with such effect that but a small share was left for him who came after me. The old traitor was not long in finding me out : I think he must have heard me sucking in the wine, for he quickly changed his plan, and placed the jar between his knees, keeping the mouth covered by his hand, and thus he thought himself quite secure against pilfering."

In a tale constructed on such lines as I have

described, there was no reason why it ever should stop, and several sequels and continuations of the story appeared. The Inquisition came down upon *Lazarillo* and purged it of much of its anti-clerical ribaldry; yet not only was edition after edition issued in Spain, but the book was almost at once published in French and Italian. In English the first version appeared anonymously in 1568, *The Marvelus Dedes and Lyf of Lazaro de Tormes*; but this edition I have never seen. Another came out in 1576, '*The Pleasant History of Lazarillo de Tormes, a Spaniard*. Imprinted at London by Henry Binneman, dwelling at Knightrider Street, at the Sign of the Mermaid.' But the best-known edition is that of David Rowland of Anglesey, published in London in 1586. Of all these, and other English editions and imitations, I shall speak in the next chapter.

I must now pass to the consideration of the development of the novel of movement in Spain itself, leaving for the present the detailed description of the picaresque novels in general, which sprang from the example of *Lazarillo de Tormes*; especially *Guzman de Alfarache* of Mateo Aleman, *Marcos de Obregon* of Espinel, *El Gran Tacaño* of Quevedo, and their many imitations in France and England.

The uncompromising realism of *Lazarillo* and its school struck a popular note, which swelled as time passed on, and as the vapid romances of chivalry became more and more extravagant. But the victory was not gained all at once. Public taste and literary traditions were slow to change, and the artificial, fanciful romance still had its votaries. In the last chapter I referred to the grafting of the pastoral form of fiction upon the stock of chivalric romance. The loves of shepherds and shepherdesses were no more real than were those of knights-errant and distressed ladies; but at the end of the sixteenth century they demanded a less copious draft upon the reader's imagination to realise their possibility. They became, in England and France particularly, for over a century a favourite vehicle of fancy; but in Spain their vogue was not long. When the great literary genius Cervantes was groping for a vehicle for his abounding wit, it was natural that he should tentatively choose the form which seemed at the moment that most in favour with readers who prided themselves upon their culture. But the pastoral form was not purely Spanish. Neither the climate nor the configuration of the country lent itself to the formation of the sparkling green pastoral lawns and rippling rills that form the background of the pastoral romance. Spain is a lean country; and fatness, not to say stodginess, is the essence of the pastoral romance. The form originally came from classic Italy, and though it spread to France and England mainly through Spain, it was never native to stern Castile.

If ever a true representative Spanish mind existed, it was that of Miguel Cervantes Saavedra. Keen, satirical, in his Iberian heart irreverent towards all things but abstract sentiment, when he elected to embody his thoughts early in his career in the pastoral form of *Galatea*, he must have felt its artificiality and have secretly laughed at it. That Cervantes was consciously following a prevailing fashion when he elected to try his first flight with pastoral wings, is seen by the knowledge he shows of the fashionable pastoral romances when the discussion is going on about the destruction of Don Quixote's library. More than a hundred stately folios of chivalric romances were condemned to be burnt, in order that they might not encourage the poor gentleman in his mad ideas. The niece then suggests the few thin little books of pastorals should also be sacrificed; for, she says, it would be no wonder if, after being cured of his chivalry disorder, my uncle, by reading these, took a fancy to turn shepherd, and ranged the woods and fields singing and piping. The curate is inclined to agree with her, but pleads that the *Diana* of Montemayor, of which I spoke in the last chapter, should be spared from the flames; only that it should be purged of all that nonsense about the sage Felicia and the magic water, and of almost all the long pieces of verse. Let it keep its prose and welcome, and the honour of being the first book of its kind; and then, one after the other, all the fashionable pastoral romances of the day are passed in review and keenly criticised by the curate, some being spared, and some burnt. That which is praised most highly is the *Pastor de Filida*, by Cervantes' friend Galvez de Montalvan, which, with the *Arcadia* of the Italian Sannazaro, inspired his own *Galatea.*

It seems strange at first sight that so consummate a realist as Cervantes should, even temporarily, have clothed his ideas in the languid, insipid artificiality of the pastoral. But he was a child of his age. The quiet, placid simplicity of the idyllic shepherds was as much a natural revulsion in form from the noisy clashing of knights and giants, as was the vulgar picaresque novel a revulsion in ethics from the superfine altruistic virtue of heroes of chivalry; and Cervantes correctly hit the taste of 1585 when *Galatea* was published— fleeting in Spain as that taste was. In any case, the form is utterly dead now; and even the genius of Cervantes cannot make these seventy odd shepherds and shepherdesses, and dozens of nymphs, otherwise than mawkish lay figures manufactured to spout interminable verse. They were abstractions never meant to be taken for reality. But though the vehicle was a poor one, of which even Cervantes could not make much, the Spanish in which *Galatea* is written, especially the prose portions, are as nearly perfect Castilian as ever was written. What is more remarkable than anything about it is that, though *Galatea* itself did not attract much attention, it was to the hour of his death a favourite with the author; and from the day it was published in 1585, until thirty

years later, on the last day of his life, the author of
Don Quixote never ceased to promise a second part.
For, by an irony of nature, Cervantes loved best, and
yearned for praise for, those things that the public did
not want of him : his dramas and his dear *Galatea*. I
will quote a short passage, chosen at random from
Galatea, in order that it may be seen how foreign the
whole tone is to the taste of to-day. Two shepherdesses, Galatea and Florisa, overhear another shepherdess, a stranger, singing a despairing love-song,
and bewailing cruel fate. They come forward and in
tears of sympathy offer her their help. After an
infinite length of florid compliment and high-flown
language, the new shepherdess of course tells the
story of her grief. It is too intolerably long to be
quoted at length, but this is how it begins :—

'Let us retire, then, said the shepherdess, from this
spot, and seek another, where, without being seen or
disturbed, I may be able to tell you what it grieves me
to have promised you, for I foresee that it will cost
more to lose the good opinion I have gained with you
than to reveal my thoughts to you, however late, if
perhaps yours have not been touched by the affliction I am suffering.

'Desirous that the shepherdess should fulfil her
promise, straightway the three arose, and betook
themselves to a secret and retired place known
already to Galatea and Florisa, where beneath the
pleasant shade of some leafy myrtles, without being

seen by anybody, all three could be seated. Forth-
with, with exquisite grace and charm, the strange
shepherdess began to speak in this wise.

'On the banks of the famous Henares, which ever
yields fresh and pleasant tribute to your golden
Tagus, most beauteous shepherdesses, was I born and
nurtured in a station not so lowly that I might count
myself the meanest of the village. My parents are
farmers and accustomed to field labour, in which
occupation I followed them, leading a flock of simple
sheep over the common pastures of our village. So
well did I adapt my thoughts to the condition in
which my lot had placed me, that nothing gave me
more joy than to see my flock multiply and increase,
and I had no other thought than how to gain for them
the richest and most fertile pastures, the clearest and
freshest waters.'

This artificiality leaves us cold, as probably it did
the mass of the Spanish public of the time in which
it was written. It was the affected cultured few,
influenced by Italian residence and travel, and proud
of classical taste, that, in Spain at least, liked to read
of shepherds and shepherdesses. The true Spaniards,
ardent and satirical, intensely realistic now, as a
reaction from the abstract transcendentalism of the
past hundred years, wished to read and to laugh
bitterly at the tricks of rogues ; to follow, as in a mirror
passing, the daily life around them, with its mean-
ness, its vice, its devotion, its hollow splendour, and

its sordid shifts. The short Italian novel of real life, free from an obtrusive moral, had become popular in Europe from the hands of Boccaccio and his followers; but in Spain nothing native of the sort yet existed, except the apologues, or moral anecdotes, I have so often mentioned, and the few incidental tales introduced into the romances of roguery—*Lazarillo de Tormes*, *Guzman de Alfarache*, and the like. So, as Cervantes himself says, he became the 'first to essay novels in the Spanish tongue.'

The first of his short novels was probably written between 1592 and 1600, and the other eleven or (according to some writers) twelve were written at various times up to 1613, when they were published for the first time under the name of *The Exemplary Novels*. The first edition of *Don Quixote* had been published eight years before; but as the *Exemplary Novels*, for the most part, represent an earlier manifestation of the author's genius, though published later, I propose to speak first of the *Exemplary Novels*, of which a good English edition has just been published in two volumes by a Scottish firm. To speak adequately of these wonderful tales would need, not the few pages I have at my disposal in a general review, but a volume by itself. They are throbbing with vitality and colour, veritable reflections of life, full of satire and observation. They are: *The Little Gipsy*, *The Liberal Lover*, *Rinconete and Cortadillo*, *The Spanish Englishwoman*, *The Licentiate of Glass*,

The Force of Blood, The Jealous Estremeñan, The Illustrious Scrubbing-Maid, The Lady Cornelia, The Deceitful Marriage, The Dogs' Colloquy, and, perhaps, *The Feigned Aunt.*

The author was already famous when they were published, and the merit of the stories was seen the moment they issued from the press. Before a year had passed they were translated into French, and the French dramatists seized upon the plots at once. *La Fuerza de la Sangre* became a French play called *La Force du Sang*; *The Little Gipsy* (*La Gitanilla*) became *La Belle Égyptienne.* As I shall point out more at length in the chapter on the Drama, the English playwrights also soon found the *Exemplary Novels* fertile of material. *The Illustrious Scrubbing-Maid* (*La Ilustre Fregona*) was made into a play by Fletcher, and called *The Fair Maid of the Inn*; *Rule a Wife and Have a Wife*, by the same dramatist, is an adaptation of *El Casamiento Engañoso*; and his *The Chances* is adapted from *The Lady Cornelia.* Beaumont and Fletcher's *A Very Woman* is taken from *The Liberal Lover* (*El Amante Liberal*). Massinger and Rowley adapted *The Force of Blood* (*La Fuerza de la Sangre*), and called it *The Queen of Corinth*; and *The Spanish Gipsy* of Middleton and Rowley was taken from *La Gitanilla*; whilst several other plays in English were derived more or less directly from these novels, as I shall have the opportunity of showing in a later chapter.

K

If the dramatists and story-tellers of England and France thus seized upon the substance of these tales, in Spain itself the same process was even more conspicuous.   Not only did the great dramatists of Spain's golden age, Lope de Vega, Tirso de Molina, and Calderon, copy and adapt them for the stage, but writers innumerable imitated them in the form of novels.   Their vogue was wonderful and widespread : Sir Walter Scott told Lockhart that it was by reading them that he was first led to write fiction, and Goethe called them 'a very treasure of delight.' But the popularity of the short story modelled on the lines of the *Exemplary Novels*, the title of which was, indeed, the last surviving tradition of the Spanish-Oriental didactic apologue, was surpassed, and overwhelmed, by the triumph of *Don Quixote* and the continued story of peripatetic adventure, which was a new development of them.   The *Exemplary Novels* nevertheless will remain one of our undying literary treasures, and now that they have for the first time been worthily translated into English by Mr. Maccoll they deserve a new lease of prosperity. The following specimen of his version will show the freedom and vigour of Cervantes' style.   It describes the first meeting of the two young vagabonds, Rinconete and Cortadillo, whose adventures with a band of thieves form the story :—

   "On one of the hot days of summer, two lads chanced to find themselves in the *Venta* of the Little

Mill, which is situated on the borders of the famous plains of Alcudia. The one was between fourteen and fifteen years of age, and the other not over seventeen, Both were engaging youths, but were very tattered, ragged, and ill clad. Neither wore a cloak, their breeches were of linen, and their stockings were bare flesh. It is true that their shoes redeemed the matter, because those of the one were sandals, as worn as they were old, and those of the other rotten and without soles, so that they served him rather as fetters than as shoes. The one wore a green sportsman's cap, the other a hat that had no band, low in the crown and with a broad flap. At the shoulder, and girt by the breast, the one had on a shirt of the colour of chamois leather, short, and gathered into one sleeve. The other was free from encumbrances and baggage, except that in his bosom was to be seen a great bundle which, as afterwards appeared, was a collar of the kind called a starched Walloon, stiffened with grease and so wholly thread-bare that it seemed all threads. In it were wrapped up and preserved sundry playing-cards of an oval shape, for by use they had become worn out, and that they might last the longer they had been pared. Both the boys were sunburnt, their nails were edged with dirt, and their hands were far from clean. The one had half a sword, and the other a knife with a yellow handle. The two stepped out to rest at a porch in front of the inn, and, sitting down opposite

each other, he who appeared to be the elder said to
the smaller, To what district does your worship
Sir Knight belong, and whithér, pray, is your worship
bound? My country, noble sir, replied the stripling
to whom the question was addressed, I do not
know, nor do I know either whither I am going.
Marry! replied the elder, your worship does not
make his appearance from heaven, and this is not a
place where one can take up one's abode, but per-
force must pass onwards. So it is, retorted the
other; yet I said the truth in what I said, for my
country is not mine, since I have nothing in it, more
than a father who does not hold me to be his son,
and a stepmother who treats me as a stepson."
And so these delicious young rascals make friends
and proceed on their predatory travels together.
Nothing could exceed the naturalness, the modernity,
of the prose of these novels, in conspicuous contrast
with the pastoral writing by the same author, of which
a specimen has been quoted in a previous page.

The following short extract from the preface of
the *Exemplary Novels*, in which Cervantes draws
his own portrait, will show how unerring was the
artistry of his pen, and how characteristically Spanish
in its vanity and yet in keen satiric observation,
even at his own expense. 'He whom you here
behold with aquiline visage, with chestnut hair,
smooth unruffled brow, with sparkling eyes, and a
nose arched, although well proportioned, a silver

beard, although not twenty years ago it was golden, large moustache, small mouth, teeth not important, for he has but six of them, and those in ill condition and worse placed, because they do not correspond one with the other; the body between two extremes, neither large nor small; the complexion bright, rather white than brown, somewhat heavy-shouldered, and not very nimble on his feet: this, I say, is the portrait of the author of the *Galatea* and of *Don Quixote de la Mancha*.' His claim in the same preface to be the originator of the Spanish short story of real life, told for its own sake and without didactic object, is emphatic. 'I am,' he says, 'the first to essay novels in the Castilian tongue, for the many novels which go about in print in Spanish are translated from foreign languages, whilst these are mine own, neither imitated nor stolen. My genius begat them, my pen gave them birth, and they go on growing in the arms of the press.'

But, fine as these short novels are in themselves, they led to something infinitely greater. The *Exemplary Novels* were, in all essentials of form, extended apologues, without the moral. Some of them in all probability were written before *Don Quixote*, and the great work, in its first inception, was intended to be another short story in comic vein like them. The thought was to show up the absurdities of the chivalric romances. The subject was crying aloud for mockery. The bubble was swelled ready for bursting. The native Spanish, mocking humour was once more asserting itself, and overcoming the exalted spiritual pride that had been for a century the nation's strength, and was now to be the nation's ruin. For over a century all literature had been saturated with this artificial obsession. It had coloured men's thoughts, it had ruled men's lives; but it was not true to nature, and it was doomed to fall, as all false things must. So Miguel Cervantes, unconscious that he was beginning a world's masterpiece, wrote the first lines of what he thought was going to be a slight skit on the already waning craze of chivalry. A mad country gentleman, full of the altruistic and exalted gallantry that much conning of chivalrous books had taught him to believe the highest nobleness, starts out in search of such adventures as had befallen Amadis and his imitators. What he meets are sights and sounds of everyday life in Spain, and his disordered brain makes windmills into giants, kitchen wenches into princesses, barbers into magicians, flocks of sheep into Moors; and him, a poor, lean, elderly squireling, into a splendid warrior, whose heroism shall conquer the world for the right. Truly it was too big a subject to be contained in a short story, and it overcame its author. This fact must also be ascribed in part to the particular framework which the burlesque demanded. The romances of chivalry, as I pointed out in a previous chapter, had depended—like the subse-

quent romances of roguery—upon the continual
movement of the hero, and his encounter with various
adventures and persons on the way. This form
encouraged continuation, because, as I have already
observed, there was practically no reason, except the
death of the hero, why it should ever stop. In any
case, Don Quixote was carried on from adventure to
adventure, from one crazy fancy to another, until,
instead of a short novel, one of the great books of
the world came to be written; and the chivalric
romance was silenced for ever by universal shouts of
laughter.

To see how *Don Quixote* thus grew from small
beginnings, we will glance at the first inception of the
story. The gentleman, doubtless a caricature of some
small local magnate named Quijada, known to Cervantes, belonged to Argamasilla de Alba, in La Mancha,
and starts out on his first journey alone. Sancho
Panza himself was an afterthought, for it was not
until the middle of the third chapter that the chance
mention by the innkeeper who was to knight Don
Quixote, that knights-errant were accompanied by
squires, that any squire at all seemed to enter the
author's head, and not until chapter seven, when the
knight starts on his second journey, that Sancho
is brought into the story. Even then he was not the
Sancho he afterwards became, for even in chapter
nine he is referred to as having long shanks. But, as
the satire proceeds, the author's hand becomes surer.

The people he described he knew in the flesh; and one by one they pass before us in their habits as they lived. For years he had ridden across those tawny plains, and lodged in those squalid inns, as the king's tithe-collector. With those stolid boors, full of sententious speech and sage proverbs, culled from the sources of ancient Hebrew and Arabic lore, to which I have directed attention in earlier chapters, he had lived. His wide travels in Spain and abroad, his vast memory and his abounding wit, gave him material enough to write a library. A true Spaniard, if ever such lived, he was a compound of the qualities, good and bad, which made the Spaniard of his day, or shortly before it, better and worse than other men. Better, because saturated still with essential nobleness of sacrifice and the sanctity of purity of aim; worse, because with an impossible high ideal ever before him he was content in most cases to let it remain an ideal, and to separate daily conduct from abstract professions. To him nothing real was sacred; his mocking laugh stopped at no barriers, so long as the ideal abstraction, quite apart from his life, was set upon a pedestal afar off for mystic worship.

The salient point of the whole work is its uncontrollable humour. The sage saws put into the mouth of Sancho are the current maxims of the unlearned Spaniards who, as I have explained in former chapters, had inherited from their forefathers the tradition of crystallising wisdom in sententious speech that passed from father to son for centuries, as guides to ideal perfection in life. But as a stylist in Castilian prose Cervantes is supreme. His style is quite unstudied, as spontaneous as his humour. He writes with point and piquancy, because he thinks and sees clearly. But, besides his gaiety, you see beneath his lines a tolerance, and an easy-going optimism, an almost contemptuous avoidance of condemnation, that shows his heart to have been as sound as his brain. It has been said well by a learned Cervantist, that there are six hundred and sixty-nine personages in *Don Quixote*, and yet not one in this motley multitude of characters is wholly bad or despicable. It is this deep humanity, this wise tenderness, this intimate appreciation of the better side of inferior natures, which have endeared Cervantes to generation after generation, to a degree unequalled by any other writer in literary history. The wonderful work seized irresistibly upon the hearts of the world, as soon as it issued from the press. The book first appeared in Spain in 1605, though probably many people had seen it in manuscript some time before ; and less than two years afterwards an edition appeared in Brussels. Then in every country in the world, at short intervals, translations were eagerly read. The fame of the book soon reached England. In 1607 George Wilkins in his play called *The Miseries of Infant Marriage* makes one of the characters speak of fighting a windmill, and Middleton's *Your Five Gallants*, of a similar date, contains a reference also to fighting a windmill. In 1609 Ben Jonson mentions Don Quixote in *The Silent Woman*, and in 1610 in the *Alchymist*. An English translation of the first part, by Shelton, was published in London in 1612; and even then Shelton says he wrote it 'long ago,' and that he knocked it off in forty days, which is difficult to believe. Fletcher wrote his *Knight of the Burning Pestle*, suggested by *Don Quixote*, as he says, in 1611, before Shelton's translation appeared. Thereafter allusions to *Don Quixote* abound in England, and I shall refer to many of them in the chapter on the Drama. One more subject for consideration in connection with *Don Quixote*, is the reason why it attracted such triumphant popularity in countries like England, where the chivalric romance had not any hold upon the public mind for centuries before, and where, one would think, the satire would fall flat. It was not read in such countries for its satire. It was read because it touched the eternal primitive springs of human feeling; because its humour was universal and for all time, just as Shakespeare's philosophy is. No local limitations can circumscribe such excellence as this, either in humour or in philosophy. There is, perhaps, another reason that may explain the instantaneous popularity and abiding vogue of the book. Europe had been pervaded, in the process I have endeavoured to describe, by the fashion of the maxim and apophthegm, which Spaniards had derived from the

Hebrews and Arabs of the Peninsula. In England, especially late in the sixteenth and early seventeenth centuries, the sententious form was considered the best literary fashion of the day. The wisdom and wit of Sancho in sparkling epigram, added to the humour and humanity that pervaded the whole book, marked *Don Quixote* as being good literary form ; and this, with its many other excellences, gave to the work in England the admiration that it more than deserved, but which, perhaps, might have been less pronounced if the sententious wisdom in it had not been so rich and abundant.

CHAPTER VI

THE PICARESQUE AND PERIPATETIC NOVELS
IN ENGLAND

In the last chapter the evolution of the novel in
Spain was followed, showing that the framework or
machinery, consisting of the movement of the hero
from place to place, and the encounter of many persons and adventures on the way, had been taken
from the Romances of Chivalry, which had inherited
the form from the personal chronicle. The special
reason why the Spanish new realistic fiction should
have been forced to adopt for its medium the representation of squalid scenes and thievish, cunning
adventurers, is to be found in the invariable rule of
reaction or revulsion when anything is carried to an
undue extreme. The tone of the Spanish romances
of chivalry had been so ineffably heroic, the personages so unselfishly noble, the surroundings so invariably regal, that the reaction had necessarily to be
exactly the opposite. I shall point out to you presently that, as the romances of chivalry had not in
the fifteenth and sixteenth centuries caught. hold of
French and English readers to the same extent as

156

Spanish, the picaresque and peripatetic novels, which afterwards became so fashionable in England and France, whilst adopting the same machinery as that used in Spain, had no need to mark reaction by insisting so much upon the background of the stories being squalid and the character of the hero dishonest. This point must be borne in mind, as marking the main difference between the Spanish and English forms.

In the last chapter there is a full account of the first Spanish realistic novel, *Lazarillo de Tormes*, the autobiography of a penniless lad who lived by his wits. It was written in 1546, and first published in 1554, and immediately became popular both in Spain and abroad, French and Italian translations appearing soon after. We shall have to consider here to what extent this book and its followers, of which I shall speak presently, influenced the development of English fiction. Up to this time English fiction had consisted mainly of the Arthurian romances, Malory's *Morte d'Arthur*, and adaptations from the Italian and French short stories, some in prose and some in verse, such as Chaucer's *Canterbury Tales*. The stories of Bandello and other Italian writers especially were translated by Painter, and furnished plots for the playwrights of Elizabeth's reign. But there was in addition to these a fugitive form of fiction, which, although it had always existed in one form or another, suddenly became popular in England about ten or twelve years after *Lazarillo* was published in Spain ; which seems to argue that, at least, one London publisher even thus early had gained some knowledge of *Lazarillo's* popularity.

The quips and cranks of professional buffoons had always been repeated, and, as happens to this day, such stories of smart answers, practical jokes, and ready shifts are apt to cluster round the name of any droll personage known to the public. Such collections of quips, as I say, had existed from time immemorial in some form or another, and it is believed that one collection, at least, had been published in England before *Lazarillo* appeared in Spain. But no copy of such early edition is known to exist; and it was not until 1565, eleven years after *Lazarillo* had appeared, that this book in a chronological form became very popular. It is called *The First and best part of Skoggin's Gests, full of witty mirth and pleasant shifts, done by him in France and other places, being a preservative against melancholy. Gathered by Andrew Borde, Doctor of Physic.* Whether Dr. Borde, who had died in 1549, really did collect these stories is now uncertain. But there is no doubt that Skoggin was a real person. He was a gentleman, poor but learned, an M.A. of Oxford, and jester to Edward IV.; and his name throughout the sixteenth century was one upon which to hang tales. Shakespeare makes Mr. Justice Shallow, when talking of his and Falstaff's hot youth, say : 'I saw him break Skogan's head at

the court gate when I was a crack not thus high.'
The point to which I am desirous of directing attention is that in the arrangement of these practical
jokes of Skoggin, published in 1565, a regular chronological sequence is followed, I believe, for the first
time, and the book thus assumes the form of a con-
tinuous roguish biography of its hero. It begins
when he is a student at Oxford, and follows him
through his pranks at court, his banishment to France,
his return to England, his tricks to force himself into
favour again, and, finally, his death and burial. I am
inclined to regard this little collection of jester's jokes
as the first manifestation in England of the picaresque
taste in fiction which had a few years before appeared
in Spain in the form of *Lazarillo*.

In order to explain my reference to the chronological arrangement of *Skoggin's Gests* in the later
edition, I will compare the book presently with
another collection published in 1566, the year after
the second edition of *Skoggin,* and tacked upon the
name of Skelton, the priest-jester and poet laureate
of Henry VII. and Henry VIII. Before doing so, a
specimen or two of *Skoggin* may be given, in order
that a comparison of them may be made with the
complete peripatetic stories in England, to which I
shall later direct attention. The artless nature of the
tricks narrated shows the probable antiquity of their
origin. *Skoggin's* first story, for instance, is entitled 'What shift Skoggin and his chamber-fellow

made to fare well in Lent,' and the device was simply
that one of them should pretend to fall ill of the
plague and the other should tend him, being entrusted
with the key of the cellar and pantry, in order to
secure isolation.   Another story tells 'What shift
Skoggin and his fellow made when they lacked
money.'   This shift was for the accomplices to separate, and for one to go towards Thame Market, and
overtake a grazier on the way, driving a flock of
sheep.   After saluting the grazier Skoggin was to
refer incidentally to the sheep as hogs, and so to
lead the man to make a bet that they were sheep,
the first person encountered to be the referee.   This
of course was the accomplice, and the mystified drover
had to pay up.   This story is a very ancient one, and
was known in Spain, and probably elsewhere, ages
before Skoggin lived.

The most famous of any of Skoggin's stories, and
one which gave rise to a common saying to denote
the search for an object in an unlikely place, was
' The Hare on the Housetop.'   The story runs that
Skoggin introduced his wife to the queen (Elizabeth
Woodville), and told each of them separately that the
other was very deaf.   The consequence was that the
two ladies bawled at each other until inquiry led to
the discovery of the trick.   The queen was so much
offended that she asked the king to banish the jester ;
and the king warned Skoggin that if he came near
the court again the hounds should be set upon him.

A few days afterwards Skoggin, having concealed beneath his coat a fleet hare, came to court; and the king, being informed of this, ordered the hounds to be let loose and set upon him. Just when the hounds were at his tail the jester slipped the hare, after which the dogs went helter-skelter, leaving Skoggin alone and safe. Being summoned before the king, the latter said: 'Thou didst cast a hare before the dogs when they were set upon thee; go and look out the same hare, or thou shalt suffer death.' Then said Skoggin: 'I can get you another quick hare, but it will be hard to find the self-same one.' 'I will have the self-same hare,' said the king. 'Why,' said Skoggin, 'I cannot tell where I shall go and look for him.' 'Thou must look for him as well where he is as where he is not,' said the king. 'Well,' said Skoggin, 'I trust I shall find him.' The sequel is that Skoggin, taking the king at his word, gets on to the roof and wellnigh brings the king's house down about his ears, tearing up the leads with a pickaxe, and knocking over the battlements; and when remonstrated with, the jester tells the courtiers that he is obeying the king's orders. When brought again before the king, Skoggin in exculpation quotes the king's words that he is to look for the hare 'as well where he is as where he is not'; and he is thereupon banished from England. He offends the King of France by similar tricks, and steals back to England, where he recommences his old life.

L

The success of this edition of *Skoggin* doubtless led to the publication in the following year, 1566, of the Skelton collection—'*Merry Tales,* newly invented and made by Master Skelton, Poet Laureat. Imprinted in London, in Fleet Street beneath the Conduit, at the sign of Saint John the Evangelist.' Skelton died in 1529, so that these tales, of which there are only fifteen, must have been merely traditionally connected with him.   There is no attempt in this case to arrange them in chronological or biographical form, and the book is doubtless the compilation of an inferior hack, who just hustled the tales together as he got them. That the success of the previous year's *Skoggin* was that which inspired the book, is seen in the first story of 'How Skelton came late home to Oxford from Abingdon,' which begins thus : ' Skelton was an Englishman born, as Skogyn was, and brought up in Oxford.'   Most of Skelton's stories have a distinctly priestly flavour, giving his sharp answers to friars and the like.   They are mentioned here mainly for the purpose of contrasting the arrangement with that of *Skoggin*—they being, in my opinion, a hasty compilation in the old manner ; [1] whilst in *Skoggin* the adoption of the quasi-biographical arrangement marks the advance in England towards the connected biographical rogue-tale originated in *Lazarillo de Tormes.*

---

[1] Collections of unconnected jests in this old manner continued to be published under various names long afterwards—*Tarleton's Jests,* 1600 ; *Merry Conceited Gestes of George Peele,* 1607 ; *Jests of Jack of Dover* (which has some attempt at a connecting plot), 1604, etc.

Before passing to the consideration of the full development of the picaresque fiction in England, I will refer again to a novel which had an extraordinary popularity and a marked effect upon the fashion in language in England. It may be called the first attempt at a modern novel which appeared in this country, and was called *Euphues*, by John Lyly. The first part was published in 1579, and it merits our attention here, in the first place, because its affected preciosity of language and far-fetched imagery was confessedly copied from the Spanish style of Guevara (of whom I spoke in a former chapter, and to whom I shall refer again), and secondly, because Lyly adopted the framework of travel upon which to hang his satires and criticisms of society. Lyly, of all things, is didactic. He makes his hero—indeed, all his characters—sermonise continually. His plot is to take a young classical Greek on his travels to Naples and afterwards to England, and everything he sees everywhere is made the text of a discourse. He teaches us some strange things about animals, philosophises endlessly about love and marriage, and denounces the extravagance of modern ladies' dress. This is what his imaginary Athenian has to say about the English ladies of Elizabeth's day:—

"Take from them their periwigs, their paintings, their jewels, their rolls, their boulstrings, and thou shalt soon perceive that a woman is the least part of herself. When they be once robbed of their robes then will they appear so odious, so ugly, so monstrous, thou wilt rather think them serpents than saints, and so like hags that thou wilt fear rather to be enchanted than enamoured.　Look at their closets, and there thou shalt find an apothecary's shop of sweet confections, a surgeon's box of sundry salves, a pedlar's pack of new fangles.　Besides all this, their shadows, their spots, their lawns, their leafkins, their ruffs, their rings, show them to be anything but modest matrons."

It will be seen by this that *Euphues* and its many imitators were rather satires, built on the framework of the peripatetic novel, than novels themselves.　To see the full effect upon English style of Lyly's affected obscure preciosity, or Euphuism, which he imitated from Guevara, we have only to read any of Queen Elizabeth's letters.　Euphuism is there carried to its extreme of absurdity.　What the queen did lesser people copied, and the correspondence of the time is often so full of obscure conceits as to be almost unintelligible to the readers of to-day.

We now come, in chronological sequence, to the first real national peripatetic novel in English, evidently inspired by *Lazarillo* and its school—namely, *Jack Wilton*, by Thomas Nash.　This brilliant young satirist, a follower and friend of Greene, who knew Spanish literature well, and took many of his dramatic plots from Spanish sources, must have had ample opportunity for reading David Rowland's translation of *Lazarillo*, which was a popular book in England at the time. He travelled abroad, and was one of the young men of Shakespeare's day who struggled hard to make a living by literature. He wrote anything and everything, from political satires to a treatise in praise of red herrings. In 1594, when Nash was twenty-seven, *Jack Wilton* appeared. I wish to direct attention here to what I have already remarked as to the difference between the two forms of picaresque novel, Spanish and English. We have seen that Lazarillo was a ragamuffin, as was Guzman de Alfarache, Pablo el Buscon, and the rest of them. But not so Jack Wilton. He is represented, it is true, as being very hard up at first, but a gentleman by birth, and a page at the court of Henry VIII. He starts his autobiography when he was quite a boy, in attendance on the king at the siege of Tournay in 1512, and carries his adventures down to the time when he has gained fame, fortune, and a beautiful wife. The scenes are not generally sordid or squalid, but there is all through the book the effort to show how keen-witted and smart Jack Wilton is. For instance, his very first adventure as a boy is when—he being short of money and wanting refreshment—he goes to an old miserly Flemish innkeeper, near the camp, who serves the English army with wine and provisions. After flattering and befooling the innkeeper by representing to him that he has come to do him a great service, he tells the poor man that he is suspected of giving in-formation to the enemy. Jack Wilton assures him that he has done the best he can for him, and will continue to do so, but nearly every one is against him, because he is so stingy of his provisions. The poor man, whose conscience pricks him, falls into a panic, and not only feasts Jack Wilton bountifully, but regales all the English soldiers who come near him with free wine and good cheer. Henry VIII., being informed of this great change in him, sends for the innkeeper and asks him the reason. He tells him the truth, and Jack Wilton gets a good whipping. This is purely picaresque, but it is not squalid. *Jack Wilton* is a true realistic novel of movement, but this and other similar novels in English approximate more to *Gil Blas* than to *Lazarillo* and *Guzman de Alfarache*, because both in France and England the violent reaction against the romances of chivalry was not felt, and sordidness of the anti-hero and of his surroundings was not needed. Altogether, *Jack Wilton* is an extremely interesting specimen of writing, the best picaresque tale in English until Defoe wrote *Moll Flanders* and *Colonel Jack*. It is here and there touched with wilful euphuistic eccentricity of language, and marred by the liberal introduction of invented words, but it deserves to be read as the first specimen of such work in English derived straight from *Lazarillo*. How popular Rowland's translation of *Lazarillo* was at the end of the sixteenth century in England is seen by the numerous references to incidents of it in the Elizabethan dramatists. Shakespeare, amongst others, shows that he had read it. In *Much Ado about Nothing* (Act ii. Scene 1) he makes Benedict say, ' *Ho! now, you strike, like the blind man: 'twas the boy that stole your meat and you'll beat the post'*—this being one of the incidents of the tale. It was inevitable that so popular a work as *Lazarillo de Tormes* should at once give rise to a flock of continuations, sequels, and imitations. The very year after its first publication in 1554, it was followed by a second part issued anonymously in Antwerp, but not in Spain. It was a wretched thing and deservedly failed, with the exception of the first chapter, which tells of Lazarillo's meeting with certain Germans in Toledo, and how he accompanied them to sea, where he is wrecked and turned into a tunny-fish. This chapter is good, and is often printed as part of the original work. The continuation was translated by William Phiston, and published in England in 1596, ten years after Rowlands's translation of the original *Lazarillo*. The best continuation of *Lazarillo*, however, and one which is usually incorporated with it, was written in Paris by the Aragonese exile, Juan de Luna, and published there in 1620 in Spanish. It is called *Vida de Lazarillo de Tormes, corregida y enmendada*, and *La Segunda parte de la Vida de Lazarillo de Tormes, sacada de las Cronicas antiguas de Toledo*. Luna was a teacher of Spanish in Paris, and modernised the original text; and he says, shocked by the silly addition about turning Lazarillo into a tunny-fish, he will tell the true adventures of Lazarillo on his expedition against the Algerines, as he has heard it told by his great-grandmother in his youth. Instead of being turned into a fish, Lazarillo is, in this version, rescued by some fishermen, who determine to turn a dishonest penny by showing him in a penny show as a merman ; and so his adventures are continued in true picaresque style. Luna's continuation is almost as good as the original, and was immediately translated into English by James Wadsworth, and ran through numerous editions under the name of *The Pursuit of the History of Lazarillo de Tormes*, and Blakeston also translated it. It was published again, 1688 (both parts) under the name of *The Witty Spaniard*, with the fish incident, as well as Luna's continuation, and with a further sequel called the *Life and Death of Young Lazarillo*, which is a hash-up of all the picaresque novels, English and Spanish, that had ever appeared. But the original *Lazarillo* still remains to this day the masterpiece, and I only mention these sequels with their English translations to show how great a hold this form of fiction had gained in this country.

But *Lazarillo* was by no means the only Spanish picaresque novel that caught on in England. *Guzman de Alfarache* of Mateo Aleman was, if anything, more famous still. Of all the brood of *Lazarillo* none approached *Guzman de Alfarache* in popularity. It was first published as *Vida del Picaro Guzman de Alfarache* in Madrid in 1599. The author was, like

Cervantes, a small government official, and, although his essay in fiction gained for him at once a world-wide fame, he remained poor, and emigrated to Mexico to better his position, where he wrote much and prosily, especially a second part of *Guzman*. Guzman de Alfarache, like Lazarillo before him, begins his story at, or rather before, his birth, which is a disgraceful one. At fourteen he leaves his mother, and starts life on his own account, and soon becomes convinced that if he is to live at all he must cheat rather than be cheated. He is led through Spain and Italy, changing his service often—now a buffoon to a cardinal, now a beggar in Italy, now a page to a French ambassador; satirising society, burlesquing types, showing up frauds, living in inns, or in the kitchens of the rich from hand to mouth, but, generally speaking, in better circumstances than Lazarillo. Forged and genuine sequels were published, and imitations innumerable, but, as they were all on the same lines, we need not further consider them. The industrious James Mabbe, 'Don Diego Puede-ser,' published a translation of both the genuine parts in London in 1622 as *The Rogue, or the Life of Guzman de Alfarache*, and numerous other editions appeared in English, French, Italian, Dutch, and German. To modern readers *Guzman* will appear tedious and discursive, notwithstanding the entertaining character of many of the incidents narrated, for the old didactic tradition still died hard in Spanish literature, and the temptation to draw a moral lesson from the iniquities of the anti-hero was rarely resisted. That this is more conspicuous in *Guzman* and other similar books that I shall mention presently than in *Lazarillo*, the first of the series by many years, is probably owing to the fact that *Lazarillo* really consisted of separate tales, strung together originally without the intention of presenting it to the public as a connected story ; whilst *Guzman* and others were, from their first inception, intended to be complete and symmetrical works, and, that being so, they had of course to adopt the traditional form, which, moreover, commended itself to the ecclesiastical censors and the authorities, who were able to make the fortune of a book or ban it.

Of the many other less famous Spanish novels of roguery little need be said in detail, since they are all founded on the same model. As a change there was a girl rogue called *La Picara Justina*, published in 1605. This became part of a book which in English became very popular under the name of *The Spanish Libertines*, translated by Captain John Stevens, and published in London in 1707. This book consisted of *Justina, the Country Jilt; Celestina, the Bawd of Madrid; Estevanillo Gonzales, the most arch and comical of scoundrels : to which is added a play call'd An Evening's Adventures.* The most characteristic of these items is the picaro Estevanillo Gonzales, who, tatterdemalion as he was, always claimed to be a gentleman. He certainly was a most entertaining

rogue. The following account of one of his escapades
will give an idea of his quality. " When I had been
there five weeks (*i.e.* in the Cardinal's service), to
reward my good service, I was preferred to be under-
sweeper below stairs. Thus men rise who conduct
themselves well in their employment, and are solicitous
to please their superiors. I was barefoot, half naked,
and as black as a collier when I entered upon my new
office, where I fared not so well as in the kitchen : for
places of honour are often not so profitable as those of
less dignity, and now nothing could stick to me but
the dust of the house, whereas before I never lacked
a sop in the pan or other perquisites. But fortune so
ordered it that the Cardinal's servants undertook to
act a play on his Eminence's birthday ; and in dis-
tributing the parts, they pitched upon me to represent
a young king of Leon, either because I was young or
for being descended from the renowned Fernan
Gonzales, who as I said before was an ancestor of
mine and Count of Castile, before there were kings in
that country. I took care to learn my part, and persuaded him that took the management of it to give
me half a pound of raisins and a couple of oranges
every day, that I might eat a small collation every
night, and rub my temples with the orange-peel in the
morning fasting, telling him that it would help my
memory, which was very weak, or else I should never
get it by heart, though the whole was not above
twenty lines ; and assuring him that I had seen this

done by the most celebrated comedians in Spain, when they acted their greatest parts. When the day of the solemnity came a stately theatre was erected in the largest room in the palace, making a wood of green boughs at the end next to the attiring room where I was to lye asleep and Moors to come and carry me away captive. My lord the Cardinal invited all the men of quality and ladies of the court to this diversion. Our Merry Andrew actors dressed themselves up like so many Jack Puddings, and all the palace was richly hung and adorned. They put me on a very fine cloth suit, half covered with rich silver loops and laced down the seams, which was good as giving me wings to take flight and be gone. Seeing myself in such guise as I had never known before, I thought not fit to return to my rags again, but resolved to shift for myself. The play began at three in the afternoon, the audience consisting of all the flower of the city. The manager of the representation was so active and watchful because he had hired my clothes, and was bound to see them forthcoming, that he never suffered me to go out of his sight. But when they came to the part where I was to appear as if I had been hunting, and then to lye down in the wood pretending weariness and sleep; I had to repeat a few verses, and those who came with me upon the stage having left me, I turned into that green copse where it cannot be said that I was caught napping, for, going in at one end, I followed a narrow path between the boughs to the other end of the stage, whence I slipped down, and creeping under it to the door of the great hall, bade those who stood about it make way, for I was about to shift my clothes. Upon this they let me pass. I made but two leaps downstairs, and flew along the street like an arrow from a bow, till I came to the sea-shore, whither I had steered my course in hopes of some conveniency to carry me off." This, of course, he finds, and begins life afresh as a gentleman of rank on the strength of his stolen clothes.

Another famous book of this sort was the *Life of the Squire Marcos de Obregon*, by Vicente de Espinel, first published in 1618. Here the moral didacticism is undisguised, though the adventures themselves are very diverting, the hero being on a somewhat higher plane than Lazarillo, Guzman, or Estevanillo. Espinel was a pious priest in Madrid, and represents himself as writing the book in his old age with a moral object in view ; and promises, ' With the help of God, I will endeavour to make the style fitting to the general taste, and so little tedious to individuals that they will not cast my book aside as tiresome, nor condemn it as ridiculous.' The story is, to my mind, much more interesting than Guzman, when you get at it ; but the good priest is so desirous of enforcing the lesson, that it must be confessed that there is a good deal of chaff to his grain. The book was at once translated into French, and was very popular ; but, so far as I know, there was no English translation until 1816. The principal reason why I have dwelt upon *The Squire Marcos de Obregon*, is that *Gil Blas*, of which I shall speak directly, appears to have been largely inspired by it : so that if *Marcos de Obregon* did not immediately affect English literature, its influence upon it, through *Gil Blas*, was very great.

Before I refer, however, to *Gil Blas*, I am anxious to speak of a previous work in Spanish, which Le Sage plagiarised so successfully as to have superseded the original work. The work itself is an inspiration, and, through Le Sage, has become one of the permanent treasures of the world. We have seen hitherto that the framework, of the wandering servant or adventurer going into many households, enabled the author to describe and satirise a great variety of persons and places. But, withal, this machinery had its limitations. The picaro could only describe what he would be likely to see and hear ; he could not portray the thoughts of his subject, nor could he be present at scenes from which a servant would be excluded. So Luis Velez de Guevara, a lawyer and favourite of the literary court of Philip IV., had the happy idea of presenting a new form in 1641. It is called *El Diablo Cojuelo*, 'The Limping Devil.' The story runs thus. Don Cleofas, an out-at-elbows student, is escaping over the roofs, from his attic window, from the bailiffs, who are hunting him. To evade them he enters the window of another attic, which happens to be the laboratory of a sorcerer. Whilst he is getting into the window he knocks over a bottle and breaks it. From it there comes a small lame demon, whom the sorcerer had confined in it, and out of gratitude for his liberation he (Asmodeus) helps Don Cleofas to fly over Madrid; and, to amuse him, he lifts the roofs from house after house, in order that the student may see what is going on within. From beggars' stews to palaces, the inner secrets, the vices, the shams, the wickedness of the city are exposed; and the result is a satire so bitter, so keen, and apparently so true, as to make this a book of the highest sociological interest. The pity is that the language is marred by the affected and tedious preciosity which had become the fashion. It will be seen that there was no limit to this satirical machinery. Every rank and every person might be scourged, if magic were called in to expose the inner-most secrets of their hearts.

And so the clever Frenchman Le Sage, keenly alive to the possibilities, and saturated with Spanish feeling and tradition by residence in Spain and study of its literature, seized upon *El Diablo Cojuelo*; and by and by all Europe, and France particularly, was tittering in scandalised whispers over *Le Diable Boiteux*, by Le Sage; and in England at *The Devil on Two Sticks*, by Swift, or some other writer still uncertain. Le Sage's adaptation of *El Diablo Cojuelo* was only one of his efforts to popularise and improve upon the picaresque novel. To him is owing the greatest and best picaresque novel of them all,

Spanish in tone and feeling, with the added keen lucidity of the French mind; and *Gil Blas de Santillana* it was, more than *Lazarillo*, or *Guzman de Alfarache*, directly, that struck the note which made the peripatetic adventurer a permanent feature of English fiction. How much of his great book was owing to Le Sage himself, it is difficult to say. The author lived in the French embassy in Madrid for some years at the end of the seventeenth and beginning of the eighteenth century, and translated *Guzman de Alfarache*, and, as we have seen, adapted the *Diablo Cojuelo*, besides writing a poor sequel of *Don Quixote*, and another picaresque book called the *Bachelor of Salamanca*. It has been urged by Spaniards, and especially by Father Isla, that a Frenchman writing about 1700 would certainly not take the trouble to pen an elaborate political satire upon events and personages that had passed away sixty years before. But it must not be forgotten that French writers and readers always leant to the romantic idea of Spain presented before their eyes at the court of Louis XIII. and Anne of Austria. Le Sage wrote *Gil Blas* when the old Spanish traditions, manners, and customs looked as if they were passing away for ever, before a new French dynasty and new French ideas in Spain. He had before him the Spanish picaresque books I have mentioned, particularly *Marcos de Obregon*, where the local colour was ready to his hand; and it would obviously be more attractive to him to place his hero in the romantic surroundings of sixty years before, than to make him a contemporary personage. It is, in my mind, at least, very doubtful whether Le Sage really cared anything about the political satire. I think he aimed simply at producing, what he did, in fact, produce, an intensely interesting picaresque novel, more amusing, because less discursive and stilted, than the Spanish books of the same sort. It is extremely likely, indeed, that a manuscript may have fallen into his hands, which supplied him with so much political gossip and detail about the person and times of Olivares, that he was tempted thus to utilise it as the background of his novel. This is the more likely, since the times of Olivares were essentially a self-conscious and memoir-writing age; and all Spaniards were, secretly or openly, writing malicious descriptions of each other. I have myself had occasion to copy some dozens of documents in various languages crammed full of local colour about the reigns of Philip III. and Philip IV., which of themselves would have sufficed to give Le Sage all the political detail he needed for his book. That Le Sage should have made use of such material for *Gil Blas* is no more extraordinary than that Victor Hugo should have utilised the *Travels of Madame D'Aulnoy* for the local colour—which, by the way, is mostly wrong—in *Ruy Blas*. However, the great point is that *Gil Blas* is one of the most amusing

M

books in the world, almost as full of proverbial
wisdom as *Don Quixote* itself; and as it presents
a view not confined to squalor and dishonesty, it
agreed with the native English form of picaresque
and peripatetic fiction, which by the end of the
seventeenth century was languishing, but took a new
lease of life from Le Sage's book.

Before passing to the consideration of the direct
effect of *Gil Blas* in reviving and perpetuating the
peripatetic rogue tradition in English fiction, I must
mention one more of the many such books that
appeared in Spain, written by one of the greatest
satirical geniuses that the Spanish race has produced
—I mean Francisco de Quevedo Villegas. The book
was first published in Saragossa in 1626, and was
called on the title-page *Historia de la Vida del
Buscon, llamado Don Pablos. Exemplo de Vagamundos
y espejo de Tacaños* (*History of the Pilferer, called
Don Pablo, Pattern of Vagabonds and Mirror of
Mumpers*). The book is a true picaresque novel.
It is not, perhaps, so fresh as *Lazarillo*, but it is
infinitely more subtle, and it is in every way superior
to *Guzman de Alfarache* and *Marcos de Obregon*. The
movement is more rapid, the narrative is closer, and
the satire with which, of course, it abounds is savage
in its ferocity; whilst its humour is unequalled by
anything but *Don Quixote*. Quevedo's lash spared
no one, not even priests; but the fun is so rapid and
so boisterous that all Spain was set laughing at *El*

Gran Tacaño, as the book soon came to be called, notwithstanding its satire. The book was promptly translated into French and called *L'aventurier Buscon*, and became very popular in France with the rest of Quevedo's works, especially the *Visions*, Scarron and his school scrupulously imitating the malicious spirit that runs through all Quevedo's works. In England they were almost as popular on the impetus of Sir Roger L'Estrange, and numberless editions of the *Visions* came out all over Europe. The first edition of the *Buscon* in English was published in London in 1657, and called *The Life and Adventures of Buscon the witty Spaniard, put into English by a person of Honour*. Another edition was printed in 1683 and called *The Pleasant Story of Paul of Segovia* (the name by which the book is still best known in England, and used in Mr. Watts's handsome edition, with Vierge's illustrations, published a few years ago). Captain Stevens also translated it in 1707, and called it *The Life of Paul the Spanish Sharper*, and evidently some of Swift's most scathing satires are inspired by this and others of Quevedo's works.

Here, then, we see that from the middle of the sixteenth century to the beginning of the eighteenth, there was a constant stream of this class of fiction passing from Spain to England. *Lazarillo, El Picaro Guzman de Alfarache, Don Quixote, Marcos de Obregon, La Picara Justina, Estevanillo Gonzales, Gil Blas*, and *La Vida del Buscon*, became part of

the ordinary reading of an English household. It
was inevitable that the form which satirised society
by exhibiting types encountered on a journey should
be naturalised in England. It was a simple and
flexible form, which lent itself to infinite variations,
and to compression or extension as might be desired.
Thus we are led from the chronologically consecutive
smart tricks of famous buffoons like Skoggin, through
Jack Wilton at the end of the sixteenth century, to
the many translations and adaptations of the Spanish
novels that amused English readers during the
seventeenth century. But until quite at the end of
the seventeenth century, little or no influence is seen
to have been exerted by these stories upon native
English novels, partly owing, no doubt, to the continued fashion for the pastoral form of romance.
When, however, satire wished to strike with a
bludgeon, and party feeling in England was stirred
by polemics, then the wishy-washy pastoral was
too weak for the purpose, the political pamphlet
was insufficient, and realism in its most savage form
was needed. Then came ready to hand the flexible
and adaptable framework I have mentioned, and
English fiction took a new flight as an aid to controversy. First in order, although it is not in prose
but in macaronic verse, we must take Samuel Butler's
Hudibras, which is closely modelled on *Don Quixote*.
It is a satire upon the rigid Presbyterians of
Cromwell's time. The burlesque knight Hudibras

is the Don Quixote of Puritanism, the redresser of imaginary wrongs done to his Dulcinea, and he has his Rozinante, and his Sancho, all complete, like his Spanish progenitor. It was, however, the polemical pamphleteer Defoe who first saw the full possibilities of the Spanish form as a satirical vehicle in prose. I am not inclined to class *Robinson Crusoe* as an indication of this, as some commentators are inclined to do. I regard that as a story inspired by fact, just as Defoe's journal of the plague year was. It simply described the incidents of travel, and made no attempt to describe types, as all the picaresque novels did. In my view, the first real picaresque and peripatetic novels purely English, after *Jack Wilton*, were *Moll Flanders*, evidently inspired by the *Picara Justina*, and *Colonel Jack*, in which probably *Gil Blas* was influential. Thenceforward the lineage is direct. Fielding's *Joseph Andrews*, originally a literary satire on Richardson's insipid *Pamela*, is picaresque and peripatetic in form and substance. Fielding called it a comic epic, and reminds his readers of *Telemachus* and the *Odyssey*. But you can guess what was at the back of his mind when he says that he is ready to call it anything but a romance. As we have seen, the picaresque novel was by its very birth a reaction from romance. Fielding also wrote a poor female Quixote which showed that he was well versed in Spanish fiction. Smollett was a Spanish scholar, and admirably trans-

lated *Don Quixote*. But before he did that he wrote
Roderick Random, a novel that was avowedly derived
from the Spanish models and purely picaresque, in
the English and French sense; that is to say, that
it did not necessarily deal with dishonest persons
or squalid scenes, but with the adventures of a poor
young man, whose wits had to supply the leanness
of his purse. *Humphry Clinker* and *Peregrine Pickle*
were inspired by the same tradition, namely, the
presentation of types encountered in travel. So,
indeed, was *Tristram Shandy* of Sterne, and *The
Sentimental Journey*, though deeply tinged by the
peculiar genius of the author. Dickens was confessedly inspired by Fielding, as Captain Marryat
obviously was by Smollett; and we have in Pickwick
and Sam Weller the early nineteenth century reflections of Don Quixote and Sancho Panza; in David
Copperfield, a sentimental and honest picaro, whose
principal adventures through life are devised not
so much to exhibit his own qualities as to show up
the types which he meets. When one mentions the
book *David Copperfield*, David Copperfield is the
last person of whom you think. You think of Uriah
Heep, of Micawber, of Traddles, of Betsy Trotwood,
of Mr. Dick; and similarly with Sir Walter Scott.
Guy Mannering or Waverley are merely lay figures
in comparison with the persons they meet and
describe; and so are Guzman de Alfarache and Gil
Blas. *Midshipman Easy* and *Japhet in Search of a*

Father are purely picaresque peripatetic tales, that would never have assumed their present form, if the Spanish novel of movement had not led the way. The same may be said of Michael Scott's *Tom Cringle's Log*, and dozens of other similar works ; and one sees in Mark Twain's *Huckleberry Finn* a transparent intention to experiment with an American picaro, as near as circumstances could make him to Lazarillo, Guzman de Alfarache, and the rest of the goodly company of sharp-witted youngsters with pockets as light as their hearts, who sprang from the Spanish genius as a reaction from the wandering knights of chivalry.

CHAPTER VII

THE LITERATURE OF TRAVEL AND OF WAR

WHEN the centre of sea power shifted from the Mediterranean, where it had remained for three thousand years, to the Atlantic, the problems of maritime supremacy in Europe were altered, and the sceptre of the sea was at the bidding of that power which should first recognise and provide successfully for the new conditions which had arisen. Galleys with the large number of hands necessary for oar propulsion, and the limited cargo and provision space possible, could not remain long enough at sea to make profitable ocean voyages without touching land, nor were they able to live in the big Atlantic rollers. This had been recognised by Prince Henry of Portugal, who in the first third of the fifteenth century inaugurated systematic Atlantic exploration, and the colonisation of the African coasts on the way to India. The type of vessel he evolved, the caravel, depending mainly upon easily trimmed small sails, and only in time of need upon oars, to some extent solved the problem, so far as the coast of Africa was concerned. But the discovery and exploration of America,

184

although effected with similar vessels to these, demonstrated that, though they might do for discovery, they were insufficient for carrying the cargoes of stores and materials needed by new colonies from the mother country, or the return freight of gold and silver, spices and drugs, that alone made discovery and colonisation profitable.

The Spaniards had to solve the problem alone, for they jealously attempted to prevent the intrusion of any other powers into the western world which they claimed as their own. The solution arrived at was not a particularly successful one, so far as the evolution of a new type of vessel was concerned. It was mainly to develop, strengthen, and arm the great, slow, lumbering store-ships, or hulks, which had always attended on galleys as supply ships. The type so evolved was heavily armed, especially fore and aft, but it was unwieldy and top hampered ; and although such great armed cargo galleons and carracks were usually convoyed by galleasses, and other smaller and quicker armed vessels, they were often practically at the mercy of any rapid, fine-built, and handy pirates or privateers which cared to attack them ; as they presented a great exposed freeboard to the enemies' fire, and were so unhandy that much smaller ships with finer lines, lower freeboards, and quicker helms, could sail round them and cripple them, whilst escaping harm themselves. There were no sailors in the world who had always had to face heavier seas than the English west-countryman; and his craft, a fisher or a trader as occasion served, was the result of centuries of experience. At dealing with the dangers and the glorious struggle of ocean sailing, the Englishman felt that he might cope successfully with any man. What a Spaniard might do and dare, so might he; and there entered into the heart of England the proud claim for equal opportunity at sea with Spaniards; that the race might be for the swift and the battle for the strong. And out of this thirst for adventure grew Britain's empire.

The discoveries and conquests of Columbus and his successors were followed in England as eagerly as they were elsewhere, and the numerous letters and pamphlets giving accounts of the earlier discoveries were translated in the form of broadsides in English almost as soon as they appeared in other languages. But it was not until the middle of the sixteenth century, sixty years after Columbus's first voyage, that public curiosity in England was satisfied by a full account of the explorations, so far as they had up to that time been published in Spain. Richard Eden it was who took the first step. He was an English scholar, who had been appointed to the household of King Philip when he married Mary Tudor in 1554; and doubtless, for the purpose of giving to Englishmen an idea of the greatness of their new king consort, Eden translated from the

Latin, in which it was written, that famous account of Columbus's voyages written by one who had known the great discoverer personally, the famous Peter Martyr Angleria, who, although an Italian by birth, was a Spaniard by adoption. *The Decades of the New World*, as Peter Martyr's book was called, first published complete in Spain in 1516, was, however, not the only book from which Richard Eden drew the material for his own *Decades*. He also utilised the books of subsequent historians of the conquest : Oviedo's *Historia General de las Indias*, and F. Lopez de Gomara's *Historia General de las Indias, con todo el descubrimiento y cosas notables, que han acaecido dende que se ganaron hasta el año* 1551. Zaragoza, 1553. Eden thus brought his story well up to date as things were managed then, by publishing his *Decades* in 1555, in England. Eden's book, although strongly in favour of Spaniards, was nevertheless considered by Bishop Gardiner to smack of heresy in some places, and the author was charged and lost his office under government.

The book, however, was seized upon and read with avidity by a public positively thirsting to have their share in the vast golden regions of the new world, which Spaniards were claiming for their own. But with Mary upon the throne, and Philip sternly controlling the English Privy Council, no public suggestion was possible that Englishmen had as much right as any others to seek for new unsettled lands beyond the western ocean. With the coming of Elizabeth all was changed. From the first year of her reign to the day of her death, the great queen never faltered in her demand that, at least, her people were not to be shut out of the new world, and that lands unsettled by Christian princes were to be the property of those whose subjects brought them under subjection. Thenceforward not curiosity alone, not love of exciting reading, but the determination of Englishmen to have their full share of ocean trade and undiscovered lands, led the adventurous spirits to scour the seas in search of plunder, trade, and discovery. Up to the time that John Hawkins, in 1562, made his first slave-dealing trip down the west coast of Africa, and across to the Spanish settlements in the West Indies to trade by force, if persuasion would not do, English voyages, with the exception of William Hawkins's run to Brazil in 1530, had not extended much beyond the coasts of Portugal, Spain, and Morocco, with a rare trip to the Levant. But from that time (1562) forward, the demand for information about the route to the west was so strong in England that authors had trouble to keep pace with it. The details of navigation west of the Azores were still practically unknown in England. Spain not only threatened to treat as pirates all foreign vessels in the West Atlantic, but jealously guarded the secrets of the currents, winds, tides, coasts, soundings, and land-lay. But the greed of the

English would brook no obstacles. Knowledge they needed and would have. And so there came from the press in London a shoal of books reproduced from the Spanish that might stir up English hearts and help Englishmen to the knowledge needed for traversing the Atlantic, and to find the golden west for themselves.

The translators sprang usually not from men of letters and learning, but from English merchants, who from residence or trading in Spain had not only become familiar with the language, but had also gained a notion of the enormous advantage that colonies, such as those of Spain, might bring to England. There were a large number of these English merchants resident in the Spanish ports, who, although professedly devout Catholics, were yet proud of their country, and ever willing to serve her interests. These were for the most part the men who now provided what their countrymen yearned for, a knowledge of the western route ; although it must be admitted that, as a rule, they were careful to put the sea between themselves and the Inquisition before their English translations came out. There was no lack of Spanish material for them, though it must be confessed that the majority of the books translated do not seem to us to convey much useful guidance for practical explorers, however interesting they may have been as books of travel. The earliest and busiest of these merchant translators was one John Frampton, who had been long a prisoner in the dungeons of the Inquisition at Seville, but had contrived to obtain his release and came to England in 1577. He began his literary labour by issuing immediately a translation of a famous book by a Spanish physician who had visited America, called *Historia Medicinal de las cosas que traen de nuestras Indias occidentales que sirven para medicina; con un tratado de la piedra Bezar: Las grandezas del Hierro y de la Nieve y del beber frio Por Nicolas Monardes*, which had been published in Seville in 1569 and 1574. Of this book, which contains not a little quackery mixed with science, Frampton issued an English version in 1577 under the title of *Joyfull Newes out of the Newe founde Worlde; wherein is declared the virtues of divers plaunts, herbes, oils, stones*, etc. In 1579 Frampton published another book, a translation of Bernardo de Escalante's accounts of the Portuguese voyages to the East Indies, which Frampton called *A Discourse of the Navigation that the Portingales doe make to the Eastern parte of the Worlde*, and soon afterwards the same industrious translator introduced the travels of Ser Marco Polo to English readers from a Spanish version. All these books were eagerly read by an England aflame with the stories of Spanish tyranny and her effective weakness on the high seas, and of the vast treasures in the holds of her lumbering unhandy ships, to be had by bold men for the grasping. Other merchant translators followed Frampton in trying to foster this spirit by producing books of exploration and travel from Spanish originals. Thomas Nicholas, a merchant in the Canaries, had, like Frampton, fallen foul of the Inquisition, and had put the high seas between him and the dominions of King Philip as soon as he could. He began to publish in England at the same time as Frampton. His first translation was a little tract from the Spanish, called *Strange and Marvellous Newes lately come from the great Kingdom of China, in a Letter sent from Mexico to Spain.* But in 1578 he issued a more important book, which is practically a translation of Lopez de Gomara's *Historia de las Indias*, which I have already mentioned that Eden in 1555 had partly utilised in his *Decades of the New World.* But this book of Nicholas's was published at a more favourable season than that of Eden, and the popularity of it was great. It is called *A Pleasant History of the Conquest of the West Indies.* Sometime afterwards Nicholas undertook to translate another famous book by one of the Conquistadores, whom he had himself met in Spain. It waš the *Conquista del Peru*, by Agustin de Zarate; and Nicholas only translated the first four books, but added thereto the final book of Zarate, giving an account of the discovery of the rich silver mines of Potosi.

There was another English merchant from the Canaries who translated similar books from Spanish originals to satisfy the desire of his countrymen for information respecting foreign lands. His name was Nichols, and several books came from his hands. When the hatred to the Spaniards grew stronger, after Drake's successful plundering voyage, and the seizure in England of the Spanish treasure, another book was published in London that caused a profound sensation. This was the famous indictment against the Spanish treatment of the native American Indians, written first by the Apostle of the Indies, the saintly Father Las Casas, whose scathing denunciation of the inhumanity of his own countrymen remains to this day one of the most powerful pieces of pleading in the world. The Spanish version was called *Brevisima Relacion de la Destruccion de las Indias*; and the English book, which was translated by an unknown author, was published under the name of *The Spanish Colony*, in 1583. To a public already incensed bitterly against Spain, this book supplied fresh pabulum for hatred, and was made use of to the full by the war party in Elizabeth's court. All these books, nevertheless, were but histories and narratives of past adventures, with slight descriptions of the new-found lands. Pleasant and exciting reading, no doubt, and likely to incite the reader to adventure his life or his money in the pursuit of similar ends.

The adventurous spirit thus spurred on, but lacking corresponding knowledge of the details of Atlantic voyaging, might undertake expeditions, but could

hardly lead them to a successful issue. Drake and
Hawkins, Cumberland, Winter, Frobisher, and the
rest of the grand seamen of the Elizabethan age, did
not launch on to the trackless Atlantic led by the
adventurous instinct alone. They had carefully
collected, by fair means and by foul, every scrap of
information that could be obtained from Spaniards
who had made the western voyage. Mariners
captured at sea were by bribes, cajolery, and threats
of torture, made to tell all they knew of the winds,
currents, tides, soundings, and coasts of the New
World. The State papers abound in such declara-
tions, and some of Drake's own memoranda have
passed through my hands, showing how patiently
he gathered and set down every item of information
that might be useful to him in his voyages. Pilots,
especially disaffected Portuguese, were heavily bribed
to conduct English expeditions. But for every big
expedition, such as those of Drake, Cumberland, or
Raleigh, there were a score of smaller adventurers,
with one little cockleshell of a boat, or two, who,
taking their lives and fortunes in their hands, set
forth to find the golden land that should give to
them and theirs luxury and ease, or a miserable death.
These men, too, not only wanted to learn something
of the perils they had to face, but the science by
which they might overcome them. The Spaniards
almost alone, as I have pointed out, possessed the
science of Atlantic navigation; and every Spanish

N

book written on the subject was eagerly translated and largely sold in England. It was only two years after Elizabeth's accession (1561) that Richard Eden published his translation of the *Arte de Navegar*, by Martin Cortés of Seville, which had originally come out ten years previously in Spain. It was reprinted again and again in England, with fresh information, and every shipmaster who dreamed of steering his bark to the new world sought to possess it as his *vade mecum*. The book is now rare, and the earliest edition known to me personally is that of 1596, revised and enlarged by the publisher, John Tapp, who subsequently for many years periodically issued fresh and revised editions. The book in English is called ' *The Arte of Navigation*, first written in the Spanish tongue by that excellent Mariner and Mathematician of these times, Martin Cortés. From thence translated into English by Richard Eden. Enlarged and Revised by John Tapp, and to be sold at his Shoppe at Saint Magnus his corner, London Bridge.' Tapp himself writes a prologue which will give an idea of the popularity enjoyed by the work. ' Courteous and friendly reader,' he says, ' you have here presented to your view *The Arte of Navigation*, being the gathering and practice of Martin Cortés, a Spaniard of whose dexterity and perfection in marine causes the work itself is sufficient to witness: for that there is no book extant in the English tongue that in so briefe and easie a method doth discover so many and rare secrets both of philosophy, astronomy, cosmography, and generally whatsoever doth belong to good and sure navigation : but because it hath been so often imprinted, some faults have crept into it, through want of overseeing and good heedtaking.' Tapp therefore boasts that he has thoroughly revised it, and provided it with new tables. The book contains minute descriptions and rules for the use of nautical instruments—the astrolabe and the compass—calendars, the names of the principal stars, much weather lore, the theory of the tides, the variations of the compass, and tables for the calculation of latitudes. There is even a description of an instrument which, so far as a landsman can understand, seems to anticipate to some extent the quadrant and sextant, which have since quite superseded the astrolabe.

Nor was Eden's version of Martin Cortés's *Navigation* the only book of its sort published in England. Pedro de Medina had published in Spain, in 1545, another : *Arte de Navegar, en que se contienen todas las Reglas, Declaraciones, Secretos y Avisos que en la buena navegacion son necesarios, y se deven saber. Fue visto y aprobado en la insigne Casa de Contratacion de las Indias por el Piloto mayor, y cosmografos de Su Majestad.* This book, which is now rare, like that of Cortés, contains a map of the Atlantic from the west coast of Africa to the West Indies and Central America, which shows how extremely hazy the notions still were of the conformation of the American coasts. Medina's book found a translator also in Frampton. In 1578 there came out in London another book on the same subject, a translation by the industrious translator from the Spanish, Edward Hellowes, Groom of the Leash, of Antonio de Guevara's *Account of the Magnetic Needle and its Inventors* (1539). Hellowes called his little book *A Book of the Invention of the Art of Navigation*.

There came, indeed, from the press in England for the last half of the sixteeth century, a perfect flood of books, either directly translated or inspired by Spanish texts, dealing with exploration and navigation, in which Englishmen were now so deeply and permanently interested. Travels to the East and to the West, of Spaniards and Portuguese, descriptions of marvels beyond human belief, of men with heads in their stomachs, of palaces of gold, of vast cities leagues in length, wild stories of half-crazed shipmen, who for years had been lost to civilisation, and had come back, dazed and confused, between imagination and fact. All were seized upon by an English public hungry for wonders, and burning with thoughts of boundless wealth easily earned in the mysterious lands afar off. A perusal of the little book of one of the greatest minds of England of the day—Sir Walter Raleigh's account of his voyage to Guiana—will prove to the reader how deeply had sunk into the mind of the nation these tales of wonder from the Spanish. Without them who knows if English imagination would have carried men away on those apparently desperate voyages in tiny, frail craft to breast Atlantic billows, and to die nobly, as Sir Humphrey Gilbert and hundreds of others did, in a hopeless quest, which, though it failed in discovering a land of El Dorado, founded the greatest empire the world has ever seen.

If Raleigh, from reading Lopez de Gomara and the other narrators of discovery, could be led to think, as he did, of the fabled land of Manoa and its mountains of gold; if these stories could lead him to risk his last penny, to pawn his wife's jewels, and stake his liberty and life, judge what effect they must have had upon ignorant, unlettered people of the same period. There need be no wonder at the enthusiasm, nay, almost the frenzy, with which Englishmen of all ranks yearned for adventure beyond the sea, as the Spaniards had done before them. A few lines from Raleigh's *Discovery of Guiana* will prove how deeply the Spanish relations had moved him. After describing in glowing words the greatness and splendour of the supposed Manoa, he continues :—' And if we compare it to that of Peru and but read the report of Francisco Lopez and others, it will seem the more credible: and, because we may judge of the one by the other, I thought good to insert part of the 120th chapter of Lopez his

General History of the Indies, wherein he describeth
the court and magnificence of Guaynacapa, ancestor
to the Emperor of Guiana, whose very words are
these: "All the service of his house, table, and
kitchen was of silver and gold, or at least of copper
and silver for the things where strength was needed.
In his antechamber he had hollow statues of gold
as great as giants, and the figures resembling in
their natural size, of all the animals, birds, trees,
and plants that the country produces, and of all
the fishes that grow in the seas and rivers that
wash it.   He had also ropes, baskets, sacks, and
wallets of gold and silver, and even logs and branches
of gold made to look like wood cut for fuel.   In fact,
there was nothing in his realm of which he had not
an imitation in gold.   It is further asserted that the
Incas had an enclosed garden on an island near
Puna where they went to enjoy the sea air, and in
it all the plants, flowers, and trees were of pure gold,
an invention such as never was seen before.   In
addition to all this, he possessed at Cuzco an infinite
quantity of rough gold and silver, which was lost at
Guascar's death because the Indians hid it, seeing
that the Spaniards took their treasure to send
to Spain." And in the 117th chapter he says:
"Francisco Pizarro caused the gold and silver of
Atahualpa to be weighed after he had taken it, which
Lopez setteth down in these words following: 'They
found fifty-two thousand marks of good silver, and

one million three hundred and twenty-six thousand and five hundred pesos of gold.'"[1]

'Now although all these reports may seem strange, yet if we consider the many millions which are daily brought out of Peru into Spain, we may easily believe the same, for we find that by the abundant treasure of that country the Spanish King vexeth all the princes of Europe, and is become in a few years, from the poor King of Castile, the greatest monarch of this part of the world, and likely every day to increase if other princes forslow the good occasions offered, and suffer him to add this empire to the rest, which far exceedeth the rest.   If his gold now endanger us, he will then be irresistible.'

Throughout the whole of this book and others by the same writer Raleigh shows how profoundly he had studied the Spanish accounts of America and the Atlantic navigation.   He was perhaps the leading mind of his time, and the books which confessedly inspired and taught him must have appealed in original and translations to thousands of his fellow-countrymen animated by a similar spirit of adventure and ambition.

All the translations of Spanish accounts of ex-ploration I have mentioned, great as was their effect upon English minds, were, as we have seen, produced by isolated publishers and translators to supply a demand.   There was but little attempt at

[1] Raleigh quotes the whole of the above in the original Spanish, but it has been considered well to translate the passages here.

correlation, and evidently there could be few men, at least until the end of the century, able to sift authorities or check statements, because previously there was scant material in English hands for testing the truth of statements made by Spaniards, who spoke as eye-witnesses of what they described. But after Drake and the hosts of privateers had harried the Spaniards nearly to death on their own seas, and Englishmen, Frenchmen, and Dutchmen were doing pretty much as they liked in the oceans which the Spaniards had endeavoured to close, the mass of knowledge grew; and a man appeared in England with a mind big enough, and an imagination strong enough, to see the importance for the future of England, that all the information obtainable about exploration and colonisation should be rendered available, and that knowledge of scientific sea-craft was as necessary as bold hearts for the foundation of a colonial empire.

Curiously enough this young clergyman, Hakluyt, whose ambition was so great and wise for England, was not of English, but of pure Dutch parentage. His services to the science of navigation and exploration are such as can never be repaid. He had published whilst very young, in 1585, a new edition of Peter Martyr's *Orbe Novo*. But by the end of the century he had matured his great project of collecting together from all sources, printed, manuscript, and verbal, descriptions of voyages in all parts of the world. The three noble volumes, as they eventually came out, presented, indeed, a complete history of exploration from the earliest times to the period of publication. From Dutch and Latin, from French and English, as well as from Spanish, Hakluyt obtained his narratives. From the lips of seamen who had returned from adventurous wanderings, from ships' log-books and captains' letters home, the learned and industrious Anglo-Dutchman got together his travellers' tales, which to this day are as valuable as they are amusing to read. But the point I am anxious to impress upon my readers is that Hakluyt's ambitious project was not entirely a literary venture. He had seen Spain outstrip the rest of the world in obtaining colonial expansion. He had seen how Englishmen, though they were born seamen, had been obliged to turn to Spanish texts and depend upon Spanish experience to learn the scientific navigation of the Atlantic ; how they had been obliged to fight for forty years, doggedly and persistently, for the right to sail their ships upon the open sea and visit lands unknown to civilisation. And Hakluyt was animated by a desire to urge his adopted countrymen to rest their future claims and action upon knowledge at first hand, rather than upon violence. That Spanish example it was that inspired his project is seen in the separate dedications of his three volumes. The dedication to Lord Admiral Howard of the first volume of the *Principal Navigations* (1599) has for its object the

enforcement of the need for the systematic teaching
of seamanship 'if England is to do her part in the
maritime world.' 'When I call to mind,' writes Hakluyt, 'how many noble ships have been lost, how
many worthy persons have been drenched in the sea,
and how greatly this realm hath been impoverished
by the loss of great ordnance and other rich commodities through ignorance of our seamen, I have
greatly wished that there was a lecture of navigation
read in this city for the banishing of our former gross
ignorance in maritime causes, and for the increase and
general multiplying of the sea knowledge of this age,
wherein God hath raised so general a desire in the
youth of this realm to discover all parts of the face
of the earth, to this realm in former ages not known.
And that it may appear that this is no vain fancy nor
device of mine, it may please your lordship to understand that the late Emperor Charles v., considering
the rawness of his seamen, and the manifold ship-
wrecks they sustained in passing and repassing
between Spain and the West Indies, with high reach
and foresight established not only a pilot major for
the examination of such as sought to take charge of
ships in that voyage, but also founded a notable
lecture of the *Art of Navigation* which is read to this
day in the Contractation House in Seville. The
readers of which lecture have not only taught and
instructed Spanish mariners by word of mouth, but
also have published sundry exact and worthy treatises

concerning maritime causes for the direction and encouragement of posterity. The learned works of such readers, namely Alonso de Chaves, Jeronimo de Chaves, and Rodrigo Zamorano, came long ago very happily into my hands, together with the great and severe examining of all such masters as desire to take charge for the West Indies. When I first read and duly considered, it seemed to me so excellent and exact a course, as I greatly wished that I might be so happy as to see the like order established here with us.' This proves beyond doubt that the very first idea of Hakluyt's work, and the priceless services he rendered to English seamanship and literature, were due to the Spanish books he had read. The continuation of his labours to their conclusion was, moreover, made possible only by the fresh Spanish material that came to his hands. Many of his narratives are direct and acknowledged translations from Spanish texts, and others relate experiences gained with Spaniards and in Spanish countries. In the dedication of his second volume Hakluyt again makes clear that the main object of his work is to provide Englishmen with the maritime knowledge possessed by Spaniards, in order that the latter might be beaten with their own weapons. After praising the seafaring career, and colonisation as a worthy outlet for the ardent energy of young Englishmen, he continues:—' There is under our very noses, in the great and ample country of Virginia, the inland of which is lately found to be so sweet and wholesome in

climate, so rich and abundant in silver mines, so apt
and capable of all commodities which Italy, France,
and Spain can afford, that the Spaniards themselves in
their own writings printed in Madrid in 1586, and within
a few months afterwards reprinted by me in Paris; and
in a secret map of those parts, made in Mexico in the
year before for the King of Spain—which original, with
many others, is in the custody of the excellent mathematician Thomas Hariot—as also in the Spanish intercepted letters come into my hand bearing date
1595, they acknowledge the inland (*i.e.* of Virginia) to
be a better and richer country than Mexico or New
Spain itself.   And on the other side their chiefest
writers, as Peter Martyr Angleria, and Francisco
Lopez de Gomara and others, acknowledge with one
consent that all that mighty tract of land from sixty-
seven degrees N. to the latitude almost of Florida was
first discovered by England, by commandment of King
Henry VII., and the south part thereof, before any
other Christian people, of late hath been planted with
divers English colonies by the royal consent of her
Sacred Majesty.'

The same insistence upon his Spanish inspiration
and his dependence upon Spanish originals are seen
in the dedication of the third volume to Sir Robert
Cecil. 'Since,' he says, 'our wars with Spain, by the
taking of their ships and sacking of their towns and
cities, most of all their secrets of the West Indies and
every part thereof are fallen into our peoples' hands—

which in former times were for the most part unknown
to us—I have used the uttermost of my best endeavours to get, and having gotten to translate out
of the Spanish, and here in this present volume to
publish, such secrets of theirs as may any way avail
us or annoy them if they drive us by their sullen
insolences to continue our course of hostility against
them.' He then goes on to expatiate upon the value
of the information collected. There is no town, port,
or river of importance in the West Indies of which
good descriptions are not given from Spanish sources,
several of which he mentions. Thus it is clear that
to Spanish literary texts the first idea of a scientific
school of English seamanship is largely owing, and
that the first literary apostle of an extended English
empire beyond the seas was inspired to undertake his
propaganda through the influence of Spanish books.

There was another science in which Spaniards in
the sixteenth century excelled all other nations: the
science of military warfare on land. There was ample
reason for this. Standing armies were unknown.
Troops were levied for a campaign, and dismissed
when peace was made. But the Spaniards had been
fighting, practically without intermission, for centuries,
first against the Moors, and then, after the accession
of the Emperor Charles, in the constant wars in Italy,
and subsequently in the wars of religion in Germany,
and the campaigns on the French Flemish frontiers.
So superior was the knowledge of Spaniards in land

warfare, that when Henry VIII., in alliance with the
Emperor, crossed the Channel with his army to besiege
Boulogne, and, it was hoped, to march on to Paris, he
had to have attached to him as an adviser a famous
Spanish general, the Duke of Albuquerque, and also
a strong body of Spanish mercenaries to stiffen his
own inexperienced Englishmen. I have related elsewhere the desperate efforts made by Henry VIII., and
even by the Protestant protector Somerset, to keep in
his pay a large body of the redoubtable Spanish men-
at-arms, who were, in fact, the flower of the soldiers of
Europe in the sixteenth century.[1] Military fashions
were adopted by other nations from Spain at the
period as naturally as the fashion of ladies' dress is
now taken from Paris, and as London dictates how
man, the civilised world over, shall attire himself. For
many centuries, with but few brief breaks, England
and Spain had been friends, and English fighting-men

---

[1] Brantôme voices the admiration of all Europe for these fine, dashing
troops. We may see in his pages how the gallant bearing of the traditional Spaniard imposed itself upon the dress, the language, the
behaviour, and manners of France, England, and Italy. When Brantôme
heard that the musketeers of the Duke of Alba were marching through
France to attack the Protestants in Holland, he tells us that he took post
for a long journey, only to have the pleasure of looking upon 'that handsome troop of brave and gallant soldiers, well chosen from the tercios of
Lombardy, of Naples, of Sicily, of Sardinia, and some of the Goleta regiment: all old veterans, so well equipped in arms and accoutrements,
most of their armour damascened, and the rest chased and engraved, so
that you might take each trooper for a captain rather than what he was;
whilst, from their arrogant and noble grace, you would have taken them
for princes.'

had had no opportunity of meeting Spanish men-at-arms in land combat. But the records of their prowess were read in Spanish, French, Italian, and occasionally in English translations. Diego de Mendoza's *Guerra de Granada*, giving an account of the war of Philip II. against the Andalusian Moriscos, was a popular and fashionable book, as were Perez de Hita's *Guerras Civiles de Granada* and Bernardino de Mendoza's *Comentarios de la Guerra de Flandes*, and Avila y Zuñiga's *Guerra de Alemania*, an account of the Lutheran wars translated by John Wilkinson into English in the reign of Philip and Mary, 1555.

In books about military affairs the same thing happened as I have pointed out in the literature of maritime exploration. The first books were historical and literary, for the purpose of conveying information with regard to the exploits of those redoubtable *tercios* of infantry which had marched victorious through Europe. But after the accession of Elizabeth, and especially after the patronage of the Netherlanders in their revolt, had sent English captains and soldiers by the thousand across the North Sea to meet those grim warriors of the school of Alba; then the need of actual knowledge of their tactics, and of the discipline and organisation that had made them what they were, came home to the Englishmen who had to do battle with them. Thereafter there came from the press in England many translations of the Spanish books that treated on military matters. The English versions are now all rare, and I have not been able to see many of them. But such as I have read are extremely suggestive, as showing how carefully military ideas in England were modelled on the Spanish teaching. Curiously enough, these books, which, as I shall point out, contain a complete system of organisation, as fully matured as our own King's regulations for the army, are presented in the form of dialogues, in which a famous general, either dead or alive, is supposed to be the person imparting the information to another person, who is seeking it. One of the principal books of this sort published in England was *The Office of Sergeant-Major*, translated anonymously from General Sancho de Londoño's book, called *Un Discurso sobre la forma de reducir la disciplina militar á mejor estado*, and it was issued in London in 1589, when, as will be recollected, the gallant Vere and his Englishmen were fighting the Spaniards in Flanders. The Spanish original was dedicated to the great Duke of Alba.

But a more important book was one that came out in London in the following year, 1590, called also *The Sergeant-Major*, which was a translation by John Thorius of Francisco de Valdés' *Espejo y Disciplina Militar*, and contains an exact description of the organisation of a regiment, which, in fact, was the system adopted in the English service, as a consequence of the publication of these books. There are two points which specially strike a modern military reader in these books, namely the supreme importance given to the office of sergeant-major, who occupied a position similar to that now filled by the senior major of a regiment and the adjutant combined, the sergeant-major having been always selected for his knowledge and experience, and never for his rank, wealth, or influence, as was very often the case with the commanding officers ; the second point being the close squadron or square formation in marching and manœuvring, and the dependence upon weight and impact rather than mobility in attack and defence. This persistence in old ideals, notwithstanding the change effected in the possibilities of warfare by the improvement in artillery, was characteristically Spanish, and through the translation of Spanish books upon military science set its mark upon tactics for two centuries longer. In naval science the appearance in England of an original genius like Drake, and the impetus given to shipbuilding by the demand for privateers, caused the recognition of the efficacy of mobility as against weight long before soldiers shook off the shackles of the Spanish tradition.

In the military books to which I am referring the most minute instructions for the management and manœuvring of a regiment are given, especially in Escalante's *Arte Militar* (1595) and in Bernardino de Mendoza's *Teorica y Practica de la Guerra*, which was translated into English by Sir Edward Hoby and published in 1597.

O

As time went on and engagements took place between Spaniards and Englishmen ashore as well as afloat, during the long irregular warfare that for forty-five years pretended to be peace, an extensive literature sprang up in England dealing with such encounters. It would be impossible to mention a tithe of the narratives translated from the Spanish, sometimes for information but oftener for refutation, that issued from the English press during the last twenty years of Elizabeth's reign. Hakluyt published several, such as that fine piece of vivid prose giving an account of the stubborn fight between the little *Revenge* and the great Spanish warships which Sir Richard Grenville obstinately and unnecessarily insisted upon fighting. This is called *A Report of the Truth of the fight about the Isles of Azores, the last of August* 1591, *between the Revenge, one of her Majesty's Ships, and the Armada of Spain, Penned by Sir Walter Ralegh, Knt.* 'Because the rumours are diversely spread, as well in England as in the Low Countries and elsewhere, of this late encounter between her Majesty's ships and the Armada of Spain, and that the Spaniards, according to their usual manner, fill the world with their vainglorious vaunts, making great appearance of victories, when, on the contrary, themselves are most commonly and shamefully beaten and dishonoured; thereby hoping to possess the ignorant multitude by false reports; it is agreeable with all good reason, for the manifestation of the truth, to overcome falsehood and untruth, that the beginning, continuance, and success of this late honourable encounter should be truly set down.'

In 1583 there came out in English two translations of the Admiral Alvaro de Bazan's account of the defeat of the Portuguese pretender's fleets, aided unofficially by England and France, by the Spaniards off Terceira; and almost every military action described by Spaniards or waged against them thenceforward claimed the attention of English readers. To mention only a few of them : there was the English attack on Lisbon in 1589, that upon Cadiz in 1596, the conquest of Portugal by Spain from the Italian of Conestaggio, and a host of others. But, as may be supposed, the defeat of the Armada gave rise to the greatest mass of this sort of literature, fugitive and polemical for the most part. It was an age when there were no newspapers, and pamphlets and broadsides gave to the reading public the only substitute for them. The accounts of the defeat from original English sources were, of course, numerous, but do not here concern us. What does come within our purview is the mass of controversial literature that sprang up at the time. The books usually took the form of real or pretended intercepted Spanish letters, from or to ambassadors of Spain, and a violent refutation of their contents. They were often called by such names as *A Pack of Spanish Lies; first printed in Spain, now ripped up, unfolded, and condemned* (1588).

Another was *An Answer to the untruths published and printed in Spain, against our English Navy* (1589), translated by J. Lea. Another was *A Copy of a Letter lately written by a Spanish Gentleman to his friend in England in refutation of sundry calumnies here falsely bruited and spread amongst the people.*

Most of these were merely squibs, for the purpose of misrepresenting an enemy. Don Bernardino de Mendoza, who up to 1584 had been ambassador in England, and was very unpopular here, was then ambassador in France, and his letters were especially attacked and held up to ridicule, as being mendacious. There is a letter of this sort which purported to have been sent to him from an English Catholic partisan of Spain, who, although professing sympathy with the objects of the Armada, condemns the untruths against England that had been set afloat with regard to it, and to the detriment of the English. It is represented as being written by one Richard Leigh, a seminary priest; but in all probability it was simply another of the polemical attacks with which, in most wars, one combatant endeavours to injure another. There are, indeed, scores of such fugitive pieces as these, in the form of pamphlets and broadsides, but they are of little importance from a literary point of view. What is important is that we have to thank Spanish inspiration for the texts intended to teach Englishmen scientific seamanship and the art of war; and also for a great mass of valuable histories of exploration and warfare. Nor did these sources cease when the countries became more harmonious. During most of the seventeenth century there flourished in England a school of Hispanophil writers who followed the fashion of the day when Spanish was the modish language, and translated amongst other books histories of wars in which Spain had been engaged. Such were *The Wars of the Commoners*, translated into English by James Wadsworth; *The Wars of Flanders*, originally written in Italian by Cardinal Bentivoglio, translated by the Earl of Monmouth; *The Wars of Philip IV.*, by Malvezzi, translated by Robert Gentilis under the name of *The Chief Events of the Monarchy of Spain*, and several others. It is thus established beyond doubt that the influence of Spanish literature in England, in matters of exploration, seamanship, and war, was powerful and enduring.

CHAPTER VIII

DEVOTIONAL, MYSTICAL, AND POLEMICAL
LITERATURE

IN the present chapter we have to deal with one of the strongest manifestations that occurred of the Spanish influence upon European thought. For the full significance of it we shall have to look to the racial character of the Peninsular peoples. From the first dawn of their history we have seen them personally self-centred as no other people were. Each soul was for himself the point around which the universe revolved. His God and himself in communion shut out from his view other considerations ; and, at some periods of the history of his country, this feeling justified in his eyes acts that a more human view than his would have condemned. The spiritual exaltation which sprang from these conditions was cleverly made use of by kings and statesmen for the purpose of forging the weapon that was to make Spain temporarily irresistible in the world. And it did so. There was no defeat possible for men who, in their heart of hearts, believed that they were fighting the enemies of God Himself; that suffering, that priva-

214

tion, that death itself were only special marks of
distinction, conferred upon them by the Most High,
to be repaid by bliss a thousandfold in the world
to come.

The soft luxury of the cultured infidels, whom they
had fought for centuries, and at last conquered, had
by mere reaction given to the Christian idea in Spain
at the end of the great struggle in the last years of
the fifteenth century an austerity and simplicity unknown in other Christian lands. The sensuous beauty,
pagan in its origin, that Italian art had called into
the service of religion, had no attraction for a people
who had only seen beauty and luxury in connection
with a civilisation which denied the truth of the Christian faith. In Spain, therefore, Christianity did not
seek to please the senses. The spirit of sacrifice that
had led Christians in the later years of the Moorish
domination to insist upon voluntary martyrdom—the
same altruistic spirit of self-immolation which had
seized like a vice upon Spain in the novels of chivalry,
made Spaniards for the first three-quarters of the
sixteenth century yearn for the maceration and
humiliation of the flesh, for the suffering incurred by
the self-denial of all that made life pleasant in a
corporeal sense, in order to realise the ecstatic communion with God, incomprehensible to grosser souls,
which seemed to lift them personally to the earthly
foretaste of the heaven to come. Such a feeling,
extended over a whole Christian people, would exalt

and purify with unselfishness their idea of Christ's teaching. When every hillside had its hermit, living, almost starving, on herbs and roots, denying himself comfort, warmth, and fellowship ; when every monastery and nunnery—and there were many thousands of them—held those within who, rapt in the ecstasy of divine contemplation, lost all sight of worldly things, and who, blameless themselves, yet lived in such self-inflicted suffering for imaginary sins, as almost to pass our understanding,—with such a leaven as this it is easy to see how ecstatic, how almost frantic, would be the form that devotion would assume.

Out of this feeling, unmatched elsewhere in Europe at the time, there arose a school of thought and a literature that powerfully appealed at different times to all Christian peoples. What is called the mystic school of religious writing, especially as applied to Spain in the sixteenth century, was not really confined either to that period or even to Spain itself. At a considerably earlier period Italian mystics had been many. Such men as the saintly Francis of Assisi and Thomas à Kempis were mystic writers, and the Spanish Jew poet, Ben Gabirol, was as pure a mystic as any of his Christian successors. The peculiarity of Spanish religious mysticism especially is, that it has little to do with theology or doctrine, and the works of Fray Luis de Granada can be read with as much edification by a Puritan as by a Roman

Catholic if once the spirit can be exalted to the level necessary to understand them. As the greatest of living Spanish critics, Menendez Pelayo, says: 'To reach the mystical inspiration it is not sufficient to be a Christian, nor a devotee, nor a great theologian, nor a saint. What is necessary is the attainment of a special psychological condition, an effervescence of the will and imagination, an intense and profound contemplation of divine things. . . . It is true that the mystic, if he happen to be orthodox, accepts the theology of his faith, and tacitly takes it as the basis of all his speculations, but at a later stage he aspires to the possession of God by the bond of divine love, and proceeds as if God and the soul were alone in the world.' This is as true as it is important.

To name but a tithe of the three hundred mystic writers who enriched Castilian literature with their rhapsodies in the sixteenth century would be of little service, and I prefer to limit myself to the mention of a few representative writers of the school, and then to consider which of them, and to what extent, and why, they exerted influence upon English thought at a period when in Spain itself the spiritual exaltation which led to mysticism was rapidly losing its power. Most of the great Spanish mystics were born between 1500 and 1550, and perhaps the first to make his mark upon the reading public was the Venerable Juan de Avila, the Apostle, as he is called, of Andalusia, who was born in 1502. When he was first ordained at Alcalá he realised his great inheritance, for he belonged to a rich family, and distributed all amongst the poor, and thenceforward in poverty lived only to save souls according to his lights. Preaching with burning eloquence from town to town, and himself living a life of rigid self-denial, his teaching from the first centred around the contemplation of the divine mystery. The teaching of the mystics had little relation with good works, or, indeed, with the possibilities of worldly life. There was no attempt, as has now become the fashion, to strike a compromise, and make the best of both worlds. The scorn of the flesh and of mundane things, and the uplifting the spirit to a stage of ecstasy that shut out the taste for worldly pleasures, was the end they sought. This passage, for instance, from a letter from Juan de Avila to a student at Salamanca sets forth the doctrine :—

'Profit to the soul must be sought more in denying our own will, and with a firm heart doing that we feel to be agreeable to the Lord, than in having a tender heart and sweet devotion : for in the former we show the true love we bear to God, which is really the perfection of Christianity ; and the latter may well conceal our own personal pride, which sullies us so much. You must not, therefore, be dismayed at the dryness of heart that you say you feel ; but must rejoice in having to travel through the desert where no green tree refreshes the sight, no foliage tempers the glare, and no brook enlivens the land. If in prayer you find no help, read for a space, pondering the while upon that which you read, mingling thus meditation and vocal prayer with your reading,—having before you the while some image of our Lord's passion, or a crucifix. Persevere in this, however arid your heart may feel, offering yourself to the Lord without cease, and He will receive you at length.'

Here is seen the invariable tendency of the mystic writers. The student is not told to go out into the highways and byways to help human trouble or assuage human suffering; not told to go and face the world of wickedness to bring it into Christ's fold, but to shut himself up until he had worked himself into a state of devotional rapture. The sweetest mystic writers, especially in devotional poetry, were the famous San Juan de la Cruz, and Fray Luis de Leon, whose fame still lingers around the University of Salamanca, where he lived and worked so long. San Juan de la Cruz, the friend and co-worker with Santa Teresa, the greatest of all mystic writers, though she was much more as well as a mystic, was called the 'ecstatic doctor'; and although he was, like Santa Teresa, a great religious reformer, he is known best as a mystic writer. His poems are said by a competent Spanish critic to be 'so angelic, celestial, and divine as to defy the possibility of literary criticism. More ardent in passion than any profane poetry, they are nevertheless so elegant and exquisite in form, so plastic, and yet so imaginative, as to be amongst the sweetest fruit of the renaissance.' Nothing, indeed, in devotional poetry is finer than some of the verses of San Juan de la Cruz.

As poetry, however, is not to be dealt with in the present volume, except in special cases where that form of Spanish writing powerfully influenced English letters, the subject of the mystical poetry is only mentioned here as evidence of the literary capacity generally of the authors, and of their power to move their contemporary countrymen.

The other sweet singer of mysticism, Fray Luis de Leon, like Juan de la Cruz, suffered persecution from the narrow-minded men, who failed to understand the exalted, all-embracing charity with which these mystics regarded religion. For translating the *Song of Songs* into Castilian, he was for four years shut up in the dungeons of the Inquisition; but for him truly could it be said that 'stone walls do not a prison make, nor iron bars a cage.' Serene and secure in his saintly philosophy, no earthly evil could distress such as him. The *Names of Christ*, by him, is perhaps the finest of all the Spanish mystical works, and this he wrote in the prison of the Holy Office at Valladolid. He thanks God in his prologue for laying the affliction of prison upon him, for without it, he says, he could not have found time to write the book he had in his heart to write. He sees things clearer, he says, in the gloom of his prison, than he did outside. Here are a few lines of the beautiful description he gives of the place on the banks of the Tormes, still reverently regarded in Salamanca, where he so often sought solitude, and where he represents the colloquy, which forms the *Names of Christ*, to have been held :—' The garden was large, and at that season, St. John's tide in June, well wooded, though the trees were scattered without formal order. This, indeed, added delight to the view, and the hour and the season completed the charm. When they had entered the garden, they walked for a little space, enjoying the freshness, and then they sat together on some benches in the shade, under a climbing trellis, by the side of a clear little spring that gushes from the verdant hillside, behind the rest-house, and runs gambolling through the garden, with a sound like the rippling laughter of children. Before them, and at no great distance, was a stately and beautiful avenue of trees ; and beyond it, but not far away, ran the river Tormes, which even in that hot season of the year filled well its banks, and stretched across the smiling plain. The day was calm and pure, the hour was fresh and cool. And when they had been silently sitting for a little while, Sabino, which is the name I give to the youngest of the students, smiling spoke thus.' The *Names of Christ*, as fine a specimen of devotional mystic writing as any in the world, has, so far as I know, not been translated into English.

Before passing on to the other mystic Spanish writer who had so great a vogue in England, a word or two must be said about Santa Teresa, one of the noblest figures of the sixteenth century. Her life was not like those of many mystics, immersed in cloistered contemplation alone. She was a great lady, a great reformer, and a great woman of affairs, as well as a mystic. To show how firmly the idea of sacrifice had seized upon the Spanish people in her youth, it will be interesting to repeat a story which she tells herself. When she was a child of seven, in 1522, she says: 'When I saw the martyrdom which the saints had suffered for God, it seemed to me that they had bought the enjoyment of God very cheaply, and I longed much to die like them, not for the love I thought I bore Him, but to enjoy as soon as possible the great treasures which I read were stored up in Heaven. Together with my brother (who was three or four years older), I discoursed how it would be possible to accomplish this. We agreed to go to the land of the Moors, begging our way for the love of God, there to be beheaded; and it seemed to me that the Lord gave us courage, even at that tender age, if we could have found means to accomplish it.' Needless to say that the children were followed and brought back home, before they had gone very far on their road to martyrdom. I cannot follow the career of this marvellous woman, who in the face of even terrible Philip and the Inquisition had her way, and purified and reformed the Carmelite order, and, through that, the whole of the conventual orders in Spain. Persistent, enduring, patient, and wise, she turned her ecstatic exaltation—hysteria some called it, even then—to the service of mankind and the church she served through good report and evil. She conquered in the end, and left religious life in Spain purer than she found it. And her teachings reached far beyond the Pyrenees; for not only was the example of her life a reproach to the cloistered religious in all countries who had fallen into laxity, but her mystic works, especially the *Road to Perfection*, has been, and still remains, a specimen of exalted religious detachment which has brought solace to thousands.

But, curiously enough, none of these mystics that I have mentioned exerted any very great or direct influence upon English thought. In the first place, when they were in greatest esteem in Spain, England for political as well as religious reasons, looked upon everything Spanish with hatred and distrust. The England of the last half of the sixteenth century, moreover, was fermenting with the new, vigorous life that the foreign policy of Elizabeth had infused into it. It was a practical, eager age, an age of discovery, of effort, and of self-seeking; and the rapt, hysterical contemplation of the divinity, without works to back the devotional intoxication which mysticism induced, would hardly of itself appeal to the Englishman of that strenuous age. But there was one mystic writer who, for special reasons which I shall mention, appealed to Englishmen, even before mysticism itself found a public ready to receive it in England. This was Fray Luis de Granada. He was born of poor people of Granada in 1504, and, being an orphan, was educated by Count de Tendilla. Like other mystics, his life was one long tale of self-sacrifice. As a sacred orator he had no equal, and his florid eloquence captured Spain completely. His rigid asceticism, his sweet reasonableness, and his all-embracing charity, as usual offended the Inquisition, and he, like other churchmen who did not stick to doctrine alone, suffered persecution. But, great as Fray Luis was, his gifts were, in their essence, oratorical, and his writings, instead of being like those of Juan de Avila and Santa Teresa, simple, austere, and direct, are modelled more upon the style of that famous Antonio de Guevara, of whom I have spoken so often, where one far-fetched conceit follows another, florid ornament is piled upon endless digression, and affectation runs riot through the printed pages. Lyly's novel *Euphues* was the first English literary outcome of this vicious taste that Guevara's writings had done so much to promote; and when Euphuism became the fashion, as it promptly did, then writing of any sort that was obscure and affected was readily accepted and admired. Luis de Granada's mystic writings therefore were welcomed in England, in the first place, because they were written in the affected style then considered good.

In 1582, just when Euphuism was getting fashionable, Granada's two principal books of devotion, *Meditaciones* and *Memorial de la Vida Cristiana*, were translated and published in Paris by one of the English Catholic refugees on the Continent, Richard Hopkins. The first of these books was called *On Prayer and Meditation, wherein are contained fourteen devout Meditations for the seven days of the week*. There was nothing that could offend a non-Catholic in either of them ; but although they passed through at least half a dozen English editions in France, and were introduced thence in numbers to England, and became very popular, they were not actually printed in England till 1592. The *Meditations* was then called *Granada's Devotion*; and thenceforward, for the next fifty years, Granada's mystical books were published again and again in England, and were, indeed, among the most popular devotional books in England at the time. There were various translators, and several different titles given to the books. *On Prayers and Meditation* (1599); *Granada's Spiritual and Heavenly Exercise, divided into seven pithy and brief Meditations, one for every day in the week*, by Waldegrave, 1600; *An Excellent Treatise of Consideration and Prayer*, by E. Alldee, 1634; *Memorial of a Christian Life*, by J. Heigham, 1625 ; and as recently as 1867, and again in 1880, new

P

versions of some of Granada's works have appeared in England.

The reason for their first popularity in England may have been, as I have pointed out, their euphuistic style, but the great favour they enjoyed in the seventeenth century came from another cause. Their main tendency, like all the Spanish mystic work, was to enforce simplicity of life, scorn of human pleasure, and direct communion with God ; and this was the feeling which became paramount in England as Puritanism grew. There was nothing specially Catholic in Granada's works. They are exhortations to patience, self-denial, and direct communion with God, stirring the instinct of devotional fervour deeper than creeds and rituals ; and it is a curious thought that the mass of exalted devotional literature that heralded and accompanied the Puritan revival in England owed much of its inspiration to the writings of a Spanish friar whose doctrinal faith was the very antithesis of Puritanism. Most of the old translations of Granada's devotional works are now difficult to read, owing to their turgid style, and in retranslating the few following lines of his, I have suppressed some of the obscurity to make them intelligible. The main idea that underlies it all is the holy ecstasy of calm, resigned communion with God, and a renunciation of the world, which renders innocuous all earthly afflictions and sorrows. Looking at such a doctrine by our present light, it appears a somewhat selfish one, since

the bliss of the devotee is held out as the object to be
gained, and an abandonment of mundane duties is
apparently the only road to it. Speaking of the need
for abandoning everything for the rapt delight of
heavenly communion, Granada in his *Guia de Peca-
dores*, called in English 'Counsels of Holiness,' repeats
the words of Christ quoted by St. Mark : 'There is no
man that hath left houses and brethren or sisters, or
father and mother, or wife or children, or lands, for
My sake and the gospel's, but he shall receive a
hundredfold now in this time, and in the world to
come eternal life'; and then proceeds to meet the
objections that may be offered to them :—

'Tell me, then, what is this hundredfold more that
is given to the righteous in this life ? For we do not
usually see great estates or riches, or temporal dig-
nities or worldly pomp given to them. On the
contrary, many of them live neglected and forgotten
by the world, in great poverty, affliction, and sickness.
How can we reconcile this with the infallible truth of
this declaration, but by confessing that God provides
them with so many and so great spiritual treasures as
suffice without any worldly glory to give them greater
happiness, greater joy, greater contentment, and
greater rest than all the possessions of the world?
Nor is this very wonderful, for, as we know, God is
not limited to giving men substance in bread alone,
but has other means of preserving them : so neither
is He restricted to giving satisfaction or contentment

to their souls with temporal gifts alone, but can do it well without them.   And so, in truth, has He dealt with all the Saints whose prayers, whose exercises, whose tears, and whose delights, have greatly exceeded all consolations, worldly joys, and pleasures.   And thus it is most true, that they receive a hundredfold more than what they left.   For false and counterfeit good things they receive true ones; for doubtful, certain; for material, spiritual; for cares, repose; for heartaches, tranquillity; for a vicious life, one that is virtuous and full of joy.   If thou hast despised worldly things for the love of Christ, thou wilt find in Him inestimable treasures.   If thou hast rejected false honours, in Him thou shalt find true.   If thou hast renounced the love of thy parents, the Eternal Father will gladden thee with more tender caresses. If thou hast put from thee pestilential and poisonous pleasures, thou wilt find in Him sweeter and more exalted joys.   And when thou hast attained this, thou wilt find that all the things that once pleased thee, not only please thee no longer, but are objects of loathing to thee.   For when the heavenly light has once shone in our eyes, all things seem new to us and changed.   That which before seemed sweet is now bitter; that which terrified now delights thee; what seemed beautiful is now unlovely.   It was so before, but thou knewest it not.   Thus is Christ's promise fulfilled.   For temporal good of the body He sub-stitutes spiritual good for the soul.   For what are called gifts of fortune, He gives us gifts of grace, incomparably greater, and more sustaining to the heart of man.' Again and again, in Granada's writings, is this thought repeated in various forms. In the *Oraciones*, called in English 'On prayers and meditations for the seven days of the week,' for instance, the contents are as follows, all tending to the one central thought of self-surrender: 'Of Death. Of the Day of Judgment. Of the Pains of Hell. Of the Bliss of Heaven. Of the Divine Blessing. Of a Knowledge of Ourselves. Of the Miseries of Human Life.'

The whole tendency of the teaching was not to inculcate good work, or indeed any work in the world, not active practical religion as it is usually understood nowadays, but to recommend a state of rapt ecstasy, self-centred, cloistered contemplation, which in certain conditions and characters might lead, as it did, to cataleptic madness, or to slothful, self-neglecting imbecility. But yet it had its uses, at a time when religion threatened to become too luxurious or too complex ; and when that was the case in any country, the natural reaction seized upon the pure devotional spirit, clear of dogma, to purify and simplify forms of faith. In dissimilar circumstances the tendency was useful both in Spain and in England, when dogma and ritual seemed to be swamping devotion.

I have mentioned that Luis de Granada's works were first translated into English by Hopkins and Heigham, two of the very numerous English Catholics

in the continental seminaries; and in the bitter controversy of creeds that took place in England during
the reign of Elizabeth, many of these Catholic exiles,
educated and maintained as they often were by
Spanish endowments at Louvain, Douai, St. Omer,
Valladolid, or elsewhere, busied themselves in the
translation and dissemination in English of devotional
or controversial works which had been produced in
Spanish. No works of the sort produced more excitement or controversy in England in the latter half of
the sixteenth century than those initiated by the
Portuguese bishop Osorio. Perhaps they hardly come
into our subject, as the author was a Portuguese, and
he wrote in Latin. But the cause and thought were
Spanish, and the theological disputes aroused by his
attacks upon Elizabeth and England, as translated by
the English Catholic exiles, profoundly stirred religious circles in this country. Osorio's reputation as
a scholar was as great as had been that of Juan Luis
Vives in the previous generation; and when his Latin
work called *Epistles to Elizabeth Queen of England
concerning Religion* appeared at Paris and Louvain in
1561, in which he exhorted the queen to renounce her
errors, it may easily be supposed that the numerous
English Catholics at home and abroad read it with
avidity. So dangerous was the work considered by
Elizabeth and Burghley, that Dr. Walter Haddon,
Master of Requests, was deputed to answer it in
another Latin epistle. Haddon lost no time, and in

1562 his answer, called *Apologetic Epistle to Jeronimo Osorio*, was issued in Paris, in order that it might reach more easily those who had so eagerly read the original attack. But the controversy could not be kept for long in Latin, and in a year or two the English seminaries translated Osorio's epistles, whilst Protestant scribes turned into English Haddon's reply. Osorio answered Haddon, and Haddon retorted to Osorio's reply ; and for twenty years the controversy was kept up busily, the main contributions being translated into English almost as soon as they appeared in Latin.

In addition to this, a perfect library of controversial pamphlets on side issues appeared in England. That Queen Elizabeth herself was deeply concerned in the polemic is seen by a remark she made to the Spanish ambassador in 1568, first published in the Spanish *State Paper Calendars* under my editorship. King Henry the Cardinal, of Portugal, she complained, had addressed a letter to her couched in disrespectful terms. 'She knew,' she said, 'whom she had to thank for this. She recognised the style of the letter to be that of Osorio's, who had written a scurrilous book about her, which Dr. Haddon had replied to.'

The English seminary exiles were not exclusively occupied in the translation of Osorio's polemics. Shacklock and Fenne, both of whom were English Catholics at Louvain, were especially busy in translating the religious and devotional works of Spanish

Jesuits—*The Mystery of the Rosary*, by Fenne, from the Spanish of Gaspar de Loarte, being in its time a favourite mystical book amongst English Catholics. But when, under the guidance of the famous Father Persons, the English Jesuits (about 1580) began their disloyal plotting to deliver England to the Spanish power, religious Spanish works were to some extent put aside for political propaganda. Writing safely from his retreat on Spanish soil, as Rector of the English College of Valladolid, and afterwards in Rome as Rector of the English College, Robert Persons, sometimes in English, sometimes in Spanish, directed a series of attacks so bitter and cruel, and so false, against England and Elizabeth, as to have disgusted even many Catholics who wished naturally for the restoration of the ancient faith. Father Allen's attacks upon Elizabeth had been severe, and, having been written in the interests, and by the orders, of the King of Spain against the writer's own country, were unworthy of a great ecclesiastic ; but Robert Persons, under various pseudonyms, surpassed in scurrility all that had gone before or came afterwards. Many of his letters to the King of Spain, whose prime adviser on English affairs he was, have passed through my hands, and the virulent bitterness against his own country, and his eager suggestions that he should use his pen in writing ever fresh books in English to forward Spanish ends, are characteristic of the man. Whether he really wrote the scurrilous *Leicester's*

Commonwealth (1584) is not certain, although it is usually attributed to him ; but even if he did not, his other writings in English are sufficient to condemn him in the eyes of all loyal Englishmen, Catholic or Protestant. Needless to say that his pupils followed his own disloyal course, and, for a time at least, until the secular priests of English birth (1597) resented the bitter Jesuit rancour that prevented religious compromise and peace, the Spanish party on the Continent were busy sending into England literature for the purpose of enforcing their own views.

Before I pass to another branch of my subject, I must refer to a Spanish influence in England that preceded the period of which I have been speaking. In my remarks upon the popularity in England of the didactic philosophy of Spanish origin, I mentioned the famous Latinist Vives, who came to England as preceptor to Princess Mary, and who, until the divorce of Catharine of Aragon, was Professor of Philosophy at Oxford. His works were to a great extent of a religious character, and were for many years very popular in England. *The Instruction of Christian Women*, which Vives had written in England about 1523, was first published in English by Richard Hyrde in 1540, and continued to be read by English ladies as an aid to devotion long after Catholicism had given way to Elizabeth's régime. In its freedom from doctrinal bias it resembled the books of the Spanish mystics, only that it laid down practical guides to daily conduct, which, although of impossible perfection, had nothing mystical about them. In the *Instruction of Christian Women*, for instance, Vives makes a list of books which women should not read, amongst which is included the famous *Celestina*, of which I had much to say in a previous chapter on the Spanish novel.

The same may be said for Vives's *Introduction to Wisdom*, translated into English by the Puritan Sir Richard Morison, and published in London in 1540.

Another instance of the freedom from dogmatic theology of Vives's works is to be found in the fact that the collection of prayers compiled by Bishop Day and John Bradford, called *Queen Elizabeth's Prayer Book*, which is still common, contains several prayers from Vives's book, as well as others from the Spanish mystics.

In passing in review the influence of Spanish devotional writings in England, we have seen that, apart from those of the Portuguese Osorio, and the polemical literature disseminated by the English Catholic refugees, the work of the Spanish mystics had to a large extent owed its acceptance in Protestant England to its avoidance of dogmatic theology, and to its visionary, unpractical sweetness. But there was another sort of Spanish religious writing at the time, which, although it exercised but little permanent influence in England, for reasons which I shall explain presently, bulked largely in the eyes of contemporaries. This was the writings of the Spanish reformers, who had taken refuge in England and Geneva from the rigours of the Inquisition in Spain. Putting aside the two Valdéses, Juan and Alonso, the pioneers of Spanish Protestantism, whose influence hardly reached England, the principal Spanish reformers who carried on their propaganda from this country were Cipriano de Valera, Juan Perez de Pineda, and Antonio Corro. They were successively received in England with two sorts of welcome. Elizabeth herself cared nothing for Spanish Protestantism, but was glad to welcome Spaniards who had quarrelled with their own king, her mortal enemy. Anything to wound Philip was a delight for her, and the Spanish Protestants in her realm were, at all events, pawns in her hands, over which she might make a bargain some day if it suited her. But very different were the views of the more rigid school of the Protestant bishops and clergy. To them the presence of a Spaniard, who acknowledged fervently the truth of Protestantism, was a confirmation of their own doctrines ; and accordingly both Valera and Corro, as well as other reformers who did not write, were welcomed in English universities and in English pulpits, and were made much of by Protestant churchmen. Cipriano de Valera wrote almost entirely in Spanish, and his works were smuggled from England extensively into Spain for many years, greatly to King Philip's indignation. Valera commenced his published works with a book in Spanish called *Two Treatises: One of the Pope, and the other of the Mass*, in 1588; and from then until 1602 his works in Spanish issued constantly from the press, at first in London, and afterwards in Geneva. There is no mincing matters with Valera. He is a Puritan of the most pronounced views, who attacked the Mass and the Papacy with vigour and effect. He showed up mercilessly, for instance, the imposture of a famous stigmatised nun, called Maria de la Visitacion, who imposed upon the saintly Luis de Granada, and was punished severely for her fraud; and Valera's vigorous polemical works generally were welcomed by English Protestants as so much material for controversy. His *Two Treatises* were published in English in 1600 by John Golbourne, under the name of *Two Treatises: the first of the Lives of the Popes and their doctrine, and the second of the Mass. Also a swarm of false miracles, wherein Maria de la Visitacion deceived many.* Cipriano de Valera, however, did not aim at Englishmen but at his own countrymen, and his fame rests not so much upon these polemical works as upon his fine translation, or rather revision of Casiodoro Reina's translation, of the Bible into Castilian.

Perez de Pineda, on the other hand, was a purely devotional writer who, although a Protestant and a Calvinist, avoided mere controversy and kept, as the mystical writers had done, to fundamental religion. His book called *Epistola Consolatoria* was translated by John Daniel, and published in English in 1576, under the name of *Excellent Comfort to all Christians*; and in the same year his *Jehova, a Free Pardon for all Sinners*, was issued in London, and these books were both very popular devotional reading with all classes. Antonio Corro, who was an Oxford professor and a popular London preacher, lived here for some years, and was the busiest of all the Spanish reformers. His writings, however, were mostly in Latin; and although some of them were polemical, like his *Address to the Protestant Pastors at Antwerp*, and his *Supplication to the most mighty Prince Philip, King of Spain*, translated into English by Fenton in 1569, most of his work was in the nature of sermons, or exegesis of passages in the Bible. Several of these were published in London, such as, in 1575, his *Epistle of St. Paul to the Romans*, his *Sermons on Ecclesiastes*, his *Solomon's Sermons*, etc. Generally speaking, however, the influence of the writing of the Spanish Protestants upon the English Reformation was not large. With the exception of Corro and Valera, they did not stay long in England, where Spaniards, from their nationality, were not popular; and the fact that Corro was a Lutheran, whilst Valera was a Calvinist of the Genevan school, divided such small force as they might have exercised. They both arrived in England too late, moreover, to convert English people, and were used more to wound Philip by facilitating the dissemination of Spanish Protestant literature in Spain, than to aid the movement in England, which was already strong enough without their help.

One writer there was who did not come to England, but whose attack and exposition of the methods and procedure of the Inquisition, when translated into English by Vincent Skinner in 1568, was seized upon by those whose main grievance was the persecution cf Protestants in Spain by the Holy Office. The writer was Ramon Gonzales Montes, or Gonzales Montano, as he is usually called, whose attack upon the Inquisition written in Heidelberg attained much popularity in England, and was the foundation upon which many other attacks against the institution were based. No less than four editions of this work appeared between 1568 and 1625. It is called '*Full, Ample, and Punctual Discovery of the Barbarous, Bloody, and Inhuman Practices of the Spanish Inquisition against Protestants. With the original thereof.* Manifested in their proceedings against sundry particular persons, as well English as others, upon whom they have executed their diabolical tyranny. A work fit for these times, serving to withdraw the affections of all good Christians from that Religion, which cannot be maintained without these Props of Hell. Printed for John Bellamy, and are to be sold at the 3 Golden Lions in Corn Hill, near the Royal Exchange, 1625.' The work commences thus :—

'Whensoever any denunciation, as they term it, or rather information, is given against any person, be it only for matters of no great importance, as nothing cometh into this court so small or simple but the parties accused are greatly damaged thereby, the Inquisitors customably use this kind of practice. First they suborn some one, out of a number such as have learned their lesson for the nonce, commonly called familiars, who of purpose shall cast himself to meet one, and being provided aforehand what to say, shall greet him on this wise: "Sir, yesterday it was my chance to be with my lords the Inquisitors, and as they happened to have speech of you, they said they had to talk with you about certain of their affairs, and so gave me charge to summon you to appear before them at such an hour." Now, the party may not (being once warned) either refuse or defer to come, but at his very great peril. Whereupon the next day he repaireth to the place where the Commissioners sit, and requireth the porter to signify unto the lords that he is come. Whereof, as soon as they have intelligence, all three, if they be present, or at least two of them, meet in a council chamber where the court is commonly kept, as at Seville in the Castle of Triana, and such-like places in other cities, and, calling the party in before them, they demand of him what his suit is. He answereth that he was warned yesterday, under their precept, to come and speak with them. They then inquire his name, which being known, they ask what he wants. "For, as for us," say they, "we wot not whether you be the same man we commanded

to be here with us. Yea or nay? Marry! since thou
hast come, if you have anything to inform us of, in
this Holy Court, either of yourself or of any other in
discharge of your conscience, let us hear it." Whereupon, the party either answereth that he hath no such
matter to inform them (as, indeed, to stand upon
that point to the end with them, who seek nothing
else but his undoing and such as he shall impeach, is
the wisest and safest way that may be taken), or else
out of mere simplicity, not knowing how he entangleth
himself, rashly and unadvisedly uttereth something of
himself or of some other. Then my lords the Inquisitors, glad that they have caught him, to the
intent more easily to afear and amaze him that thus
foolishly hath made himself so fit a morsel for them to
prey upon, cast looks one upon another, and rejoicing
as though they had smelt the rat, all at once fix their
eyes upon him and behold him earnestly, and whisper-
ing together a little while, I wot not whether they say
ought or nought, at last either award him to prison if
the matter that he discloseth seemeth in any way
weighty, or if he chance to confess nothing at all they
will let him depart, pretending they know not, without
better information, whether he be the same party they
commanded to appear before them or not.' The
author then continues to narrate that the informer and
a familiar are hidden behind the arras during this
interview, and that the victim is thenceforward closely
watched day and night. 'Jolly mates,' he says, 'are

always near him, to spy and listen and worm themselves into his confidence, and then, perhaps after
years of observation, the suspected person is suddenly
pounced upon and is known to the outer world no
more.' The book abounds in tales of horrible cruelty,
and, in its original and translated forms, was evidently
designed to arouse hatred of the papacy and the
Roman Catholic form of Christianity. This work,
which was popular in England and Protestant
countries, and undoubtedly fed the irritation in this
country against Spain and its religion, almost as soon
as it appeared in Latin in Germany, was only translated into Spanish in 1851. An edition of it in
English was reprinted in 1857 by Mr. Wiffen.

I have already mentioned that the works of Juan
de Valdés, the first of the Spanish reformers, and the
finest Castilian prosodist of his day, did not reach
England until a century after his time. His most
famous religious book is *Ciento y Diez Conside-
raciones divinas*, and it was not translated into English
until 1638, by Nicolas Ferrar. Notwithstanding its
fame in foreign countries, it has never to this day
been published entire in Spanish. The reason for its
tardy appearance even in England is to be sought in
its rigid puritanic tone, which tends not a little to
unitarianism. It was not until the Puritan reaction
that such a tone was welcome in England. The
gentle Puritan poet, George Herbert, it was who in
the seventeenth century stood sponsor to the work

Q

and made it popular, and in our own day Mr. Wiffen, that industrious and enlightened Quaker, who made Spanish protestantism his especial province, has revived the vogue for the works of Juan de Valdés.

The mention of Juan de Valdés brings me to another school of writing in which Spaniards of the sixteenth and seventeenth centuries influenced English letters and English taste. I mean the political works, which had grown out of those instructions for young princes to which in an earlier chapter I called attention as being specially a Spanish form of sententious didacticism in the thirteenth, fourteenth, and fifteenth centuries. In the form of a dialogue Juan de Valdés wrote in 1528 a supposed conversation between Mercury and Charon, in which the methods of government are bitterly and brilliantly satirised. This form of attack, in which reform is suggested in a way which carries with it the condemnation of existing methods, became for the next hundred years a favourite vehicle for the attack and criticism of political affairs. Guevara in his *Dial of Princes* and his *Familiar Epistles*, both translated, as I have already said, by Edward Hellowes, and extremely popular in England, had previously adopted this form to some extent, and he was followed, with scathing effect, by the persecuted and exiled secretary of Philip II., Antonio Perez, who, in the safe retreat of Essex House, and in Paris, indited his venomous sugar-coated aphorisms and political letters, which pretended to give good counsel, but really attacked the system and the person for whose ostensible benefit the advice was given. Perez's witty sayings and bitter-sweet epigrams, euphuistic as they were, were the fashion in England and France from 1591 to 1598 ; and all the young bloods who followed the footsteps of the splendid Earl of Essex, sought to imitate the quips and obscurities of 'Master Antonio,' whose affected manners they laughed at. I point out in the next chapter that Shakespeare himself was not oblivious of the mingled charm and absurdity of Antonio Perez. How insidious were the political books I refer to, and how difficult to suppress without seeming injustice, is seen in Furio de Ceriol's book *El Consejo y Consejeros de un Principe*, which is addressed *Al gran Catolico de España D. Felipe II.*, and is, to all appearance, intended to be effusively loyal. But just a little beneath the surface its malice is apparent. If it were not, it would certainly not have been welcomed in English dress, as it was in 1570, translated by Thomas Blundeville. If Ceriol's advice had been adopted, Philip would have found himself a cipher in his own government. He is told, moreover, in words plainly to be understood, that his court is corrupt, that his favourites are bought and sold, and that ineptitude rules supreme in his government.

It must have been dangerous, nevertheless, for any Spaniard to have written this in the realm of Philip II., advocating toleration :—

'It is a very certain sign of a torpid genius to speak ill or with prejudice against an adversary, or against the enemies of one's prince, or of those who belong to a different sect, or foreigners, be they Moors, Heathens, or Christians; for true genius finds in all countries seven leagues of bad road: in all parts there are good and bad: the good he lauds, and cordially receives; the bad he denounces and rejects, but it is foolish of him if he abuse the nation in which the bad are found.'

The accession of James I., and the renewed political friendship with Spain in the first quarter of the seventeenth century, introduced a new element in the connection between the two countries. James Stuart's idea had always been to curry favour with the power which he, like the rest of the world, over-rated. His subservience to Gondomar, and his plans to marry his son to a Spanish princess, drew to him a school of courtiers who had always been well affected towards Spain. Sir Francis Godolphin, Digby, Earl of Bristol, and for a time, even the powerful Buckingham himself, were strongly Spanish in sympathy, and with the hair-brained trip of the Prince of Wales to Madrid, the fashion for Spanish things, Spanish language, and Spanish literature reached its height in England. Charles's friend, Endymion Porter, was half a Spaniard, and he, like the courtiers already mentioned, industriously turned Spanish verses and songs into English. James Howell, too, was a busy propagator of Spanish books and letters. But with the failure of the Spanish match, and the marriage of Charles I. with a French princess, the direct Spanish courtly influence in England declined, and we must seek for Spanish influence upon English letters in another direction.

CHAPTER IX

THE SPANISH THEATRE AND THE
ENGLISH DRAMATISTS

IN Spain, as in the rest of the world, the profane drama largely derived from the ecclesiastical miracle plays, and it happens that the earliest specimen of Castilian literature now known is a dramatic fragment to which I directed attention in the opening chapter of this book. This fragment is called *El Auto de los Reyes Magos*, and already in it the vivid dramatic instinct of the Spanish race is conspicuous. The language is lilting but terse; the story of the Kings of the East and their visit to the Child Christ, their first incredulity, and subsequent conversion, being developed quite naturally on dramatic lines, although the little drama cannot have been written later than the twelfth century, and is known to have been represented at Toledo Cathedral early in the thirteenth. The Provençal troubadours at that time were flocking into Spain, partly in consequence of the Albigensian wars; and the juglars, in competition with each other, naturally tried to give dramatic value to their songs by added appropriate music and action. The famous code of laws, the *Siete Partidas* of Alfonso X., to which I referred in my first chapter, contains a set of regulations which show how soon the juglars and buffoons had introduced profane elements even in the sacred mystery plays, Judas and the devil being usually treated as characters would be in an old-fashioned knockabout farce. Speaking of the clergy, the thirteenth century code says: 'Nor must they be performers in scurrilous plays for people to go and see, as they do; and if other men should perform such, priests may not attend them, because the performers do many lewd and scandalous acts in them. Nor should any person whatever do such things in churches. On the contrary, we declare that they must be cast out with reprobation, for the church belongs to God.' In Catalonia, as being more directly under the French and Italian influence, the confessedly profane drama appeared earlier than in Castile; and at the poetical court of John I. of Aragon, late in the fourteenth century, the king's brother, Prince Henry, a great patron of letters, founded a regular academy or corporation for the promotion of all sorts of poetic compositions, one result of which, at least, we know to have been a regular tragedy, performed before the king in 1394, called *The Man in Love and the Contented Woman.* The first really dramatic secular piece that we know of in Castile was written by a converted Toledan Jew called Rodrigo de Cota, about 1470. It is in the form of a dialogue between love and an old man. The latter, frightened by Cupid, retires into a neglected garden, where a palace of pleasure lies in ruins. Here he shuts himself up in a poor hut, to escape the pursuit of love. But Cupid comes in such humble guise to reason with him, that a conversation ensues, with the result, of course, that love conquers, and the old man is subdued. The dialogue was adapted for representation, but probably it was recited by one person only with changes of voice and action. The same may be said of the contemporary satirical poem in eclogue form called *Mingo Revulgo*, in which a courtier and a rustic discuss the abuses of the court and the misgovernment of the country. But these dialogue poems were mere harbingers, and, if they were represented scenically at all, they had little of the characteristics of the modern drama.

But it was quite otherwise when that great work which I mentioned at some length in my remarks on the novel appeared—I mean *Celestina*, or, to give it its original name, *The tragi-comedy of Calisto and Melibea*, which was written late in the fifteenth century, probably by another Jew, Fernando de Rojas. It was, to all intents and purposes, a novel in dramatic form ; and, as it consisted of twenty-two acts, it was impossible of representation in its entirety. But it was a true dramatic work for all that, telling the tragic tale with the inevitable moral, of how desires attained by licentious and vicious means turn to dust and ashes in the mouth. At the same period as *Celestina*, the poet Juan de Encina wrote numerous eclogues, or pastoral dialogues for recitation, full of dramatic spirit ; and we have details of frequent representations of these little pastoral plays. For instance, in the year 1495, there was represented one of Juan de Encina's eclogues with the following elaborate title :—'*Eclogue represented on the last night of the Carnival, where there are introduced four shepherds called Benito, Blas, Pedruelo, and Llorente.* First Benito enters into the saloon where the duke and duchess are, and begins to lament very much, because it is rumoured that the Duke (of Alba), his lord, has to go to the war in France. Then Blas enters and asks him the cause of his grief, which they discuss together. Then they call Pedruelo in, and he brings the glad news of peace; Llorente then comes in, and joins in the final song of rejoicing.' This, it will be remarked, is a little drama of simple motive, without any of the complicated characterisation and action of *Celestina*; so that probably we shall be correct in assuming that at this period (the end of the fifteenth century) the dramas actually intended for representation on a stage only dealt thus with very simple themes easily followed by unlearned persons.

The next step forward was taken by one Bartolomé de Torres Naharro, a Spanish soldier of fortune, who lived mostly in Italy. Copying from the Italian dramatic works he saw, he wrote eight comedies, which were not only really adapted for stage production, but were divided into five regular divisions, which he called 'journeys,' and developed an intelligible tale by the action of several personages. These plays were at first represented at Naples (which belonged to Spain), and soon found their way to Spain itself. This was in the first third of the sixteenth century, when the fiscal and commercial policy of Ferdinand and Isabel, together with the discovery of America and the final conquest of Granada, had sown the seed of luxury and idle self-indulgence in the Spanish people. Soon there spread a perfect craze for comedies. Those of Torres Naharro led the way; and then came the licentious farces of Castillejo, which wittily laughed and scoffed at the Italian innovations. The plays were performed before a blanket in a courtyard, and without any attempt at appropriate costume until late in the sixteenth century, and every village in Spain thenceforward was constantly visited by strolling players, with comedies adapted for the ignorant and the rude, for as yet the court stood aloof from such frivolity. Out of the ruck of leaders of such wandering troops of players there arose one Lope de Rueda, a silversmith's hammerman of Seville, who wrote his own plays, and, like Shakespeare, acted in them himself. He was in his way a genius; a keen observer of life, with the true Spanish malicious, satirical wit, and he invented what afterwards became in the hands, or rather heads, of his greatest successors, a characteristic vehicle for the manifestation of the Spanish literary genius, and remains to this day a popular dramatic form, namely, those bustling farces which are called *pasos* or *entremeses*. One, for instance, *La Caratula*, recounts the story of a silly rustic servant finding a mask, and his master making him believe that it is the face of a hermit named Diego Sanchez that has been cut off by murderous thieves. The poor servant, in a fright, lest he should be prosecuted for the murder, becomes a hermit himself in the cell and garb of the one who has been murdered, and his master frightens him into all sorts of absurdities and simple talk by pretending to be the hermit's ghost.

Lope de Rueda's plays were very popular, and he had many imitators, one in particular—Juan de la Cueva, who, in the third quarter of the sixteenth century, introduced into Spanish plays that which afterwards became so characteristic of them generally : the dashing, soldierly element that we call '*capa y espada*,' ' cape and sword '—a natural result of the spirit engendered by the long wars of the emperor throughout Europe, and the elevation of arms and adventure as the most honourable professional means of livelihood. The drama was thenceforward popular and prosperous all over Spain. In 1582 two permanent companies of players were established in Madrid, playing in courtyards specially leased and kept for the purpose. Twenty years before this, there had been born a boy in Madrid, the child of a basket-maker, who later became one of the most extraordinary literary geniuses the world has ever seen : a man whose facility of production was so marvellous as to be almost incredible, whose most rapid trifles are so crammed with invention, wit, and verbal felicity, that a week of his work would suffice to make the lifelong reputation of another man, as in fact three sonnets stolen from him do mainly make the poetical fame of the Frenchman Scarron. I refer to him whom his friend Cervantes called the 'prodigy of Nature,' Lope de Vega Carpio. The life of this genius, whose brain without effort wove intrigue which amused all Europe for a century and a half, and left deep traces upon the drama down to our own day, was as full of adventure as that of Gil Blas or Guzman de Alfarache. Dissolute in his youth and prime ; immoral, even in his age ; a brawler and a debauchee ; in and out of prison ; banished and proscribed, only to come back insolent in the knowledge of his genius, that he knew no man could withstand ; a soldier in the Spanish Armada against England, and, during even that catastrophe in the rough seas of the north, able to write verses by the hundred—a great epic amongst other things : his life was, until old age made him outwardly decent, as became a familiar

of the Inquisition and a priest, one tale of unblush-
ing vice and indulgence. But for twenty years or
more before the end his genius conquered. The
dramatic pieces which he looked upon as mere play-
things, and of which he confessed to have written
fifteen hundred, carried him from triumph to triumph,
and all Spain, very soon all Europe, was dazzled by
his boundless invention and his brilliant wit. He was
one of the sights of Madrid. As he returned from
his priestly duties in the hospital of charity, men and
women clustered around him to crave his blessing,
and admiring crowds followed him. His daily walk
was a procession, and prints of his portrait adorned
almost every dwelling in the capital.[1] In his old
age, from 1625 to 1635, when he was between sixty
and seventy, Lope de Vega produced on an average
seventy plays a year.

To say that they were all masterpieces would be
absurd, for not more than five hundred are now known
to exist, and most of these are no more than names
to us; but we can judge of the man's excellence by
those few of his plays which are still household words,
and we can understand by them the qualities that
made their author the supreme master of the Spanish
stage for at least forty-five years, and before whose
dramatic ability the great Cervantes himself was obliged
to retire abashed and defeated. Lope wrote a book
that professed to instruct people 'how to do it.' But,

[1] J. Fitzmaurice-Kelly, *Taylorian Oxford Lecture*, 1902.

whilst he lays down his rules, he coolly confesses that
he does not follow them. In fact, Lope was in his
very essence creative, and was no critic in any sense.
He wrote by instinct, as all true writers must, and
not by rule. He pictured contemporary modes and
humours with unflagging vivacity and unshrinking
truth; his characters were no longer mere gramo-
phones to repeat speeches, but men and women to
do things that forwarded the story he had to tell.
For the telling of the story was Lope's object, and
in this both he and his successors, as I shall point
out later, differed from Shakespeare and his school,
whose object was the dramatic exposition of passion
and character.

The Spanish drama and the contemporary drama
in English had this in common, if nothing else, namely,
that they broke with the classical tradition, and
adopted a modern and more colloquial presentation;
but in most other points they were dissimilar, because
the national character is dissimilar. Reverie and
speculation, cogitation with oneself, musing on things
seen, are the natural bent of the English nature. An
Englishman wants to get at the springs that turn the
human wheels of life round; he wants to understand
the works, to sound the reasons for action. The
Spaniards, like most semi-Latin peoples, care little for
that. They wish to see and participate in the movement itself; to talk, to enjoy the surface of things
whilst they may: in short, to follow the story, to weep

with the afflicted heroine, to see themselves reflected in the unselfish bravery of the hero, to laugh at the buffoon, and to curse the villain.

As an instance of this we will take one of Lope's most famous quasi-historical plays, *La Estrella de Sevilla* (*The Star of Seville*). The story, though containing many strong situations, is very simple. Sancho IV. of Castile is visiting Seville for the first time, and falls in love with a lady named Estrella, the sister of Bustos Tavera, a young noble of the city.[1] The lady is in love with, and is loved by, a gentleman named Sancho Ortiz, her brother's inseparable friend. When the king's chamberlain, Arias, hears that his master is in love with Estrella, he suggests that the lady's brother, Bustos Tavera, should be brought to the palace and flattered as a means of gaining his sister for the king.

When Bustos Tavera arrives before the king, ignorant of the reason for his summons, he throws himself at his sovereign's feet, and, when bidden to rise, says :—

> 'Que si el Rey se ha de tratar
> Como á Santo en el altar.
> Digno lugar escogi.'

> 'If sacred kings, like saints upon a shrine,
> Ador'd should be, this place is surely mine.'

The king, pretending to be struck by his loyalty, tells him he will make him Alcalde of Seville, a post which

[1] The digest of the story given here is partly condensed from G. H. Lewes's *Spanish Drama.*

is just vacant, and is much sought. Bustos Tavera
says that others are more deserving of the post than
he, and refuses it. The king, loud still in his praises,
offers to procure a splendid match for his (Bustos')
sister, and gives to Bustos Tavera himself the privilege
of access at all hours to the royal chamber. But
Bustos Tavera is ill at ease. What can this royal
favour mean?—

> 'Sospechoso voy. Quererme ;
> Y sin conocerme honrarme,
> Mas parece sobornar mi
> Honor, que favorecerme.'

> 'These sudden favours with mistrust I view :
> Why should he love a man he never knew?
> Such honours savour more of bribes than meeds,
> To gain my virtue, not reward my deeds.'[1]

Arias, the king's evil counsellor, persuades the king
to allow him to bribe Estrella's servant to give him
access to her chamber, and the king is at length
admitted incognito into the house. Just as he is
parleying with the false servant, Bustos Tavera comes
home and overhears the plot to compromise his sister.
He at once draws his sword, and the king, to save his
own life, reveals who he is. Bustos Tavera, in a fine
scene, pretends to disbelieve him, but with scathing
words lashes his dishonourable course. He allows
the king to escape, and in deep shame and anger
Sancho returns to his palace, telling the chamberlain

[1] G. H. Lewes.

Arias how he has been foiled. Arias instigates him to have Bustos Tavera executed ; but the king dares not do this openly, for Bustos is popular, and has committed no crime. Arias then advises him to kill two birds with one stone, and to order Sancho Ortiz, the betrothed of Estrella, to murder her brother Bustos Tavera, his dearest friend. Ortiz is summoned, and told to kill a person unnamed for an offence against the sovereign. With much repugnance and remonstrance he consents to do so, and then, to his dismay, reads in the secret paper given to him that the man he is to murder is his friend, the brother of his betrothed. Compelled by his promise to the king, but in an anguish of despair, he commits the crime, and at once proclaims his guilt. Before he can kill himself, as he intended, he is seized, but refuses to save himself by avowing the king's orders. The king, in remorse, learns this, and commands him to divulge it on pain of death. Estrella demands of the king the ancient right to dispose of her brother's murderer, and the weak king, struck by her grief and beauty, hands to her the pass-key of the prison. Instead of at once wreaking vengeance upon Ortiz, she offers the latter his liberty, which he refuses to accept; and when the judges condemn him to death, notwithstanding the king's efforts in his favour, the king orders the prisoner to be brought to him. He appears with Estrella, and throws himself at the king's feet. Then follows this striking dialogue, which I have

R

translated almost literally, and without any attempt
at rhyme :—

'ORTIZ. Great Lord.　Why finish not the tale of my distress?
　　By death wipe out the blackness of my crime?
　　I killed Bustos Tavera ; kill thou me !
　　For he who kills, 'tis meet that he should die.
　　My liege ! do justice, for 'twill mercy be.
KING. Wait ! Wait ! Who ordered thee the deed to do?
ORTIZ. A paper.
KING. From whom ?
ORTIZ. If paper spake, the paper should ye tell.
　　But since a crumpled leaf is hard of speech,
　　Enough that with this hand I killed my friend,
　　To keep my word ; and kneeling here I pray
　　To thee, dear heart, Estrella, end my life :
　　A little vengeance for so dire a sin.
KING. Estrella ! thee have I betrothed
　　To one, a noble, of my royal house,
　　As young and handsome as in all Castile
　　There be.　Powerful and rich.
　　I crave for payment of the boon I give,
　　Mercy and pardon for the evil done
　　By this poor soul, who pity well deserves.
ESTRELLA. My liege ! since thou hast bidden me to wed,
　　Let Sancho Ortiz go.　I seek no life,
　　No vengeance, for my brother's loss.
ORTIZ (to ESTRELLA). The pardon givest thou because the king
　　Hath married thee so nobly and so high.
ESTRELLA. 'Tis true : for that I pardon thee.
ORTIZ. And is my sin for this condoned ?
ESTRELLA. It is, and pardoned quite.
ORTIZ. Thy hopes I will not break,
　　If by living I can them fulfil,
　　Much as I wished to die.
KING. Then thou mayest go ! farewell.
JUDGES. But, sire, Seville will not forgive !
　　The man must die.

KING (*aside, to* ARIAS). What shall I do?
  These people frighten me.
ARIAS. Speak——
KING. Seville! 'Tis I whom thou must kill!
  I was the cause of this foul deed.
  I it was who ordered it, and this
  Should free the man from blame.
ORTIZ. I only prayed for this discharge.
  The king it was who gave me the command
  To kill my friend : for no behest
  On earth but his would I have done the deed.'

The king, struck by such loyalty, offers to allow
Estrella and Ortiz to marry; but the lady shrinks,
naturally, at being tied for life to the murderer of her
brother, and declines. Ortiz then goes to the Moorish
wars in the hope of being killed, and Estrella to her
loveless marriage, hoping soon to die of grief.

Although I have not been able to give more than
a small scrap of one play of Lope's, this is a fairly
representative one of its class. It will be observed that
the characters in the play are not so much persons as
personified qualities. They are ticketed unmistakably with their characteristics the moment they
appear on the stage, and they are invariable throughout. The king is weak and impressionable, Bustos
Tavera is magnanimity personified, Sancho Ortiz is
steadfast loyalty, Arias is temptation, and Estrella is
gentle love. The story is developed by these primal
passions personified. As we know, persons are swayed
in real life by many circumstances that complicate
their primal passions; and the varying phases of a

story should develop fresh manifestations of character. But this needs introspection, patient thought and study on the part of the author, which neither Lope nor Calderon, his successor—and, as some think, a greater than he—could give, or indeed their public desired.

Calderon, who died in 1681 at a great age, is certainly more subtle and introspective than Lope. This more especially is seen in *La Vida es Sueño*, where the mystery and philosophy of human life are touched ; the plot of the play being the drugging of a prince, imprisoned since his birth, and testing him by putting him into his proper place on the throne, telling him that his life-long solitary imprisonment has been a dream. When he turns out to be a cruel tyrant he is drugged again, and wakes once more in prison, to be told that his regal state was a dream. This machinery, it will be recollected, is like the Christopher Sly incident in *The Taming of the Shrew*; but it was not an uncommon device in ancient Oriental tales. Perhaps the most characteristic of Calderon's plays is the fine *Alcalde de Zalamea*, which, with several other of his plays, was so eloquently translated by Edward FitzGerald. Crespo, the peasant head-man of the village of Zalamea, has to welcome a company of the king's soldiers to his village, and lodges the captain, Don Alvaro, in his own house. His son, Juan, is indignant that his rich peasant father should submit to have soldiers billeted upon him. 'How should I avoid it?' asks Crespo.

'By purchasing a patent of nobility,' says the son. Crespo, with rough dignity, says: 'Is there any one ignorant of what I am? That I am an honest man, sprung from an honest stock. No. Then what should I gain by letters of nobility, if I could not also purchase noble blood? Should I be thought better than I am? No. People would point at me and say that I was ennobled for six hundred reals. That would prove me rich—not honourable. Honour, my son, is neither bought nor sold. I want none that is not mine by nature. My father was a peasant—my grandfather was a peasant—and my children shall be peasants too.' The captain, Alvaro, repays the peasant's hospitality by inventing a ruse to get a sight of his pretty daughter; and the mayor and his son find the captain in the girl's room paying her high-flown compliments. The son understands the intent, and is indignant; he quarrels with the captain, who spurns him as a peasant, and the general, Don Lope, appears greatly angry that peasants should dare to quarrel with the king's officer. The captain's servant, however, blurts out the whole story of the ruse, and the captain is sent to lodge elsewhere, the general himself staying in Crespo's house. Here a vigorous conversation takes place in which Crespo shows that he is a match in pride for any noble. In the next act the captain, Alvaro, abducts Isabel, Crespo's daughter, after tying her father to a tree and gagging him. The captain is wounded by Crespo's son, and the outraged daughter returns to her despairing father, now sternly resolved on vengeance for his wounded honour. News is brought him that he has been appointed Alcalde, and that the king will enter the village next day. In the meanwhile he, as mayor, has to sit in judgment on his son for the attempted murder of the captain. Here, too, is his opportunity for vengeance. He goes to the wounded captain, and in a magnificent speech appeals to his chivalry. Eloquently, and with beautiful dignity, he says that he is only a peasant; but an honest man, and rich. He will give all he possesses, and leave his home a beggar, if only the captain will marry the daughter whose honour he has compromised. The captain scornfully treats it as a joke that he, a noble, should marry a peasant's daughter; and then Crespo, rising in his wrath, exercises his duty as a magistrate, and orders the captain's arrest for the abduction of his daughter. Whilst he is about to judge the man who has ruined his happiness, the general, Don Lope, arrives, and is indignant that a king's officer should be submitted to a village judge. But Crespo is obdurate; and when the king himself arrives the case is submitted to him, and he decides that, although the captain is guilty, the Alcalde must not sentence one of the royal officers, a noble. This is a truly dramatic situation. The peasant-mayor, firm as a rock, and as dignified, bows his head to his sovereign; and, turning round, tears aside a curtain to show the strangled body of the captain, and that the peasant-mayor of Zalamea, with his own hands, has already done justice to his injurer. What matters it who executes the sentence, he asks, if the crime is admitted and proved? And the king, struck with his strength of character, makes him Alcalde for life.

Although Crespo is one of the best-developed characters of the Spanish drama, here again the same tendency is observed. The characters are all personifications of fixed qualities, not human beings swayed by complex emotions. Crespo is innate nobleness in a rustic garb ; Don Alvaro, the captain, is dissolute privilege ; Juan, Crespo's son, is rash hot-headedness ; Isabel is rustic innocence, and so on. They all do what they are bound to do, seeing their fixed characters, and the story is worked out, not by the development of character, but by the operation of primal passions dressed like human beings. Compare this treatment with that adopted by Shakespeare and his English contemporaries. Take what is called the comic relief first. The *graciosos* in all the Spanish dramas of the best period, of which I am speaking, are roguish servants, brought in to serve as foils to their masters by their shrewd, vulgar wit. There is no differentiation of them. They are all turned out of the same mould, and from the beginning of the play to the end, whatever happens, they never change. They come on when required, and say their boorish smart things, and that is all. But, take some of

Shakespeare's comic relief, and see the difference. Look how infinite are the moods of Falstaff. How different the tone with which he humours Master Shallow from that he uses to his boon companions at the 'Boar's Head.' How dignified, withal, when the new king dashes all his hopes by turning his back upon him, and sending him to prison. He does not go out with a wry-mouthed quip, as a common clown would do, but puts a brave face upon it to Justice Shallow, and bears himself like a gentleman. And, again, look at the drunken, vicious roisterers at the 'Boar's Head,' when Falstaff dies. How tenderly they tell of Falstaff's death! Surely one of the most moving passages in English writing is the hostess's reference to her dead customer. The cap and bells are hidden, and a sigh shows the clown is human. Take Bottom, the stage-struck weaver; his bemused surprise, and unwillingness to tell of his temporary bewitchment into an ass by the fairies. No verbal smartness is this, but the development of a man's character. His quaint simplicity in the play scenes would be meaningless without our seeing how muddle-brained the man naturally was. Even more clearly, because more directly bearing upon the story told, is to be seen the personality of Shakespeare's heroes. Hamlet, for instance, is a creature of moods, and each new mood he shows has its influence upon the development of the story. He is not ticketed beforehand with a permanent character, like Calderon's Sigismundo in

La Vida es Sueño, or like Sancho Ortiz in Lope's *Estrella de Sevilla*, but is moved by circumstances as live men are ; and his changes react upon the story that surrounds him. Look at Macbeth. We know the Thane to be a weakly ambitious man, easily led and uxorious. See how his character develops with the urging of his stronger wife. See how his fears and his hopes, alternately, rule him ; how he sways from side to side in his instability, whilst you feel that the issue of the story depends upon the irresolute will, which is being unfolded before you. Then, after the crime is done, the remorse, and how his native courage flickers up, and he becomes momentarily great, when manly deeds are to be done in facing the English and his foes. So is it, too, in the comedies. The timid, shrinking Portia, under the influence of her love for Bassanio, sways the whole tale to its dramatic end, by casting aside her maidenly reserve and appearing as a young advocate, with all the outward attributes of a young man, not a woman in disguise. What is true of Shakespeare is true, in a degree, of his contemporaries and followers—Beaumont and Fletcher, Massinger, Ben Jonson, and the rest of them. They wrote for a public which desired to watch the springs of action, as well as to see the action itself; and human character is utilised to develop the story they have to tell.

It was inevitable that, when Spain, the most powerful and fashionable country in the sixteenth century, produced a drama so fresh, so abundant, and so witty, Europe should turn to Spain for dramatic material. For the last ten years of the sixteenth, and first forty years of the seventeenth century, all Spain was stage-struck, poetry was an obsession. The king, Philip IV., was one of the greatest patrons of the drama that ever lived; and, in his court, literature, and particularly dramatic literature, was the fashionable pursuit. It is true that the direct influence of Spanish drama upon France was greater than upon England, where the Italian *novelle* ruled, although I shall show later that at a subsequent period the influence was passed from France to England through Molière and his contemporaries. But at present I wish more particularly to direct attention to the considerable use made by the English dramatists of Shakespeare's day of the stories invented or adapted by Spaniards. As I have already pointed out, the debt was mainly for stories and plots, or pieces of intrigue; for the characterisation was much stronger in the English plays than in Spanish originals, although Englishmen could not weave the plots. It is impossible to point out more than a few of the instances of such indebtedness, even of those we know, and a diligent study of the immense mass of material in both languages would certainly reveal many others—especially at the later period of which I shall speak presently. Perhaps of all the great English playwrights of the Elizabethan and Jacobean period, Shakespeare has borrowed least, directly, from the Spaniards. In two instances, to which I referred in a former chapter, he took his plots from Spanish sources : *The Two Gentlemen of Verona* from the Felismena incident in the *Diana* of Montemayor, and the *Taming of the Shrew* from one of the tales of Count Lucanor, which I have given almost at length in a previous chapter. But it has no doubt struck readers how often he introduces personages of Spanish name, and with Spanish characteristics, in his plays, which, if it does nothing else, shows the influence of Spanish upon literary production generally. But, more than this, although there is no reason to believe that Shakespeare had more than the fashionable smattering of a few phrases in Spanish, it is curious to see how frequently he introduces such phrases into his plays. To take only one instance, that of the Ancient (or Ensign) Pistol, the swashbuckling soldier who had picked up Spanish in the wars, and interlards his boastful vaunts with it. Indeed, it is more than probable that the whole character of Pistol was an intentional burlesque upon a type that was considered to represent Spaniards at the time, and was known throughout Europe, both in real life and in the grandiose Spanish drama—namely, the ostentatious Spanish captain, loud in his claims for personal distinction, vain and showy, pompous and grandiloquent. When Shakespeare wrote *Henry V.*, such a burlesque could not fail to be popular in England, for the feeling against Spain was still very bitter, and the Spanish swashbuckler was an accepted type of boastfulness. He is made to pile quotation upon quotation, to indulge in outlandish oaths and strange threats; but, of course, is represented as an abject coward, and eats Fluellen's leek like a babe, for England was still at war with Spain, and enemies are rarely represented as heroes.

But, to my mind, at least, another character in Shakespeare bears signs not only of being a caricature upon the heroic pretensions, the chivalrous pose, and the extravagant language, which were supposed to mark Spaniards in general, but of being intended for a burlesque upon a particular person. I mean the character of the Spaniard, Don Adriano Armado, in *Love's Labour's Lost*. I wish to dwell upon this point with some little attention, because, so far as I know, my theory is a new one, and I have formed it because I have had perhaps as good opportunities for studying the details of the person who, I think, was caricatured, as I suppose any Englishman. I mean Antonio Perez, the exiled Spanish Secretary of State. *Love's Labour's Lost* cannot originally have been written later than 1591, and Perez did not escape from Spain into France until November of that year ; so that, if I am correct in my supposition, the points upon which I rely cannot have been introduced into the play until it was enlarged and partially rewritten for a court performance in 1597. Perez arrived in England in the autumn of 1593; and whilst he was, of course, made much of by the war party of Essex, he was greatly disliked and distrusted by Burghley and the moderates, as well as at first by Elizabeth herself. By all he was laughed at for his affectation, and envied for his malicious wit. Lady Bacon was violently angry that her son Francis should be so friendly with him: 'A proud, profane, costly fellow, whose being about him I verily believe the Lord God doth mislike'; and one of Anthony Bacon's agents writes of him in 1594: 'Surely he is, as we say, an odd man, and hath his full sight everywhere. . . . I have hardly heard of him, and yet, I know not how, I begin to admire him already.' He lived on the bounty of the Earl of Essex until Henry IV. became jealous, and insisted upon his coming back to him in the summer of 1595. In France and in England, as in Spain, he betrayed and sold every one who trusted him. He had been spoilt and pampered to such an extent by Henry IV. and by his English friends, that his presumption and caprice became unbearable. When he met Essex at Dover in 1596 he finally disgusted and offended the ·earl, and thenceforward his star in England had set. In France he was still endured, though he finally tired out even Henry IV., who had treated him with almost royal honours. So that if we assume that the special touches of caricature that identify Don Antonio Armado with Perez were introduced into the play when it was recast for the court performance in 1597, the reason for the skit upon Essex's fallen favourite becomes at once apparent. The court, and the court only, would see the joke, which no one would have dared to make when Perez was in favour three years before, for then Perez would have struck back with the sharp claws beneath his velvet paw.

No one can read Perez's many published letters, and the famous *Relaciones* written whilst he was in England, without identifying numerous affected turns of speech with those put into the mouth of Don Adriano Armado; and the description given of Don Adriano by the King of Navarre, in the play, tallies exactly with the word-portraits remaining to us of Antonio Perez drawn from his own writings and those of his contemporaries. 'Our court, you know, is haunted,' says the king,

> ' With a refined traveller of Spain,
> A man in all the world's new fashion planted,
> That hath a mint of phrases in his brain :
> One whom the music of his own vain tongue
> Doth ravish, like enchanting harmony ;
> A man of complements, whom right and wrong
> Have chose as umpire of their mutiny :
> This child of fancy, that Armado hight,
> For interim to our studies, shall relate,
> In high-born words, the worth of many a knight
> From tawny Spain, lost in the world's debate.
> How you delight, my lords, I know not, I ;
> But, I protest, I love to hear him lie,
> And I will use him for my minstrelsy.'

The Constable then hands to the king Don Adriano's letter, giving an account of the clown Costard's
violation of the king's order that there is to be no
love-making in his court. Leaving out the inter-
jections of the clown, the Spaniard's letter runs
thus: 'Great deputy, the welkin's vice-regent and
sole dominator of Navarre, my soul's earth's God,
and body's fostering patron. So it is, besieged by
sable-coloured melancholy, I did commend the black-
oppressing humour to the most wholesome physic
of thy health-giving air; and, as I am a gentleman,
betook myself to walk. The time when? About the
sixth hour, when beasts most graze, birds best peck,
and men sit down to that nourishment which is
called supper. So much for the time when. Now
for the ground which; which, I mean, I walked upon:
it is yclept thy park. Then for the place where;
where, I mean, I did encounter that most obscene
and preposterous event, that draweth from my snow-
white pen the ebon-coloured ink, which here thou
viewest, beholdest, seest.' . . . And then follows, in
equally bombastic strain, his account of his appre-
hension of the clown Costard, for flirting with
Jaquenetta. This letter, absurd as its diction is, is
hardly an exaggeration of Perez's usual epistolary
style. For instance, this is a short extract taken at
random from one of his letters written to Henry IV.
of France from England, saying he will return to
France because he has left his soul behind him

with the king, and without it he cannot live :—' Pardon me, sire,' he says, 'for the boldness of the compliment; but the soul, sire, has its loves, and uses compliments as the body does—compliments which break and pass all bounds of earthly respect. I write, too, that your Majesty may entertain yourself with the Spanish language, of which you say that I am to be your master. Surely, sire, you have chosen a pretty barbarian for a master, barbarous in idea, in word, in all things. I understand, rather, sire, that you will be my master; and from your sweet hand this rough pebble will marvellously receive polish; for great artificers thus show their cunning on the coarsest materials; even as royal souls imitate the acts of God in repairing that which is destroyed by others, who dare to show their sinister power by usurping the functions of the omnipotent.' To Essex's sister, Lady Rich, Perez sends a pair of gloves, with this letter :—' I have been so troubled not to have the dog's skin gloves your ladyship desires, that, pending the time when they shall arrive, I have resolved to sacrifice myself to your service, and flay a piece of my own skin from the most tender part of my body, if such an uncouth carcass as mine can have any tender skin. To this length can love and wish to serve a lady be carried, that a man should flay himself to make gloves for his lady. But in my case this is as nothing, for even the soul will skin itself for the person it loves.' . . . And then Perez for two or three pages continues to ring the wearisome changes upon dogs and skins and souls, in a way that Don Adriano Armado himself could not have bettered. But there is another reason besides similarity of epistolary style that seems to support my belief that Shakespeare was personally caricaturing Perez in Don Adriano Armado. Perez gave himself several nicknames; but he had one favourite, one that he never tired of from first to last, and under which he wrote his book. This name was 'Peregrino,' 'El Peregrino,' or 'Rafael Peregrino.' He signed himself thus in countless letters, and his affected play upon the word was ceaseless. Peregrinate is, and always has been, an extremely rarely used English word, so that its introduction by Shakespeare, especially applied to Don Adriano Armado, is significant. The two pedantic scholars are discussing Armado, and between them they describe Antonio Perez to the life thus :—

'SIR NATHANIEL. I did converse this quondam day with a companion of the king's, who is intituled, nominated, or called, Don Adriano de Armado.

'HOLOFERNES. *Novi hominem tanquam te:* his humour is lofty, his discourse peremptory, his tongue filed, his eye ambitious, his gait majestical, and his general behaviour vain, ridiculous, and thrasonical. He is too picked, too spruce, too affected, too odd, as it were, too *peregrinate*, as I may call it.

'SIR NATHANIEL.   A most singular and choice epithet.'

When Armado enters, and boasts to the pedants of his intimacy with the King of Navarre,[1] he says, 'I must tell thee, it will please his grace, by the world, sometime to lean upon my poor shoulder, and with his royal finger, thus, dally with my excrement—my moustachio—but let that pass. By the world, I recount no fable : some certain special honour it pleaseth his greatness to impart to Armado, a soldier, a man of travel, that hath seen the world ; but let that pass.'

At the period that the play was represented at court (1597), Antonio Perez was so much favoured by Henry IV., that the king would hardly let him out of his sight, and Essex had been deeply offended with the ingratitude of Perez in preferring to remain in France; so that it is easily understood that a burlesque upon Henry's affection for him would not be displeasing to Shakespeare's patron at the time. It has already been suggested by Shakespearian scholars, that the character of the Jew Shylock may have been taken from that celebrated Jew, Dr. Ruy Lopez, Queen Elizabeth's physician, who after many years of favour entangled himself in politics, and was executed for a supposed design to poison the queen in the interests of Spain. The Earl of Essex

---

[1] It must not be forgotten that Henry IV. of France was King of Navarre, and had been so called until the death of Henry III.

was his bitter enemy, and the cause of his death in
1594; anything that presented a Jew like Lopez
in an odious light would please the earl and his
set. Lopez certainly figured in other plays soon
after his death—in Marlowe's *Jew of Malta*, and *Dr.
Faustus*; in Dekker's *Lady of Babylon*, and in Middleton's *Game at Chess*. *The Merchant of Venice* was
first seen on the stage two months after Lopez's
execution (7th June 1594), when all the country was
ringing with the news of the unpopular Jew's fate.
Everybody had known that Lopez was an avaricious,
greedy man, and a poisoner by profession, and that
he had outwardly conformed to Christianity. It will
be recollected that, when Portia in the trial scene
demands that Shylock shall become a Christian, he
makes no demur whatever. Lopez, indeed, was fond
of dwelling upon his Christianity, and constantly
speaks in his letters to the Spanish agents of the
'great remedy for Christendom' that is to be effected
by his means. On the scaffold, even, he made a
despairing reference to his love of Christ. Probably
Shakespeare had this in his mind when he puts these
words into Antonio's mouth :—

> 'The Devil can cite Scripture for his purpose.
> An evil soul producing holy witness
> Is like a villain with a smiling cheek,
> A goodly apple rotten at the heart.'

But, however much or little Shakespeare himself
may have been influenced by Spanish thought or

Spanish models, there is no question that the other playwrights of his time depended very largely upon Spain for their plots. This was especially the case with Fletcher and Ben Jonson. To show how rapidly Spanish literature reached England at the time, *Don Quixote* was first printed in Spain in 1605, and in Brussels in 1607. In that same year, 1607, George Wilkins the dramatist produced in London a play called *The Miseries of Infant Marriage*, in which the fighting of a windmill is mentioned, and Middleton's *Five Gallants*, in the same year, also refers to it. Ben Jonson, who knew Spanish well, constantly refers to *Quixote* before Shelton's translation was published in 1612. *The Silent Woman*, for instance, was written in 1609, and in it Dauphin asks Truewit how he knows so well the secrets of ladies' wiles, and begs him to tell him how to learn. Truewit replies: 'Yes, but you must leave to live in your chamber, then, a month together upon *Amadis of Gaul* and *Don Quixote*, as you are wont to, and come abroad, where matter is frequent; to court, to tiltings, to public shows, and to church sometimes.' In the *Alchymist*, again, reference is made to *Don Quixote*. Fletcher, of course, knew of *Don Quixote* as soon as any one, for he was a good Spanish scholar. He burlesqued it, indeed, in his play *The Knight of the Burning Pestle*, which was written before Shelton's translation appeared in London. Fletcher depended very largely for his plots upon Cervantes' *Novelas Ejemplares*.

His *Fair Maid of the Inn* was from the *Ilustre Fregona*; *The Chances* from *La Señora Cordelia*; *Rule a Wife and Have a Wife*, from *El Casamiento Engañoso*. *A Very Woman*, by Fletcher and Massinger, was taken from *El Amante Liberal*. *Love's Pilgrimage* is a dramatisation of *Las dos Doncellas*. With Middleton and Rowley, they turned *La Fuerza de la Sangre* into *The Queen of Corinth*. Middleton and Rowley, again, dramatised Cervantes' *Gitanilla* as *The Spanish Gipsy*. Shirley's *Young Admiral* is taken from Lope de Vega's *Don Lope de Cardona*; and Webster's gloomy play *The Duchess of Amalfi* was either taken direct from Bandello's Italian novel of the same name, or from Lope de Vega's dramatisation of it.

One is struck, too, by the very frequent use of Spanish scenes and personages in plays of the English Elizabethan and Jacobean dramatists, which, although they are not always traceable to a known source—for at least a thousand plays of Lope de Vega alone have been lost—suggest a Spanish origin. Kyd's *Geronimo* and *Spanish Tragedy* are both saturated with Spanish feeling; so is Fletcher's *Spanish Curate*. Ben Jonson in his *Alchymist* introduces a scene where one of the characters, a member of a gang of swindlers, is made up as a Spanish nobleman, for the purpose of imposing upon a foolish young man and his widowed sister, who is to be married to the supposed Spaniard for the sake of her fortune. The scene is played half in Spanish, and very good Spanish it is, considering; and when the pretended count is introduced, the poor, innocent lady who is to be deluded, asks, when she is told that she is to be a Spanish countess, 'Why! is it better than an English countess?' After an expression of indignant surprise at so foolish a question, the led captain who is carrying through the swindle replies: 'Ask from your courtier, from your Inns of Court man, from your mere milliner; they will tell you all. . . . Your Spanish jennet is the best horse, your Spanish stoup the best garb, your Spanish beard the best cut, your Spanish ruffs the best wear, your Spanish pavan the best dance, your Spanish titillation in a glove the best perfume; and as for your Spanish pike and Spanish blade, let your poor captain speak.' This will give an idea of the extent to which the fashion for things Spanish had pervaded the English court in the early part of the seventeenth century, and how dramatists, amongst others, took their inspiration from Spain. To such an extent must this have been done, that they were sometimes inclined to apologise to English audiences for pilfering so largely from a nation then so unpopular as Spain; or, as an alternative, they were fond of making the most markedly Spanish characters despicable, and of flattering English vanity by showing how much superior English morality was to Spanish. For instance, in Fletcher's *Rule a Wife and Have a Wife*, the prologue thus excuses the origin of the play and its tendency :—

'Pleasure attend ye, and about ye sit
The springs of mirth, of fancy, delight, and wit,
To stir you up : do not your looks let fall,
Nor to remembrance our late errors call.
Because to-day we're Spaniards all again,
The story of our play, our scene, in Spain.
The errors, too, do not for this cause hate,
Now we present their wit, and not their State.
Nor, ladies, be not angry if you see
A young, fresh beauty, wanton and too free,
Seek to abuse her husband :—still 'tis Spain—
No such gross errors in *your* kingdom reign.'

Thus it is clear that in the palmiest days of the English drama, the plots were almost as frequently taken from Spanish as from Italian sources, and especially from the former in cases where a drama was the origin instead of a tale. The tradition, founded, it must be admitted, on solid fact, that the Spanish writers were unrivalled as inventors of intrigues and imbroglios for the stage, lingered long after the craze for things Spanish in general had disappeared from England. Navarro's company of Spanish players visited and represented in England during the reign of Charles I., and the Hispanophil writers of his court, some of whom I have mentioned in a former chapter, and shall refer to again, kept alive the literary cult of Spanish until the flood of the great rebellion swept away for a time all such vanities as stage plays, and darkness fell upon the Spanish stories of amorous intrigue that had amused Englishmen for sixty years.

CHAPTER X

THE SPANISH THEATRE AND THE ENGLISH STAGE
AFTER THE RESTORATION—CONCLUSION

In the previous chapters I have traced the evolution of Spanish letters, showing the marvellous fecundity of idea and invention, the proud, almost disdainful, abundance of literary resource, which at certain periods possessed this interesting people. From the circumstances of their history and topography, they had been more isolated from outside influences than other European peoples. They had retained old characteristics longer than most continental nations ; the chivalric idea which in the fourteenth, fifteenth, and sixteenth centuries seized upon their imaginations, and the long wars and moving adventures in far countries, had made Spaniards in the sixteenth and seventeenth centuries pompous, proud, and self-centred, with higher ideals of honour and religion, though with lower real standards of personal conduct, than others. Their costume matched their professions. After the death of Philip II. in 1598, their dress, which before had been splendid, became extravagant and bizarre in its exaggerated magnificence.

280

No court, perhaps, was ever more sumptuously attired than that of Philip III. under Lerma. Great spreading lace ruffs, enormous extended trunk-hose, velvets, satins, cloth of bullion, and glittering gew-gaws on every available spot; enormous rapiers, with damascened hilts and jewelled scabbards: all this, added to natural stateliness of gait and pompous self-assertion, made the Spaniard in the palmy days of his dramatic literary period, when Lope de Vega, Calderon, Alarcon, and Tirso de Molina wrote, different from other Europeans, both in appearance and manners.

Spain was already in full decline, but men as yet hardly recognised the fact. The assertion of superiority, and the tradition of overwhelming strength, were still so constant and strong that they carried conviction, in the face of the obvious fact that Spain was an overgrown giant with no stamina of its own. James I., in one of his fits of constitutional self-abasement, told Gondomar, in 1618, that he well knew that the King of Spain was greater than all the rest of the Christian princes put together; but yet at that very time Philip III., at the end of his resources, had to send round officers to beg from door to door in the capital for contributions, over and above the oppressive and squandered taxes, to keep him and his household in food. We have seen how this tradition of Spanish preponderance had produced throughout Europe an idea that everything Spanish was better than that of other countries. In 1612 and 1615 events occurred that gave an enormous impetus to the fashion in Europe for Spain and Spanish things. The betrothal and marriage of the heir of Spain, afterwards Philip IV., with the daughter of Henry IV. of France, and the simultaneous marriage of Louis XIII., King of France, with Anne of Austria, daughter of Philip III., brought scores of the French nobles to the frontier and into Spain, and sent Spanish grandees to Paris. Anne of Austria throughout her life kept a Spanish court, with Spanish actors and authors; and for the next forty years at least, until the predominance of French influence in Europe was gained under Louis XIV., everything Spanish was the rage in France—Spanish dress was the fashion. The Spanish gallant air was not only adopted, but its name, and dozens of other Spanish terms, were naturalised in France. The games, the dances, the terms of endearment, the favourite dishes, all had Spanish names. Cervantes, writing in 1616, says: 'No man or woman in France fails to learn Castilian.' In fact, Spaniards were regarded in France in the seventeenth century much as Englishmen in the nineteenth; that is to say, they were derided, their dress and appearance were caricatured, and their demeanour lampooned; but they were imitated both in garb and manners as nearly as the Frenchmen could manage to do it.

It was pointed out in the last chapter how the plots

of the Spaniards had been utilised by the Elizabethan and Jacobean dramatists, and how, under the influence of the proposed marriage of Charles, Prince of Wales, with the Infanta, the English Hispanophils had translated many works into English, and had, to some extent, introduced Spanish fashions and manners. But this direct influence upon England was of no long duration. Lord Bristol, who had been ambassador in Spain when the marriage treaty fell through, translated Calderon's *Mejor está que estaba*, under the name of *Better 'tis than it Was*, and *Peor esta que estaba*, under the name of *Worse and Worse*; but both English plays have disappeared. Lord Bristol's very amusing play *Elvira* remains with us, and that is an adaptation of Calderon's *No siempre lo peor es cierlo*. Sir Richard Fanshawe, a great Spanish scholar and an adherent of Charles I., translated Antonio de Mendoza's *Querer por solo querer* (*Love for Love's Sake*) when he was in prison after the battle of Worcester; and several other translations and adaptations of this sort were made direct in Charles I.'s time from the Spanish drama. The main characteristic of all such dramas, and what really was the Spanish invention, was the machinery of the intrigue — rooms with hidden doors, secret staircases with facilities for the exchange of one personality for another, the ringing of changes on two or more pairs of lovers. All this was unknown to the classic drama; and to this day, when we see what

is called a bustling farce—now rather out of fashion—
which depends upon the fortuitous appearance and
disappearance of the personages through many doorways, and the hiding of characters in incongruous
places, it may with confidence be said that the original
initiative of it came from Spain.   I mentioned in a
former chapter that Juan Navarro and his company
of Spanish players were popular in London in 1635,
and on the 23rd December of that year received
£10 for playing before the king.   But all the efforts
of English sympathisers of Spain, to introduce the
Spanish drama directly to England, were swamped by
the blood of the great rebellion and the prohibition
of all stage plays and such like vanities for the next
twenty years and more.

In the meanwhile, during that period, France was
saturated with Spanish fashions.   Under Richelieu, during the regency of Anne of Austria, and during the youth
of Louis XIV., especially after he, in his turn, married
a Spanish princess, the swaggering *espadachin*, with his
great trunk-hose extended with cotton, his vast ruff,
and his plumed hat, was the model copied by soldiers
and young bloods, such as may be recognised now in
Dumas' revival of the taste in *The Three Musketeers*,
and in Stanley Weyman's novels of the same period.
It was no wonder that the stilted aloofness of the
classical drama should be to some extent supplanted
in France by the lively drama of intrigue, and by the
tragic historical plays, which were pouring out of

Spanish writers of the time with the inexhaustible abundance and freshness of a mountain spring.

The pioneer in France to popularise the new taste was a playwright of a fertility of production almost rivalling that of Lope himself, Hardy, who borrowed plots wholesale from Spanish dramas. But it was not until a man of genuine genius in France, Pierre Corneille, cast his eye upon the Spanish plays and transformed them somewhat to suit French taste and tradition, that the movement became powerful enough to penetrate all Europe, through France. So long as Spanish plays had been simply translated, or their intrigues copied, they remained necessarily exotic, because the Spanish view of honour, of love, of conduct, of morality, of religion, was different from that of France or of England ; and many of the points and scruples upon which the action turned were incomprehensible to people of other nationalities. But in 1636 Pierre Corneille, already a famous dramatist of the classical school, presented his great drama *Le Cid*. His writings were already deeply imbued with the prevailing Spanish taste for bombastic and inflated language, especially in tragedy. He had, moreover, introduced in others of his plays two characters taken straight from the Spanish drama—the swashbuckling mercenary Captain Matamore, and the Picaro. He was therefore a fit man to blend in his own writing the romantic, chivalrous spirit of Spain with the classical traditions which were still strong in France. Cor-

neille was recommended by a Spanish officer in the
suite of Anne of Austria to read a play by a second-
rate Spanish writer, Guillem de Castro, called *Las
Mocedades del Cid*, a semi-historical play, founded on
an ancient poem. The result was one of the highest
importance to the future of dramatic art, for Corneille's *Le Cid* proved that Spanish dramas in the
hands of a writer of genius might, without losing their
vigour, be naturalised to the tastes of other countries.
Corneille's *Cid* is known to every one, and is still acted
by the Comédie Française. At its first appearance
in the last days of 1636 it was an astounding triumph,
and its popularity in France has never ceased. To
Spaniards, and indeed to Englishmen, it appears
artificial and stilted to the last degree, but that was
a concession to the old French taste. The language
is less terse and natural than it is in Spanish, but,
when all is said, it is a grand historical drama,
bristling with strong situations; and not even the
barbarous transformation of Spanish names to French
like *Shimène* for *Ximena*, and Don *Diègue* for *Diego*,
can mar its splendour.

Corneille, of course, was attacked bitterly by his
contemporaries for departing, even to the extent he
did, from the classical traditions, and grafting the
modern romanticism upon the machinery of the Greek
and Roman drama; but Spanish romanticism was in
the air; and, although purists might protest, the
public wished for some degree of naturalness, and

Corneille triumphed. He took another step forward in 1644, and wrote a comedy which took Paris by storm. It was called *Le Menteur* (*The Liar*); and in the prologue to it he says that, having scaled the heights of tragedy, he would not attempt to descend to comedy without a hand to guide him, so he has taken as his model the famous Lope de Vega. The curious fact, however, is that he really did not follow Lope de Vega at all. The comedy from which *Le Menteur* is taken is called *La Verdad Sospechosa*, and tells of a young man just returned from college to his home, who is so much given to lying, that when he tells the truth no one will believe him. The complications that he brings upon himself by his infirmity are infinite: he is engaged to be married, first to one lady and then to the other; misunderstandings, scrapes, and all sorts of troubles and intrigues are the result, and it is one of the most perplexing, as well as the most amusing, of any of the Spanish comedies. It is not by Lope de Vega, however, but by Alarcon. In the book that Corneille took it from, it was bound up with Lope's works, and it was not until 1660, when Corneille saw it ascribed correctly to Alarcon, that he corrected his error, which he did carefully in later editions. The amusing part of it is that when in the eighteenth century Sir Richard Steele translated the play into English under the name of *The Lying Lover*, he ascribes it to Lope de Vega (Sire de Vega, as he calls him), oblivious of

the fact that eighty years previously its real author-
ship had been known. Corneille's adaptation of *La
Verdad Sospechosa* makes the personages French, and
the scene Paris, and suppresses some scenes which
would have clashed with his traditions. But he
weakens the play considerably thereby as a drama,
and particularly by his altering of the end. The
Spanish drama, written mostly, you will recall, by
churchmen, shared with all other Spanish writing that
tendency to didacticism which I have traced from the
very earliest birth of the literature, and when vice
is represented it is almost invariably punished. In
Alarcon's play the Liar is married to the wrong girl,
and the one he loves is married before his eyes to
another man, as a result of his falsehoods. But the
French tradition was that only tragedies must end
unhappily, and all comedies must finish happily, so
Corneille makes his fibber triumph in the end.

Corneille wrote another play from the Spanish,
called *Don Sanche d'Aragon*; but on the *Cid* and *Le
Menteur* his fame rests, and to these two emanations
of his genius we owe the perpetuation of the Spanish
spirit into the modern theatre. But it was a greater
than Corneille that was the conductor through whom
the current ran. Jean Baptiste Poquelin Molière
himself tells us that he decided to write plays, and
become an actor, owing to his reading *Le Cid*.
Already, when he was in his prime, the Spanish
force in literature was on the wane. Like a maple

forest in the autumn, Spanish letters were dying in a blaze of glory. Calderon and Quevedo were still writing, and a half-hundred other poets and playwrights, headed by King Philip himself, kept all Madrid in idle amusement, as witty as it was profitless. But Molière, bettering the instruction of Corneille, threw aside both the worn-out classical traditions, and the remaining exotic traces in the personages and plots of Spanish dramas; adapted the intrigues to French surroundings, and founded a modern drama in which the language and personages were those of everyday Parisian life. He, like most geniuses, borrowed where he pleased; and the origin of every part of his plays is difficult to trace. He was not content, like other inferior men, to adapt a Spanish play entire, but took a situation here, a character there, and an intrigue somewhere else; but, withal, his great comedies, upon which his fame mainly rests, are all more or less founded on Spanish originals. *Tartuffe*, for instance, which Colley Cibber turned into the *Nonjuror* in England, would not have been written as it was unless the author had seen Lope's *Perro de Hortelano* (*Dog in the Manger*), in which a lady was in love with her secretary, and was too proud to marry him, and yet too jealous to let him marry any one else.

Le Médecin malgré Lui (*The Mock Doctor*, as Fielding's version is called) owes its origin to Lope's *Acero de Madrid*, where a lover assumes the garb of

T

a physician to forward his amorous aims. *L'Amour Médecin*, another of Molière's plays, is generally believed to have been taken from Cyrano de Bergerac's *Pédant Joué*; but probably Molière did not know that the famous poet with the prodigious nose, Cyrano de Bergerac, himself had plundered the plot from Lope's *Robo de Elena*.

What Molière did in the way of borrowing, his rivals and followers imitated. It would be profitless for me to enumerate the many known imitations by French dramatists of the late seventeenth century of Spanish authors; and, of course, there are immense numbers of instances that are untraced. It will suffice to point out a few instances of how, and in what form, the influence was transmitted to England. On the return of Charles II. to England from his long exile in 1660, he found a people ready once more for gaiety. The reaction from Puritan dulness and austerity was bound to occur, and Charles II. came in at the top of the wave. With him, and around him, were courtiers, many of whom had, like himself, lived in foreign countries for years. Foreign mistresses accompanied him; he himself was half a Frenchman, with a love for frivolous amusements as great as that of Philip IV. himself. It was no wonder, therefore, that a public, hungry for stage-plays, should have greeted his coming with a great outcry for the restoration of the theatre. They did not have to wait long; nor was fashion tardy in taking to the play, as may be seen by the vivacious confessions of Mr. Pepys.

The English exiles who had lived in Paris had come back full of Molière and his charming comedies, but alas! the art of writing blank verse had been lost in England. There were no more Beaumont and Fletchers, no more Shakespeares, and the facile versification of the Spanish drama, and of Molière, had to be replaced in England by dramas in prose, with lyrics and poems introduced. Before the indirect adaptation of Spanish intrigue through the French had become the fashion under Charles II.—for it took some time for Dryden and his followers to get to work and hit the taste of the court and public— a direct adaptation from the Spanish was made of one play, which attained a success, as it seems to us now, out of all proportion to its merits. But, however that may be, it was practically a reintroduction to the eager, English public of that Spanish comedy of intrigue which, from that day to this, has never left the English stage: the comedy of contrary purposes, of mistaken personalities, and of mixed-up lovers, ultimately sorted out to everybody's satisfaction. This play, which was hailed by all men as a work of genius, was called *The Adventures of Five Hours*. The author was an Essex gentleman, named Samuel Tuke, who had been a Royalist leader during the Civil War, and had afterwards lived abroad. He evidently understood Spanish, and to judge by the prologue, which I shall quote presently, the king appears to have told him how much he enjoyed the Spanish play upon which the *Adventures of Five Hours* was founded, and recommended Tuke to translate it. Tuke was at this time (1662) elderly, and had intended to retire to live quietly in the country ; but in obedience to the king's hint he adapted the play from the Spanish—it is said with the assistance of the Earl of Bristol, who, as I have already said, had himself translated three of Lope's plays. Tuke's *Adventures of Five Hours* was first represented at the court of Whitehall in 1663, and afterwards in the Duke's Theatre, Lincoln's Inn Fields, where it had then the unheard-of run of thirteen consecutive nights. Pepys, of course, went to see it ; and the first time he read it he declares that 'it is the best play that ever I read in my life'; and a few days afterwards he gives the astounding judgment that 'the *Adventures of Five Hours* makes *Othello* seem a mean thing.' Others, and perhaps more competent critics than Samuel Pepys, pronounced the play to be the best specimen of the comedy of intrigue that had ever been seen in England.

It is complicated enough, in all conscience. Broadly it tells the story of a rough, passionate, young Spanish noble, burdened by the guardianship of a marriageable sister, whom he has betrothed to a Spanish noble officer, who has long been absent in the Flemish wars, and has never seen his future bride. She, being

secretly promised to another man, bewails her fate
to her girl-friend, who says that her trouble is greater
still, since she has fallen desperately in love with a
man whose name she does not know, and only saw
for a moment, when he rescued her from an ambush
and capture by brigands in Flanders. By a series
of most complicated misunderstandings, the two young
ladies are taken for each other; and after an infinity
of adventure and intrigue each eventually gets the
husband she wants. Reading it now in English, the
play seems not much better, if no worse, than dozens
of Lope's and Calderon's plays, and far behind the
best of them; but the London public at the time
was unjaded, perhaps uncritical, and the play was
accepted as a work of genius. I must confess that
personally I have not been able to satisfy myself as
to the Spanish original of this famous successful play.
Every text-book and authority that has been written
on the subject, says that Tuke's play is an adaptation
of Coello's *Empeños de Seis Horas* (*The Undertakings
of Six Hours*). Authorities and text-books, however,
have a somewhat misleading habit of copying each
other on minor points without much investigation,
and so one mistake may make many. I have myself
been unable to obtain Coello's *Empeños de Seis Horas*,
so that I do not know if Tuke's play resembles it;
but I do know that Tuke himself repeats, more than
once, that he translated the play from one of Calderon's
comedies. I see, moreover, that the British Museum

Catalogue, as if to make confusion worse confounded, says that the *Adventures of Five Hours* is adapted from Calderon's *El Escondido y la Tapada*; but a careful perusal of both plays does not suggest, to my mind, any connection between them.   This is what Sir Samuel Tuke (he was made a baronet soon after the play was produced) wrote in his preface to the third printed edition of the play.   After apologising for the garb in which the work is presented, he continues: 'This refers to the dress only; for certainly the plot needs no apology.   It was taken out of Don Pedro Calderon, a celebrated Spanish author; the nation in the world who are happiest in the force and delicacy of their inventions; and recommended to me by his sacred Majesty as an excellent design, whose judgment is no more to be doubted than his commands are to be disobeyed; and therefore it might seem a great presumption in me to enter my sentiments with his Majesty's royal suffrage.   But as Secretaries of State sign their names to the mandates of their prince, so at the bottom of the leaf I take the boldness to subscribe my opinion that this is incomparably the best play I ever met with.'

In the spoken prologue, when the play was produced at the Duke's Theatre, the author makes a similar declaration after apologising for the novelty of the style of writing:—

'They're in the right, for I make bold to say,
The English stage ne'er had so new a play.

The dress, the author, and the scene are new.
This ye have seen before, ye say! 'tis true.
But tell me, gentlemen, who ever saw
A deep intrigue confined to five hours' law?
Such as for close contrivance yields to none,
A modest man may praise what's not his own.
'Tis true the dress is his, which he submits
To those who are, and those who would be, wits.
Ne'er spare him, gentlemen, to speak the truth,
He has a per'lous censurer been in's youth ;
And now grown bald with age, doting on praise,
He thinks to get a periwig of bays.
Teach him what 'tis in this discerning age,
To bring his heavy genius on the stage,
Where you have seen such nimble wits appear,
That passed so soon, one scarce can say they're here.
Yet, after our discoveries of late,
Of their designs, who would subvert the State.
You'll wonder much, if it should prove his lot,
To take all England with a Spanish plot.
But, if through his ill-conduct or hard fate,
This foreign plot, like that of eighty-eight,
Should suffer shipwreck in your narrow seas,
You'll give your modern poet writ of ease.
For, by th' example of the King of Spain,
He resolves ne'er to trouble you again.'

Tuke's success spurred others on in the same field ;
but not many could obtain Spanish plays direct, or
could understand them if they did. Probably Dryden
read Spanish, and almost certainly several of his plays
were inspired by Lope de Vega, either directly or
through some French translator. Dryden's *Evening
Love*, for instance, is certainly taken from Calderon's
Astrologo Fingido, through the translation of Corneille's brother Thomas. To please the licentious

court of Charles II., Dryden produced plays on the
Spanish lines, in which the bombastic and impossible
heroism of the principal personage, the valour and
prowess, the high-faluting grandiloquence of the characters, outdid the originals, and became supremely
ridiculous; whilst his coarseness was quite bereft of
the satirical fun that gilded suggestiveness, both in
Spanish and in French. Dryden could, and did, do
infinitely better things than write pot-boiling comedies
in prose, which he produced to please a vicious king
and court. But, badly or well written, the framework of these comedies of Dryden and his followers is
purely Spanish. The absurdity of the inflated style,
natural in Spain, when turned into English was evident even then to men with a keen sense of humour ;
and Buckingham's famous parody of Dryden's attempts
to acclimatise Spanish diction, as well as Spanish
intrigue, set all the court laughing. It is called *The
Rehearsal*, and the poet himself is brought upon the
stage to superintend the rehearsal of his piece. He
is made to appear prodigiously vain and fatuous, and
to commit himself to the opinion that the more extravagant a piece is, the better it is. Every resource of
Buckingham's malicious wit is used to pour ridicule
upon a style which only Corneille's genius and the
staid classical tradition of the French stage had made
tolerable even in France.

But, when Dryden was content to take his cue from
Molière, as Wycherley did, then things were better

and more natural; and with Dryden's *Sir Martin
Mar-all*, taken from *L'Étourdi*, and Wycherley's
Plain Dealer, taken from *Le Misanthrope*, the modern
English comedy of manners may be said to have
commenced. It is impossible to trace every play from
the Restoration to the age of Anne to distinct Spanish
sources, but it is not too much to say that hardly one
of them was free from signs of Spanish inspiration.
Many, of course, are traceable, such as those I have
mentioned : Wycherley's *Gentleman Dancing-Master* to
Calderon's *Maestro de Danzar*; *The Parson's Wedding*, of
Killigrew, was Calderon's *Dama Duende*; Sir Richard
Steele's *Lying Lover* is *La Verdad Sospechosa*, through
Corneille's *Menteur*. Indeed, at the end of the seventeenth century, French power and French culture,
French fashion and French literature, had triumphed
over the Spanish. The inexhaustible ingenuity of the
Spanish plots was taken wholesale, but the plays that
resulted were French now, and not Spanish.

The death, in 1700, of the last Spanish king of the
house of Austria, and the accession of a French king,
after years of civil war and foreign invasion had swept
over Spain, finally revealed to the world the utter
decadence of native Spanish letters. The English
stage, flourishing and excellent, took its impetus from
France, in ignorance that the invention that animated
it was Spanish, divested of Spanish exaggeration and
the verbal heroism that had grown out of the development of Spanish letters, as I have tried to lay it before

the reader. The immortal *Don Quixote*, and the picaresque novels—especially *Gil Blas*—still kept alive in England the recollection of the Spanish tradition, and permanently left their mark upon the form of English fiction; but with this exception, the dawn of the eighteenth century saw the disappearance of the conscious influence of Spanish models and modes of thought in England. The tradition of the apophthegm, or moral sentence, survived strongly, and was Spanish to the core, though few now recognised the fact; the comedy of intrigue in English dress depended more than ever upon the substitution of one person for another, the mixing and re-sorting of lovers, and upon the existence of a multiplicity of doors and convenient hiding-places. The public laughed and applauded at the amusing tangle, without dreaming that it was all as Spanish as could be, though it had reached England in a French garb.

It is said that a sound uttered echoes for all eternity through space. Certain it is that a literary influence, like an hereditary taint, lasts ages after the memory of its origin has passed from the minds of men. The philosophical literary historian seeks to trace back to their birth the varying currents which, combined, make the mighty river of a national literature. But the historian can do no more than convey hints and point directions. There is no possibility of a student gaining a real knowledge of the influences that have dominated the literature of his own country, unless he reads for himself the masterpieces of it, and then studies, so far as his circumstances permit, the great literatures that have grown up before and simultaneously with it. I have sometimes been tempted to think that text-books are the bane of precise knowledge. I will not, however, say so much as that, because text-books, used as they should be used, simply as finger-posts, are useful; but the misuse of text-books, and particularly literary text-books, by students who think that they are a substitute for the study of originals, is an unmixed evil, and does more than anything I know to produce the shallow superficiality which is the hall-mark of modern so-called scholarship.

Once more in the history of Spain, a period of social and political decadence had been marked by an irresistible flood of over-florid literary production. In the poetical, artistic, and theatrical court of Philip IV., the arts ran riot in their rank luxuriance. Every man who aspired to culture at all, wrote verses, satires, political squibs, novels, or dramas, born one day to die the next. The out-at-elbows, famished man of letters, real or pretended; the sham student, who with his wooden spoon stuck in his cap lived upon doles of soup and bread given at the monastery gates; the gangs of idlers, who flocked into the church and crowded the religious houses; and the mixed multitude of copper-captains, adventurers, bullies, swindlers, and lackeys, who sauntered up and down the Calle Mayor

of Madrid the livelong day, and thronged Liars'
Parade on the steps of St. Philip: all these, as well as
great nobles, sought to attract attention to themselves
by writing something. In these circumstances, of
course, 'Conceptism,' or Euphuism, as it was called in
English, was rampant; affectation and extravagance
reigned supreme again, as it had done in the later
romances of chivalry, and with a similar result. If
a man had not the soaring wit to excel his fellows
in his writings, at least he could make people stare
and wonder what he meant by far-fetched obscurity.
Gongora, a really great poet, had followed Guevara,
and had made what was called the cultured style
fashionable. Lope de Vega declaimed against the
absurdity savagely, and himself sinned as badly as
any one. Quevedo sneered and scoffed at it, called it
by the barbarous names of *Latiniparla, Cultigracia,*
and the like; but if an endeavour be made to read
in the original any of Quevedo's social satires, the
reader will find himself entangled in a net of preciosity
almost impossible to follow lucidly. And so, as
Velasquez and Murillo dwindled first to Manzanedo
and Claudio Coello, and then to crowds of daubers
who simply spoilt good canvas, so did the literary
Spanish giants, with their over-facility and fertility,
bring Spanish letters to utter contempt; and what had
been a finely cultured garden was, by the end of the
seventeenth century, a dense jungle of dying weeds.

For years the War of Succession raged in Spain, and

when at last the French king, Philip V., found himself established upon the throne (1713), he looked over a land in which industry, literature, and art were apparently dead. Social and political decadence and corruption had rendered the upper classes powerless to regenerate institutions; and in all departments of life the impetus towards renascence had to come from abroad. Whence could it come but from France, the native land of the new dynasty? French finance ministers and administrators took in hand the nation's exchequer, French engineers planned and started productive public works, and French enterprises and capital re-established flourishing industries, worked by French labour. When the king and court dressed in French garb and read French books, it is not to be wondered at that Spanish literature, which once more began to raise its drooping head, looked across the Pyrenees for the inspiration which was to give it fresh life. For in the struggle of civilisations, that long series of wars between Spain and France under Louis XIV., in which, at length, the inflated Spanish claims of supremacy had been faced and destroyed, French culture had conquered the Spanish form, just as the French military power had triumphed over the once invincible armies of Spain; and not Spain alone, but all Christendom, was now receiving its civilisation coloured by French influence.

We have seen how, at an earlier period, French writers had borrowed much, especially in plot and incident, from Spanish novels and plays. We have seen how, for the first forty years of the seventeenth century, the traditional Spanish bearing and tone had dominated society and literature in France; but we have also seen how, first, in the hands of Corneille, the classical French traditions had somewhat modified the Spanish plots and their treatment, and how, secondly, under the modernising genius of Molière, the plots and personages themselves had been naturalised and had become French. The impetus that now reached Spain from France had therefore lost nearly all traces of Spanish origin, and was still impregnated with the classical Greek traditions which, in consequence of the more recent Oriental antecedents of Spanish literature which I have described, were quite foreign and antagonistic to Spanish tastes. Philip V. did his best to make the new Spanish literature a native one. He founded the Royal Spanish Academy, in imitation of the Académie Francaise, and the Royal Academy of History, and other similar corporations followed. But the very constitution of these Academies, following that of their French originals, made it inevitable that the standard of excellence erected by them should be the classical one.

There were, it is true, Spaniards who struggled against the tide in literature, as others did against the introduction of French fashions in dress and manners ; but the great mass of the Spanish people now did not

read at all, and culture was almost entirely confined
to the upper classes, who naturally followed the
official Academies and the court, and adopted readily
the new tone introduced from France. But, withal,
the Spanish literary bent was naturally too strong to
be destroyed permanently, and before the end of the
eighteenth century the old traditions had begun to
show head again, with new force behind them now,
because they embodied the resistance offered by the
Church and all the conservative elements of the
nation to the iconoclastic ideas of the French Revolution. The first name that stands out distinctly in
this Spanish revival is that of the elder Moratin
(Nicolas Moratin), a lyric and epic poet whose works
are really more Spanish in their spirit than French.
His comedies are inferior to those of his son; but
Guzman el Bueno and *La Petimetra*, and especially his
epic *Fiesta de Toros en Madrid*, mark the first awaken-
ing of Spanish letters from the classical French night-
mare. Tomas Yriarte, the poet, shortly afterwards
made another step forward with a revival of the old
Spanish didacticism in verse in his famous *Fabulas
Literarias*, which, although evidently owing for their
existence much to the immediate inspiration of La
Fontaine, are quite Spanish in treatment and subject.
His famous fable of *The Donkey Flautist* (*El Burro
Flautista*), which inculcates the moral that a writer
may succeed by chance once, but can only succeed
permanently by patient work, may be quoted here

entire to show how distinct the style is in the hands of an original Spaniard from that of the French fabulists :—

'Este fabulilla,
Salga bien ó mal,
Me ha ocurrido ahora
Por casualidad.

Cerca de unos prados
Que hay en mi lugar,
Pasaba un borrico
Por casualidad.

Una flauta en ellos,
Halló, que un zagal
Se dejó olvidado,
Por casualidad.

Acercó-se á olerla,
El dicho animal,
Y dió un resoplido
Por casualidad.

En la flauta el aire
Se hubo de colar,
Y sonó la flauta
Por casualidad.

Oh ! dijo el borrico,
Que bien sé tocar.
Y dican que es mala,
La musica asnal.

Sin reglas del arte,
Borriquitos hay,
Que una vez aciertan
Por casualidad.'

In the last third of the eighteenth century, and the first few years of the nineteenth, Spain produced a worthy group of serious writers who, though Spanish in manner, were all more or less impregnated with French spirit, and most of them imbued with the speculative tendency of the French Revolution, and consequently frowned upon by the Church and conservative Spaniards :—Mayans y Siscar, a great critic and editor of Spanish masterpieces ; Father Florez, the historian of the Catholic queens ; Forner, another notable critic and editor ; Sempere, the political economist ; Father Feijoo, the critic ; the great Jovellanos ; and, above all, Father Isla, the humorist and reformer, abounding with wit which stuck at nothing ; and the reviver of the Spanish stage, Leandro Moratin.

But once more Spain was swept clean of the arts of peace, by a scourge of war so terrible as to throw in the shade all other visitations that had afflicted her. For five years hostile armies made Spanish land the battlefield upon which the fate of the world was to be decided for a hundred years. Not this alone ; but what we in England call the Peninsular War (1808-1813) set Spaniard against Spaniard in bitter hate. With one party, and that the largest, all that was French in the slightest degree was anathema. *Afrancesado* was a term of opprobrium worse than that of murderer, and, however great the merits of literary men, if they sided with the invader or the ideas he represented to the public mind, obloquy, exile, or persecution was their lot when the French domination

U

fell. This is what happened to Moratin. His *Origines del Teatro español*, a work of immense research and sound criticism, reproducing the principal plays in the Spanish language, has been of incalculable value to students. His famous comedies, *El Sí de las Niñas* (*The Maid's Consent*) and *La Mojigata* (*The Hypocrite*), still hold the stage, but Moratin was, notwithstanding his purely Spanish nature, sullied with the name of *Afrancesado*, and he died in poverty and exile. Far different at first was the fate of those literary lights who opposed the French and advocated parliamentary and liberal institutions, like Jovellanos and Father Isla. They were the idols of the populace, and their writings were applauded not alone by their own countrymen, but in England, where they were largely read. With the restoration of Ferdinand VII. and the flight of all men of progressive ideas a new Spanish influence was introduced into England and France, whither most of the reformers fled, an influence which subsequently had for its complement a curious reaction upon Spain itself. For years, with short intervals until the death of Ferdinand and the disappearance for ever of the old order, the best minds of Spain were in exile. Count Toreno, the historian of the Revolution ; Quintana and Espronceda, the poets ; the Duke of Rivas, Zorilla, and a score of others passed their exile in the pursuit or practice of literature in the country of their adoption. When the death of the tyrant at length allowed these men to return to their own land, and the government of the new queen was forced to look to the progressive party alone to support her against Carlism, the literary views of the liberal leaders became the fashion in Spain. The régime of Ferdinand had crushed out literature in the country, and the exiles had brought back with them the spirit they had imbibed through their study of Byron, Scott, Hugo, and Schiller. The result was that for years to come the literature of Spain was mainly imitative. Espronceda copied Byron almost slavishly. Sir Walter Scott was the model for the national historical novel that now became popular in Spain. Victor Hugo, in his prologue to *Hernani*, remarks that romanticism is 'liberalism in literature'; and it is possible to reverse the dictum by saying that for nearly forty years, from 1830 to 1868, liberalism in politics in Spain meant romanticism in literature, the old Spanish romanticism filtered through a foreign medium, and so much transformed as to be almost unrecognisable, reintroduced from abroad to the country of its birth. As usual in Spain, the finest and most characteristic results were seen in the theatre. The Duke of Rivas produced some historical dramas worthy of the great times of the Spanish stage, such as *La Fuerza del Sino* and the *Faro de Malta*. Breton de los Herreros still holds the stage with his *Marcela*, *Un Tercero en Discordia*, *Muerete! y verás*, and other romantic dramas; whilst Zorilla, with *El Zapatero y el Rey* (*Cobbler and King*) and *Don Juan Tenorio*, both powerful but gloomy, romantic melodramas, exhibited unmistakably his own literary genius, his knowledge of old Spanish legends, and his faithful study of the French modern romancist school of Dumas.

But the presence of the Spanish liberals in England and France for so many years had effects in literature of a wider character than the introduction on their return to Spain of a taste for Byronic poetry and Scott's national romance. The interest and sympathy excited in Europe by the dramatic events in Spain in the first third of the nineteenth century, added to the writings of the exiles in England and France, revived the chivalric idea of Spain that had predominated in Europe in the seventeenth century. Romances with a Spanish setting, tales of impossible love adventures, and soul-moving tragedies, in an equally impossible land, where men wore doublets and trunks, and serenaded their lady-loves in the intervals of stabbing their rivals, were fashionable in England. But it was in France where the great romantic revival really struck strong root. Victor Hugo's father had been a general in Spain, and there the poet was born. Hugo was saturated with the Spanish literary tradition, and there came from his pen in the days of his greatest power play after play, in which picturesque Spanish local colour was laid on lavishly. Spanish legends and romantic historical episodes were placed under contribution, and the characteristics which had been traditionally those of Spaniards two hundred years before were again presented as being true to life. The consequence is seen even to the present day, when many untravelled Englishmen, and more especially Frenchmen, persist in the superstition that modern dress and manners stop at the Pyrenees, and that in crossing the frontier the traveller steps into the seventeenth century.

The flood-time came with Alexandre Dumas. He was half a negro, with Spanish blood in his veins, flamboyant as a Spaniard of old himself, and the romantic school of fiction and drama under his vivid pen seized hold of France, and thence spread to England. *The Three Musketeers, Monte Cristo,* and the whole series of slashing, vaunting, florid stories, and the plays made from them, are old Spanish to the core, and entirely untrue to French nature in general, for even the Gascon, although a great talker, really loves his ease better than swashbuckling adventure. But the school served its turn. It was exciting, it was rapid and full of invention, and from France it spread to England. The numerous tales of G. P. R. James that amused our fathers in their youth are turned out of the same mould, and, though infinitely superior to these, *The Fortunes of Nigel* and *Quentin Durward* have as direct a Spanish descent as they, through a French medium. Not only were England and France thus dominated, but the influence was carried back to Spain again by the writings of Dumas and his school, and a revival of the old French view of Spanish character was made fashionable in Spain itself. There was nothing natural in the taste. The extravagant, boastful posturer which the French adopted as the Spanish type was never true to nature, except perhaps in the case of the Spanish soldiers of fortune in the sixteenth century, and certainly for the last two hundred years is absurdly wide of the mark.

Like all artificial things, the French conception of Spain is ephemeral, especially in Spain where its falsity was felt; but it dies hard because of the persistence of travellers in keeping up the fiction, and repeating what other people have told them, instead of judging for themselves. In Spain itself the romantic school of fiction is, for the present, dead. The works of fiction most in demand, apart from the somewhat slight, but interesting, political historical novels, made popular by Señor Perez Galdos, are the provincial novels of manners, representing the surviving provincial life of a few years ago; the reproduction of local and provincial legends, tales, and poetry, and, indeed, provincialism generally. But the tendency most recently discernible is that towards solid didacticism in the form, mostly, of translations of English and German scientific and philosophical works. Spain has once more entered upon one of its periods of sober reticence. Florid eccentricity and volubility, for the moment, are not the fashion in literature; and, to judge from the past literary history of the country, we may look for an improving and increasing production of solid, good work in history, science, and the serious drama ; to be succeeded gradually by mordant satire, fertility of invention, over-production, exuberance, and afterwards, decay. But that is not yet, for the revival of good literature is only yet commencing, and it will take years to teach its apogee. At the present moment Spanish literature cannot be said to exert any influence whatever in England.

I have briefly traced Castilian letters in these pages from their very birth, and have tried my best to show that at certain stages of their history they exerted powerful and salutary influence upon our own literature. The didactic proverb and sententious maxim from the Jews of Cordova have left their mark for good upon the thought and literary form of the whole civilised world ; the literatures of history and of travel bear upon them to-day the indelible traces of the Spanish chronicles and stories of personal adventure which sprang therefrom. The poetry of the whole world still carries upon it the tint of knightly sacrifice and of pastoral simplicity, as a revolt against the sordid struggle for daily existence and the blighting corruption of great cities ; and this spirit, when it was dying elsewhere, received new birth in Spain by the altruistic romances of *Amadis of Gaul* and its hundred imitators. The novels of Fielding, of Smollett, and of Dickens, remain to show us that the picaresque tales born in Spain have left their progeny in our own land; and the costume drama imitated from the French, with the swashbuckling stories of adventure, to which so many English novelists are now devoting their energies, proves that the traditional Spanish type of the sixteenth century still survives, thanks to the boisterous gaiety and vitality which always appeals to youth.

Spanish literature, in its higher sense, may be dead beyond resurrection, as some critics say, though I, for one, do not believe that it is; but even if it be, it may still claim to have stamped indelibly its seal upon all the living European literatures of the present and the future. The object of this brief review has been to trace its influence especially upon the development of English letters, and to point out the marks of it that still survive. If I have been successful in interesting any number of my readers to the extent of leading them to study in the original the masterpieces of this fine and forceful literature, so long neglected by my countrymen, my efforts will have been richly rewarded.

INDEX

313